STRANDED
IN THE JUNGLE

STRANDED IN THE JUNGLE

JERRY NOLAN'S WILD RIDE—
A Tale of Drugs, Fashion, the New York Dolls, and Punk Rock

CURT WEISS

Backbeat Books

An Imprint of Hal Leonard LLC

Published in 2017 by Backbeat Books
An Imprint of Hal Leonard LLC
7777 West Bluemound Road
Milwaukee, WI 53213

Trade Book Division Editorial Offices
33 Plymouth St., Montclair, NJ 07042

Front cover photograph of Jerry Nolan © Alain Dister
Book design by Kristina Rolander

Printed in the United States of America

Library of Congress Cataloging-in-Publication Data

Names: Weiss, Curt.
Title: Stranded in the jungle : Jerry Nolan's wild ride--a tale of drugs, fashion, the New York Dolls, and punk rock / Curt Weiss.
Description: Montclair, NJ : Backbeat Books, 2017. | Includes bibliographical references and index.
Identifiers: LCCN 2017017453 | ISBN 9781495050817
Subjects: LCSH: Nolan, Jerry, 1946-1992. | Drummers (Musicians)--United States--Biography. | Punk rock musicians--United States--Biography. | New York Dolls (Musical group) | Heartbreakers (Musical group : Johnny Thunders)
Classification: LCC ML419.N58 W45 2017 | DDC 786.9/166092 [B] --dc23
LC record available at https://lccn.loc.gov/2017017453

www.backbeatbooks.com

CONTENTS

CONTENTS

FOREWORD

Going to art school in New York City in the seventies introduced me to lots of things, amongst them: Eric Emerson and the Magic Tramps, Urban chaos, and the New York Dolls. The first time I saw them was when I went to the Mercer Arts Center to see Eric and the Tramps open for them. I quickly realized the Dolls were the Lower East Side's own version of the Stones in that they were locally ubiquitous. But they also reflected that same rebellion I'd embraced as a kid growing up in Brooklyn: loud, longhaired, intelligent, and antiestablishment. They were raw, but they were still great and, most of all, familiar. After their first drummer Billy Murcia died, people thought they were gone forever. But they returned with a ringer on drums—Jerry! Everyone knew that now they'd get a record deal. But once I saw that cover, I grew skeptical about their immediate possibilities, regardless of how good the record was. The cover, a shot of the Doll's in semi drag, was too strong for the time. It only took Mötley Crüe and Whitesnake another ten years to make any money off a reworking of the Dolls' style. But the Dolls were bigger than that, opening a door for the rest of us to walk through. Jerry was part of that excitement, and this book gives us a little glimpse into what it was like to live through. Sadly, he didn't make it through to the other side, but his legacy is still with us.

Chris Stein
2017

PART I
BLAME IT ON MOM

 BABY TALK

IT'S THE SUMMER OF 1980 AND AN AVOCADO-GREEN MID-'70S station wagon is lumbering down a nondescript American highway in the dead of night. It's dragging a black trailer behind it, filled with guitars, drums, a stand-up bass, and luggage for eight; three roadies, a bass player, a singer, two guitarists, and a drummer. Half of those in the vehicle are under twenty-five, and all are under thirty except for the drummer. He's been through hell and back the last few years, living a junkie's life of lying, sometimes stealing, and playing shitty gigs just to make the rent, but at one time he was living the sweet life—limousines, champagne, cameras flashing, women, and drugs. Lots of drugs. He still has a way with women, there's no denying that, even to the women's dismay. Junkie romance rarely ends well.

On top of his morning dose of methadone, he shot a speedball—a heroin and cocaine cocktail—after the evening's gig. He's now in fine fettle for the long drive to the next city.

No one else in the station wagon is having fun though. The band is always moving—they can never stick around for the pretty girls and after-show parties. They have to pack up quickly and get out on the road to arrive in the next town early enough to hit the methadone clinic before it closes. Clinics are early-morning affairs, a musician's nightmare, but if your drummer is a heroin addict, you don't have much choice.

But the drummer doesn't mind the summer heat, or the close quarters, which accentuate the wafting body odors. He's floating on opiated air with an additional cocaine kick, leaving him as tight as a snare drum.

But when he's high and happy, he likes to talk. Sometimes he might talk about his old band, the New York Dolls—they were legends, legit punk rock originals—or Johnny Thunders, Richard Hell, or the other Heartbreakers. That was his family, dysfunctional as it might have been.

He can share stories about everyone in New York: Debbie Harry, Willy DeVille, Dee Dee Ramone, most anyone who ever played Max's Kansas City or CBGB. He was on the notorious Anarchy tour, with the Sex Pistols and the Clash. He can tell you stories about being in street gangs and watching people get stabbed to death, making a zip gun from a car aerial, or a hypodermic needle from a paper clip and a ballpoint pen, prison style. He loves talking about seeing Elvis Presley and his original trio, or Eddie Cochran, or Little Richard, or the trips he made to the Brooklyn Paramount to see Alan Freed's rock 'n' roll shows with his childhood pal Peter Criss, from Kiss. He can talk about living in Detroit with leather-clad glam queen Suzi Quatro and her family, or dating Bette Midler in New York. He's met Jimi Hendrix and Marc Bolan, and he even carries a scrapbook of photos with him that includes his most prized possession, a photo of him as a boy with his lifelong idol, Gene Krupa.

His name is Jerry Nolan. He is the ultimate New Yorker: wisecracking, cocky, confident, streetwise, moody, hip, and one of the greatest drummers in the history of the sport. His life has been one of largesse and legend. He used to be a contender.

* * *

JERRY NOLAN'S LEGACY REVELS IN MYTH.

He was born in Manhattan, May 7, 1946, at 895 West End Avenue, in the building where his father worked as superintendent. Jerry also had an older brother, Billy, and an older sister named Rose.

Their father, William Sr., also known as Billy, had other jobs besides being the building super. As many did during the Depression, he gravitated toward any opportunity to make a few extra dollars, honest or otherwise.

During the Prohibition years of 1920 to 1933, speakeasies flourished in New York. On weekends, after he'd spent the bulk of his time selling fruits and vegetables from a horse-drawn wagon, Billy bartended at a speakeasy in the Canarsie area of Brooklyn, where his wife-to-be, Jerry's mother, Charlotte lived.

"They had them beer rackets every Saturday night," Charlotte recalls. "I loved ballroom dancing and so did he. So . . . I saw him quite often."

Charlotte was born Charlotte Beers in Williamsburg, Brooklyn, in 1914, and grew up in the area between Scholes Street and Ten Eyck, an area primarily made up of two-family houses. Williamsburg is now the epicenter of hipster cool, but back then it was mostly a Hasidic enclave peppered with European immigrants. Her mother's family were Irish, her father's Anglo-Saxon. Her husband, William Nolan, was also Irish.

Jerry Nolan got his first taste of ignominy before he was even born: William was not actually Jerry's father. Jerry's son John tells the tale: "[Charlotte] was with several different people. The man who raised Jerry was not actually his biological father." Jerry's friend Luke Harris recalls Jerry telling him that his biological father was a "hustler."

Charlotte's side of the family was musically inclined. Her mother enjoyed singing, and her father was a self-taught piano, guitar, and mandolin player. Like his grandparents, baby Jerry showed an interest in music—and had no interest in his toys, not even a toy drum. "He threw it aside," Charlotte said. "Ya know what he done? He took my pots and pans! Even though he was [barely] walking, he knew the difference. He had my big pot that I would cook a ham in. And he would have another pot that I'd cook potatoes in and then another one with vegetables. He knew that there was a different sound in each pot. It didn't pay me to buy him any toys. His father would come home with a new toy once a week or so. He didn't want it. Just my pots and pans. And when he was able to walk . . . I had no pots and pans. Even my frying pan!"

Even banging on her cookware, little Jerry was the apple of his mother's eye. He could do no wrong as far as she was concerned, and he quickly realized that she was the only one that he could depend on. Her husband was an alcoholic, and prone to fits of abusive rage and violence, which led to the couple's divorcing by the time Jerry was six.

Charlotte wanted the children to stay with her. Her husband wanted the children too—but only "his" children. They went with him, except for Jerry, who moved with Charlotte back to Williamsburg.

In the years since Charlotte had left Williamsburg, it had changed mostly for the better. Depression-era public housing projects had replaced crumbling old buildings, providing a step up the economic ladder for immigrants, many exiting the crowded tenements of Manhattan's Lower East Side. With the Williamsburg Bridge allowing easy access to Manhattan, and local industries like the Domino Sugar factory, the Brooklyn Navy Yard, and the Brooklyn Eastern District Terminal providing plentiful employment, Williamsburg in the early 1950s offered good middle-class opportunities.

But the era also saw a challenge to that stability: Street gangs started appearing in Williamsburg and the surrounding areas. Different ethnic groups had their own gangs: Puerto Ricans had the Mau Maus and the Hellburners; the Italians had the Sand Street Angels; the Jokers were both Irish and Polish; blacks had the Bishops, the Robins, and the Fort Greene Chaplains.

Each gang had their own style of clothing. According to Paul Kendall in his book *50 Years of West Side Story: The Real Gangs of New York*, "Many had special sweaters which featured their gang's insignia—such as a crimson 'MM' for the Mau Maus—on the breast. The Beavers . . . favoured black, felt hats, for example, while the Tiny Tims wore blue berets."[1] Marlon Brando's iconic character in the 1953 film *The Wild One* made leather jackets and Levi's a more common choice for gang members. Kendall continues: "Hair was meticulously brushed into a pompadour and the whole gang culture was influenced heavily by bebop and rock 'n' roll. Fighting was known as 'bopping,' and walking 'bop style' meant to walk with a swagger, swinging your shoulders and hips."[2]

Gangs provided community and family for their young members. They were easily identifiable groups whose members looked out for one another, defending their territory, and each other, to the death, looking cool all the while. Jerry, while too young to join a gang, took notice, picking up style tips and affectations that stayed with him throughout his life.

Brother Billy continued to visit Jerry and his mother when he could, taking Jerry out to Coney Island and teaching him to play stickball. After joining the merchant marines and moving to New England, Billy saw less of Jerry. After 1968 he never saw Jerry again, but by the end of 1955, sister Rose had decided to move back in with Jerry and his mother. Little Jerry was now surrounded by two loving women.

Charlotte worked as a switchboard operator at the Hotel Astor on Broadway and Forty-Fifth Street in Manhattan. These were the days when telephone calls in and out of hotels were routed manually by an operator who connected callers through a bank of wires and jacks. Hotels also offered personal services to guests, including valet service. It was here that Jerry got his first job, assisting the valet and learning to sew clothing.

Charlotte soon met her second husband, an army sergeant named William Gray, also known as Billy. After the pair married in Brooklyn, Sergeant Gray prepared to ship out for Pearl Harbor on the Hawaiian island of Oahu, where he'd been stationed since March 1955. Charlotte, Rose, and Jerry met him a few months later in their new home in Pearl City in Honolulu.

Jerry was ambivalent about moving, even to Hawaii. As far as he was concerned, life in Brooklyn was fine. His mother spoiled him rotten and he had friends, including a kid from down the street named Peter

Criscuola, another future rock-star drummer—later he'd be known as Peter Criss, the "Catman" who played the drums in Kiss. Jerry and Peter were like family. Said Charlotte of Peter, "I practically brought him up. Peter loved me as a mother and loved Jerry as a brother."

As adolescents, the pair were not particularly interested in music. Said lifelong friend and saxophone player Buddy Bowzer, "At this point, neither one of these cats were really serious about playing any music or . . . drums." Music was on the radio but so was *The Lone Ranger* and *Amos 'n' Andy*. Fantasizing about cowboys or motorcycles was more important to them than music.

Jerry's new family—the Grays—lived a picturesque life in Pearl City. Unlike in New York, the weather was always warm and the pace was slow. Jerry tried to fit in by getting a crew cut, but he was still an outsider. Knowing this, his stepfather pursued shared interests to ease the boy's loneliness. According to Buddy, "Jerry was a marksman [and] a member of a gun club." Jerry won awards and commendations for his marksmanship.

His sister Rose was also a gun enthusiast, described as an "Annie Oakley type." But shooting guns wasn't the only thing on her mind. Rose, who Jerry claimed was in a gang during the time they spent in Williamsburg, was into rock 'n' roll, and took Jerry to see his first concert, which featured Frankie Lymon and the Teenagers.

Now Rose had fallen for a new singer, with dark, greasy hair, sideburns, and dance steps that drove girls wild. Jerry was curious and listened to his records. His name was Elvis Presley.

On November 11, 1957, Elvis performed at the Schofield Barracks' Conroy Bowl, also known as the Boxing Bowl, in Honolulu. Off-duty soldiers used the facility to watch boxing matches, roller derbies, and basketball games as well as movies and concerts. Bob Hope's famous USO shows made stops there in 1950 and '57 (and later in 1971). Now, the singer Rose and Jerry had seen on TV and in films was coming to their town.

Jerry and Rose waited in line all day to sit as close as they could to Elvis, ending up in the first few rows. This watershed moment was an epiphany for Jerry, who would grow starry-eyed speaking about it throughout his life. Jerry could recount the details of Elvis's clothing, from the stitching of his shirt to the type of shoes he sported, and even the way he wore his belt. He remembered the impact it made on his sister, who was overwhelmed by Elvis in a way that Jerry had never witnessed before. Elvis made her crazy.

Jerry was also taken by a hole in the sole of Elvis's shoe, and spoke of feeling pity for Elvis, as if the singer were poor. Elvis had grown up poor, but by the time Jerry saw the twenty-two-year-old perform, he was anything but, selling twenty-five million records, appearing in several successful films, and commanding concert appearance fees in the five-figure category. Elvis was a millionaire.

But even at eleven, Jerry may have seen through to the core of Elvis: a poor boy at heart, alone in a world where a celebrity can never truly know if someone loves him for who he really is. After losing his father and siblings in Brooklyn, along with his Brooklyn friends, Jerry was lonely. Elvis made him feel less so.

Deep-seated feelings about Elvis influenced Jerry throughout his life, as evidenced by his love of clothes, his love of music, and his desire to rise above his difficult beginnings and be someone—someone who wasn't alone.

Charlotte returned to New York periodically to see her son Billy and her extended family. Jerry came along, checking in with his friend Peter. With Rose, the two boys made forays to the Brooklyn Paramount and the Fox Theatre to catch Alan Freed's rock 'n' roll revues. They saw Eddie Cochran, Bo Diddley, Chuck Berry, Dion and the Belmonts, and Little Richard. Seeing these early rock 'n' rollers had a profound impact on Jerry, which he would refer to again and again throughout his life.

All of these performers impressed Jerry not only with their music but with their presentation. Like Elvis, whom he saw in '57, they all dressed immaculately and were impeccably coiffed. And, like Elvis, they all seemed like real people. The gap-toothed Bo and Bronx-born Dion could just as well have been kids he went to school with a few years before.

Jerry never acclimated to Hawaii. Charlotte and Billy loved it, but Charlotte recalled that Jerry felt there was "no activity there." But, as for most military families, home was temporary. Soon it would be time to ship out for new "exotic" surroundings: Fort Sill, in Lawton, Oklahoma.

* * *

NATIVE AMERICAN CULTURE WAS PERVASIVE IN LAWTON, WHICH had been inhabited by members of the Wichita and Caddo tribes for over a thousand years. The city was named for Major General Henry W. Lawton, who, as quartermaster at Fort Sill, had taken part in tracking down the great Apache leader Geronimo.

Lawton was fortunate in that its proximity to Fort Sill kept its economy stable through the difficult years of the Depression. But, with a population of sixty thousand, compared to bustling New York, it was dullsville.

By now, Jerry was emulating rock 'n' roll musicians, styling his dirty-blond hair in a greasy, exaggerated pompadour, and dressing in New York "hep cat" clothing. But Lawton wasn't cosmopolitan New York. His pompadour and clothing made him an outsider, ridiculed by the locals.

To raise Jerry's spirits, his mother bought him a gift. Recalling his joy in playing pots and pans, she found a "fella that had a drum set but gave it up. He kept the bass drum. I couldn't afford drums at that time so I gave Jerry this big bass drum. And Jerry added cymbals to it."

Jerry managed to find other abandoned drums, cobbling together his first drum set and trying to play by imitating what he heard on the radio and records. But just banging along to the radio wasn't cutting it. He needed someone to teach him the basics. Keeping an eye out for anyone to show him how to play properly, he spied someone at a local high school football game—a soldier named Otis, who would beat on a drum to cheer on fans of the local team, the Dragons. Jerry befriended Otis, sitting by him at every game, absorbing all he could about drumming. Otis would let him bang on his drum whenever the Dragons scored, and gave him rudimentary lessons in his barracks. They were an odd pair, not only because of the age difference, but because Otis was black. To Jerry though, it made no difference. To him, Otis was a god.[†]

Buddy Bowzer later described a local Lawton drummer, very likely Jerry's Otis. "We heard about this one drummer. He was a rock 'n' roll star . . . in all the surrounding area because he was the best drummer of all the drummers that played in these rock 'n' roll bands. They'd have football games, and after the game, they would have a big rock 'n' roll hop, a teen hop. This one cat was like a James Dean on the drums. He kicked ass on his drums, and plus he kicked ass when he got off the drums. If somebody tried to jump him, he's jumping them! I told Jerry about this guy. So Jerry went out to meet him and naturally got jumped by a bunch of fucking punks, because his hair was too long."

---

† Jerry claimed he met Otis in Hawaii. However, research uncovered only one Hawaiian high school football team named the Dragons, a team from the Honokaa area on Hawaii's "Big Island," more than 180 miles from Pearl City. As Honokaa is on a completely different island, and high school football teams traveled by bus, it would be impossible for them to get to the island of Oahu, where Pearl City was. However, the city of Purcell, Oklahoma, a little over 80 miles from Lawton, also had a high school football team named the Dragons. It seems reasonable for a team to travel two hours by bus for a weekend football game, making Lawton, Oklahoma, the more likely place where Jerry met Otis.

Life was tough for Jerry. He was the new kid at school with a strange haircut. He didn't excel academically or in sports. "He's got a bad attitude," said Buddy. "He's got this big pompadour, and nobody likes him. With his . . . New York attitude, he wasn't gonna get too far in this hick town. He was always getting . . . in and out of fights left and right."

Being an outsider at school led to playing hooky. As Jerry told author Nina Antonia: "I used to play hooky a lot, and one day . . . *The Gene Krupa Story* was playing in this theater in Lawton, Oklahoma. I went in at twelve o'clock when it opened, and I stayed and came out at twelve o'clock at night. It totally changed my life."[3]

In 1961, as a student of Lawton's Central Junior High School, Jerry joined the school marching band. Though he might play a marching drum, he was often relegated to playing cymbals due to his inability to read musical notation. The times where the cymbals crashed were more obvious to a musical neophyte. This is where another army brat, Buddy Bowzer (then known as Otis Dupree), first took notice of him. The band director also took notice, and didn't like what he saw.

Buddy: "[Jerry] had this Brooklyn accent, and he came on like a tough guy, chewing gum on the bandstand." The band director "told him to put the gum on his nose and stand in the corner. When Jerry refused . . . he kicked him out of the school band."

Buddy liked that Jerry stood up to an authority figure. After packing up his saxophone, Buddy asked Jerry if he wanted to help him form a "rock 'n' roll, rhythm and blues band." Jerry agreed. They called themselves the Strangers.

With Buddy on tenor saxophone, the struggling novices began figuring out what to play and how to play it. They also had to figure out what to wear.

They perused magazines for the coolest threads and tried finding them in Lawton. It wasn't always possible. They had two ways of acquiring clothing. One was "to go down to the store that sold to black folk, and white folk inclined," said Buddy. But mostly, "in order to get anything that was stylish, you had to order that. They had catalogs." And of course, Jerry's mother would come through with a check.

"Number one, we had to have pointed-toe shoes," recalled Buddy. "They had perforated ones, [and] they had plain ones with fancy little somethins on the side." As for his jacket, Jerry found what Buddy called a "profiling jacket. It's a leather jacket. It's casual, not like a suit jacket. But it's got knitted sleeves on the side, and a nice high collar. It's pure Elvis, [a] 1950s outdoor jacket with knitted accessories."

As for the music, there was an unexpected source: jazz.

Fort Sill had the United Service Organizations (USO) as a resource, where veterans and their families could play pool or read magazines. Buddy and Jerry used it to borrow records and musical instruments. They loved listening to Benny Goodman's "Sing, Sing, Sing," with Gene Krupa on drums. "People go, 'You guys came up doing that rock 'n' roll, man.' No, we came up studying jazz. Cozy Cole, Gene Krupa, man!"

Continuing their jazz instruction, Jerry and Buddy had another impactful experience when Louis Armstrong and his band came to town. Buddy: "His whole band is decked out! They're all in tuxedos with patent-leather shoes on, bow ties, the whole bit, man! And not only are they looking cool, these guys are kicking ass onstage."

The lesson the boys learned was that in music, "if you want a career, you better go onstage fuckin' looking good."

* * *

THE GRAYS WERE DOING WELL, LIVING IN A SIMPLE BUT NEWER three-bedroom, one-bath home off base at 609 Glendale Drive. Sergeant Gray drove a brand-new metallic red Pontiac station wagon, which he parked in the driveway, allowing the boys the garage for rehearsals. After they told the sergeant that they wanted to record themselves, he came up with a tape recorder. Additionally, Buddy's dad gave them the use of a Quonset hut. The Strangers now had their very own recording studio.

Still, despite his revelation after seeing *The Gene Krupa Story*, Jerry was less committed to music than Buddy was. He wanted a motorcycle. Buddy was having none of it, telling him he needed to get a new set of drums instead. "He was playing on some John Philip Sousa's marching band tubs. You could barely see his head over the fuckin' bass drum."

Jerry was persuaded, but, like clothing, drums also had to be ordered through a catalog. "We used to look at the [catalog] every night in his house. We'd pick out . . . each drum separately and ordered the whole set." The boys chose a set of red Slingerland drums. It combined two things: the color of Sergeant Gray's station wagon, and the brand Gene Krupa played.

And, as with the cool threads, Mom was left to figure out how to pay the bill. A local music store ordered the chosen drums, and Charlotte paid on an installment plan.

The Strangers continued rehearsing for their first gig at a school assembly, adding a second tenor sax player named Junior Candelaria, a Puerto Rican neighbor of Jerry's. The threesome's entire repertoire consisted of the instrumental hits "Night Train" by Buddy Morrow and

"Swingin' Shepherd Blues" by the Moe Koffman Septet. Buddy described the band as "a rock 'n' roll, bebop kind of a thing."

Although Central Junior High was integrated, much of Lawton was not. Whether it was the desperation of a lonely teenager, or just happenstance, Jerry, a white kid of Irish descent, had for his musical compatriots a black kid and a Puerto Rican kid. In 1961, and in Lawton, Oklahoma, this must have been shocking. But, in a dynamic that would reappear throughout his life, Jerry's dedication to his band and bandmates was total. "A band should be as tight as a fist" was a phrase he offered to anyone who would listen. It was like a gang. A family.

Jerry's adherence to this ethic was demonstrated one hot summer day when Jerry and Buddy wanted to cool off with some ice cream. Pooling their few pennies, they put their order in at the local ice cream shop, only to find that the proprietor would only serve Jerry, not his black friend. Just like the school band director who Jerry refused to bow down to, Jerry told the clerk to stick his ice cream where the sun didn't shine. In Jerry's mind, that was what friends did for one another.

Jerry's life as an outsider continued. He'd pursue his own path, wearing the clothes he wanted, playing the music he wanted, and having the friends he wanted. But then everything changed, with a single school assembly. Sixteen-year-old Jerry was already feeling his youthful hormones and fell for a girl in his math class named Kathy Brill. He wanted to ask her to the prom but was too shy. He told Nina Antonia:

> She used to have this beautiful hairstyle . . . teased up in the back, and an extremely exaggerated DA. She looked like Kim Novak with black hair and I was shy and nervous because of my grades.
>
> Finally, I learned to play a full set of drums and we played the school assembly talent show. We tore the place up. Buddy said, "Let's go in the hallway and get a drink of water," so we went in and everyone was coming up to us, saying it was great. That changed my whole life. I wasn't ashamed anymore, I could finally do something real good . . . and that girl, Kathy, I got her for a girlfriend.

Now Jerry was committed. He gained self-esteem, confidence, and a girlfriend. Music gave those things to him.[4]

* * *

JERRY AND BUDDY DECIDED THEY NEEDED TO ADD GUITARS TO their sound. Buddy found someone who was into Bo Diddley, describing him as a "country boy." The only issue was, he was on crutches due to polio. Neither Buddy nor Jerry cared. "So we bring this cripple guy onstage with us along with another hillbilly. . . . We were a big hit in junior high school, and word started getting on out. Then we went on a couple of TV shows. We're barely into our teens."

Buddy also credits the guitarist's Bo Diddley fixation with Jerry learning another skill: the syncopated Bo Diddley drum beat. As far as Jerry was concerned, it was just another version of Gene Krupa's part on "Sing, Sing, Sing," which he played over and over in the USO. "That was our theme song," said Buddy. Even twenty years after its release, the raw "jungle beat" still resonated with Jerry.

Jerry began to play with other groups in Lawton, instrumental combos with names like the Naturals and the Vibetones. Still, the Strangers with his pal Buddy was his favorite.

Jerry kept in touch with his Williamsburg pal Peter Criscuola, telling him tales of the Strangers and their "success," his pal Buddy, and his girlfriend Kathy. Jerry's newfound joy was infectious. Buddy: "[Peter] came to Oklahoma and hung out for a while. When he came back to Brooklyn, he got himself a set of drums."

Jerry had gone from sad loner to happy and popular. A few years before, he'd been abandoned by his father and left with no siblings. He was an army brat with few friends, with all the loneliness and loss that accompanies constantly being the new kid in town. He had now found himself. As he told Nina Antonia: "The whole idea, the way musicians looked in books, made me feel like 'Wow!' There's something more to music than just being a musician."[5]

TEENAGE NEWS

2

FOR THE FIRST TIME IN FIVE YEARS, JERRY WAS HAPPY AND CONTENT. He had friends, a girlfriend, a band that played gigs, and a beautiful red Slingerland drum kit. He was wearing the clothes he craved, and had hair like a teen idol. He had a mom who'd give him the world, a step-dad who went the extra mile for him, and a loving sister. Life was good.

His mother had different issues though. Sergeant Gray had a few secrets. One was drinking. The other was knitting. "I never knew it!" Charlotte confessed, "until one night he got really drunk and he started beating on me [with knitting needles] and I called the MPs." It became too much and she left, taking Jerry and Rose with her back to New York.

Having finally come around to liking Oklahoma, Jerry now had to leave. For him, this was as big a letdown as a sixteen-year-old could experience. He'd just learned to trust a father figure after being abandoned by the first.

The family's first stop after Oklahoma was an apartment in Sunnyside, Queens, on Fortieth Street between Queens Boulevard and Forty-Seventh Avenue. Jerry decided to check out the new neighborhood and happened upon a fourteen-year-old neighborhood girl named Corinne Healy. "He was so cute and good-looking . . . and he had a good sense of humor." She would be Jerry's main squeeze for the next ten years.

"In 1962 I was fourteen," recalled Corinne. "He was sixteen." While Jerry hadn't been to church since his first Communion in 1953, Corinne attended St. Michael Academy on West Thirty-Third Street in Manhattan, where Jerry would whistle to her from the street below. "A couple of the nuns thought that was fun and cute. We were sweet." The nuns weren't as pleased with the ankle bracelet Jerry bought Corinne, though, telling her not to wear it to school. When she did, they took it away until the end of the school year. "I was a very defiant girl."

His birthday was May 7, and hers was May 8. "He could never forget mine, and I could never forget his." By early 1963, they were a steady couple of teenage lovers, choosing as their song "He's So Fine" by the Chiffons.

While Jerry was happy to find a girlfriend, Charlotte's concern was supporting her family. She quickly found two jobs, working nine to five as an office clerk and then, from seven to one, back at the Hotel Astor switchboard. These two jobs paid for a homier spot than the Sunnyside apartment: a four-bedroom, two-bath duplex in East Brooklyn at 189 Pine Street. There was plenty of room for all of them, plus Jerry's drum set. But Jerry could only store his drums there—or pose for pictures with them. Per Charlotte, "We never were able to have him practice in the house. I would have to pay different stores that would let them kids go in at night and play."

Now, someone else wanted to move in—one of the only male "someones" (he also trusted Peter) Jerry felt he could trust: Buddy. His dad was transferring to Okinawa and, as at Fort Sill, blacks had to live on base. Base life didn't come close to offering the comforts the Nolans enjoyed in their off-base home. Buddy decided he wanted to live off base too . . . in New York, with Jerry.

Jerry got the go-ahead from his mom and was overjoyed.

Buddy: "Little did they know . . . the neighborhood wouldn't allow it."

Charlotte was beside herself: "My landlord called me and told me, 'You have to get rid of him.' He was black . . . and they were Italians." She didn't know how to tell Jerry, but reluctantly, she did.

Buddy: "Jerry couldn't deal with it because he never dealt with anything like that. The only thing we dealt with was our goddamn ice cream in Oklahoma."

In the previous decade, over 165,000 blacks had moved into Brooklyn, while 280,000 whites departed. "White flight" to the suburbs was in full swing. Many landlords withheld tenancy from blacks for fear it would lower property values or rental income. This was the milieu Buddy, Jerry, and Charlotte were caught up in.

Buddy found a job, and a coworker let him room with him uptown in Harlem. Buddy and the Nolans acquiesced as a matter of survival. As a result, both Jerry and Buddy lost another layer of their youthful innocence.

With his best pal up in Harlem, Jerry spent more time with his old Brooklyn companion Peter. Like Jerry, Peter started playing drums on an old beat-up, hand-me-down set, which he purchased from his boss at a butcher shop, working off the debt over time. Unlike Jerry, he didn't have an Otis to teach him the basics. That was Jerry's job. They would play face-to-face, with Peter attempting to match Jerry's every move. As Peter was a righty and Jerry a lefty, sometimes they'd set up side by side, sharing a floor tom.

Peter credits Jerry with not only giving him his first lessons, but also pushing him forward through sheer jealousy. Said Peter, "My father thought he was like Gene Krupa. . . . He'd go 'Jerry this' and 'Jerry that.' I was so jealous that he thought Jerry was better than me."[1]

Meanwhile, Buddy was finding New York less welcoming. He heard from his father that his dad was being shipped out to Indonesia and was going to receive better treatment befitting an officer, in off-base housing. Off Buddy went, leaving even more bonding time for Jerry and Peter.

* * *

IN 1959, 335 AMERICAN RADIO DISC JOCKEYS ADMITTED TO TAKING money in exchange for playing particular songs on their radio programs. Among those caught up in what was to become known as the radio payola scandal was Alan Freed, credited as the first white DJ to popularize rock 'n' roll music. After Freed lost his popular radio and TV slots, Murray the K became the hot DJ in New York. Like Freed, he hosted his own rock 'n' roll shows in New York theaters from 1960 through 1967. Jerry and Peter recalled attending various Murray the K shows featuring Jan and Dean, Dionne Warwick, the Crystals, the Ronettes, and "Little" Stevie Wonder.

Like Jerry, Peter was also drawn to gangs. However, it was really about self-preservation. If you weren't in a gang, you were on your own, getting robbed or beaten up. The Phantom Lords became Jerry and Peter's gang. But first they had to serve an apprenticeship as Young Lords.

"We were really like wannabes,"[2] said Peter. "They let us fight next to them, but we weren't as badass as these Puerto Rican guys."[3]

Each of them saw their share of knife fights and learned how to create their own makeshift firearms from car aerials or rubber bands called zip guns. With their attention turning to girls, the gangs became less interested in fighting and more interested in their clothing.

As different styles took hold during the '60s, the sea change was reflected in the clothing worn by Jerry and the other members of his gang. He later told the *Village Voice*'s Doug Simmons, "At first my gang were greasers, but then we started wearing suits."[4]

The greasy pompadour was gone, replaced by a parted and fluffy style. But if a gang member's hair wasn't done just right, he might wear a porkpie hat, with a thin, "stingy" brim. Sometimes they'd wear trench coats and carry umbrellas, regardless of whether rain was expected or not. Continental suits with narrow lapels, often with black velvet collars and skintight pants, were preferred. The same suited style had been employed by pop stars Dion and the Belmonts, whose lead singer, Dion DiMucci, was a member of the Bronx-based gang the Fordham Baldies. Sometimes their shoes had buckles but they were always pointed. They too were called Continental. A few years later, both the suits and the ankle-high version of the boots without buckles would be worn by the Beatles.

Jerry hid his gang activity from his mother and girlfriend Corinne, who swore, "He was never in a gang. They used to have a place called the Bamboo Lounge, and it was like a storefront. People just hung out and they played nice music. The Paragons and the Jesters. You know . . . *grinding* music."

The Bamboo Lounge, which Peter recalled as Club Gentlemen, was a rented storefront paid for by members' dues and jukebox income, conveniently supplied by the mob, who gladly got their piece of the pie. Said Peter, "Jerry designed a logo with a top hat, a cane, and two white gloves."[5]

They'd black out the windows and leave a small peephole in the door through which members could be identified. A little paint and a few couches, and presto, you had a social club. After contributing to the Police Athletic League (PAL), the boys got a PAL sticker to put in the window, giving the police the impression they were good, wholesome youngsters. The reality was a little different. As Jerry told Pete Frame in 1977, "We could sniff glue, smoke pot and fuck bitches in the cellar."[6]

Peter and Jerry would pool their money to buy one-dollar joints from someone they called "the Dirty Swede," smoking them in the club's basement. "Immediately that eerie smell would hit you and you knew you were doing something forbidden. You feared that you might get addicted and get into heroin: All that propaganda was out then. I didn't even get high the first time we did it, but the second time was the charm. Jerry and I just laughed and ate a million Twinkies and listened to the jukebox. Music had never sounded so good before."[7]

As for the "bitches," Jerry's main squeeze was still Corinne, but he wasn't always faithful. Corinne: "I wasn't the jealous type. I know he probably cheated on me. . . . It didn't bother me, because he was coming home to me."

While Jerry enjoyed the social club scene and dreamed of becoming a musician, he still had a future to think about. His mother convinced him to pursue his other great interest, fashion.

Corinne recalled when he entered New York's High School of Fashion Industries. "He was always ahead of his time when it came to clothes. People would be into something; he was on to the next thing."

Despite being surrounded by fashion and acquiring skills he would call upon throughout his life, the regimentation of school was still too stifling for Jerry. He left Fashion Industries and decided to enter another pursuit. Charlotte: "I put him through barber school thinkin' that's what he wanted. It cost me a lotta money for his uniforms and his scissors."

Corinne saw it as something Charlotte wanted more than Jerry. "His mother made him [do it] so he would have some kind of a trade. But he hated it." Charlotte realized with a hint of resignation that this was not the life for her little Jerry: "He didn't want people to tell him what to do. So that was the end of barberin'."

Corinne: "He could do anything creative, but he just wanted to be a musician and that was it. I envied that about him because he knew from the time I met him what he wanted to do."

With both boys now in full pursuit of lives as professional musicians, Peter depended on Jerry's fashion sense to help him look like a musician. "We knew that image was everything, so we'd sit in front of a tanning lamp, then give ourselves facials with the creams and lotions that Jerry had. . . . He'd razor-cut my hair. We looked like two gigolos!"[8]

"Our first love was jazz. We'd dress up in our three-piece suits and slick back our hair and go to the Village Vanguard to see people like [Dave] Brubeck and [Charles] Mingus and [Thelonius] Monk . . . Miles Davis and Cal Tjader."[9]

Both boys felt without question that the greatest jazz drummer of all was Gene Krupa. They would have given anything to meet the master himself. As usual, Charlotte was there to give her Jerry just what he wanted.

Krupa had a regular gig at the Metropole Cafe on Seventh Avenue and Forty-Ninth Street in Manhattan. The windows of the club were wide-open, so passerby could hear the music and see the band. Charlotte made a point of bringing Jerry to the Metropole to not only see and hear Gene but to meet him.

"We used to go to the Metropole," said Charlotte, "and stand outside because Jerry was under age to go in. So this here man that I was with knew him and hollered . . . from outside. So Gene, when he got through, he came out and he invited us up to his room. So of course, Jerry was thrilled. We had a picture taken of Jerry and Gene. So we became friends."

Gene, wearing patent-leather shoes and a silver-gray iridescent suit drenched in sweat, talked drums with Jerry. The accomplished drummer told Jerry he could come talk to him anytime he wanted. Jerry went back multiple times and started bringing Peter with him.

According to Peter, they were like groupies, but without the sex. The two of them "would bother Gene to show us whatever he could. 'Drum Boogie,' 'Sing, Sing, Sing.' Then it would be 'Tell us stories: What was it like to play with Benny Goodman, Teddy Wilson, and Lionel Hampton?' He was amazed that these young guys knew about this stuff. Now and then we'd get there early and he'd show us a couple of cool licks and we'd go home and try to play them. Then we'd go back—we were a couple of pains in the butt—and he'd show us more."[10]

These one-on-one lessons were the equivalent of a master class in drumming. But watching from the street, they would see a show that only Gene could put on; the way he'd move his arms, often raising them above his head for visual effect, almost telegraphing the musical accent to come; hunching his shoulders when playing quieter tones, then darting upright to announce an upcoming sound explosion; rearing back, like a pitcher winding up to throw a fastball, while blasting out a snare drum roll; bobbing his head, chin extended, deeply entranced by the music.

In addition to grasping a sense of stagecraft and theatricality from Gene, Jerry also found inspiration. Gene was just a normal guy, who dressed and played great, but he could have a conversation with you, making you feel like he was your pal. He was an approachable god. If a "normal" guy like Gene could be successful, then it was reasonable to think that Jerry could too.

Corinne: "Jerry never wanted to do anything but play drums. There's actors . . . they'll wait tables and stuff like that. He didn't want to do any of that."

* * *

JERRY'S PURSUIT OF STARDOM WAS NOT WITHOUT ITS interruptions and false starts. It was 1965, and American involvement in the Vietnam War intensified, with troop commitments growing from 16,000 in January to over 180,000 by year's end. Peter and Jerry were both over eighteen and eligible for the draft.

To avoid conscription, the pair concocted a host of stories, including that they were gay or junkies, supposedly pricking their arms with pins as evidence of heroin use. Neither ruse was needed. Peter got out due to his flat feet. As his brother Billy was a merchant marine, Jerry was the only son living with his single mother, and deemed safe. Corinne: "I remember Charlotte writing to the service. God forbid, the love of her life would have to go."

Despite constantly asking her for money, Jerry could do no wrong in his mother's eyes. He understood he possessed the ability to manipulate her for his own means. Elvera Bakas, a friend of Jerry's since his days living in Williamsburg, said, "He was always bothering her for money. He never held down a full-time job his whole life. Never." Corinne remembered, "He got to sleep all day. . . . He wouldn't even soak a dish."

Charlotte, though annoyed at Jerry's lack of consideration for her efforts on his behalf, never wavered in her support of him. "I worked two jobs. I had no time for my kids. That's what I regret to this day. I was on my own . . . but I gave them what they wanted. When Jerry needed another new set of drums, I hadda go pay $800. I never neglected them . . . because they were good kids. I had no worryment."

Corinne: "She kind of made it worse by doting on him. He was always able to turn to her for anything. He always had this thing that women wanted to take care of him."

Yes, he could get women to do most anything for him, and perhaps that lulled him into a state of dithering procrastination at times. Jerry was no longer a teenager, though, and he needed some real motivation. What happened next would shock him into adulthood quickly. Corinne was pregnant. "We had a son together . . . John. I was nineteen when I had him."

Corinne was devastated when she realized she was pregnant. She'd lost contact with her parents, Jerry and his mom acting as her only family. Luckily, Charlotte helped her enter the Angel Guardian Home in Brooklyn, which took in orphans and offered services to unwed teenage mothers. Corinne stayed at the home for several months until the child was born on July 29, 1967. "His name was Gerard, Gerard Stephen Nolan, like Jerry, but *they* changed it to John instead. They at least kept 'Stephen.' John Stephen O'Hanlon is his birth name."

The "they" Corinne refers to were the O'Hanlons of Massapequa, Long Island, who arranged to adopt the child soon after birth.

Charlotte was against the adoption, pressuring Jerry and Corinne to keep the child. The parents-to-be were adamant in their opposition. "She thought that she would work nights, and I would work days, and we'd work something out," said Corinne. "I wanted him to have a chance of having parents and a normal life. And it worked out. I never had any regrets."

Before giving John up to his new family, Jerry, Corinne, and Peter's girlfriend Lydia DiLeonardo took the infant child to Central Park. All involved were dressed up as if it was an important occasion, Jerry wearing a double-breasted mod suit. It was the last time Jerry would ever see his only son. Just as all his "fathers" had abandoned him, Jerry was now carrying on that same, sad family tradition.

ARE YOU
3 EXPERIENCED?

JERRY NEVER WANTED TO BE IN THE POSITION OF NOT BEING ABLE to support a child again. But he also didn't want to get a straight job. He had to get busy at becoming the star he had dreamed of becoming since seeing Elvis ten years earlier.

He had finally caught on to playing Top 40 music in bar bands, and learned where all the hot spots in town were: Steve Paul's the Scene, the Cafe au Go Go, and Cafe Wha?, where Bob Dylan and Jimi Hendrix had made their marks. Jerry played them all, albeit on the low end of the professional totem pole. The clubs shifted quickly through the many styles of the era, from the twist to folk and onward, and Jerry had to keep up with whatever was the style of the day.

Jerry was very much aware of the British Invasion, but claimed to never be swept up by it. "I'm sorta before the Beatles, I'm a little too old,"[1] he declared, adding that it was "nothing new at all to me."[2] He said he "got into rhythm and blues and soul, all that 'gotta gotta,'"[3] using Otis Redding's favorite phrase to describe the music. He still preferred older-style rock 'n' roll, but his ear was to the ground for new sounds to get hip to.

In the summer of 1967, psychedelia was happening. Songs and hair were getting longer, and lapels and trouser cuffs were getting wider. One band making the transition to the new style was called the Peepl. They were previously a Top 40 cover band, playing up and down the East Coast. "We were burnt out playing Top 40 and trying to do songs with horns," said original member Joseph De Jesus. The new rock was guitar-based. This was what the Peepl wanted to do.

They were managed by Peter Glick, who later managed Looking Glass, whose 1972 hit "Brandy" hit number one. Seeing Jerry playing at the Cafe Wha? one night, Glick convinced him to audition for the Peepl, who needed a drummer. "Jerry was young," recalls De Jesus. "He was eager. He was really cool. He wasn't like us. Jerry would show up with the suit and the tie . . . squeaky clean . . . compared to the ratty guys that we were back then." While the band acquired what De Jesus described as "Gary Puckett and the Union Gap–type suits," Jerry was just fine the way he was.

In their Top 40 days, the band made a living from music. Now, trying their hand at their own thing, they barely made $10 a show. "We didn't care, because we were playing original material," said De Jesus.

Jerry's style was harder than the previous drummer, who was described by Joseph as more "light" and "airy." Joseph thought "it was perfect."

Glick got them a deal with Kama Sutra Productions, who produced sides for their own Kama Sutra Records as well as for major labels. That summer, Kama Sutra capped a fiscal year of over seven million records sold, including the Lovin' Spoonful's number-one hit "Summer in the City." All involved felt they were with the right people to turn them into stars.

The Peepl's deal was for a single, which would act as a demo for Glick to shop the band to a major label. If it had promise, they'd continue working together. The song chosen as the A side was called "Freedom." With an intro melody reminiscent of the 1962 hit "Sealed with a Kiss," the track featured chiming, twelve-string guitars, angelic vocal harmonies, and competent, if unremarkable, accompaniment from Jerry. Awash in reverb and slap-back echo, the chorus had Jerry going back and forth on his crash cymbals between drums rolls, accentuating the voices, emulating ringing bells.

The B side, "Please Take My Life," was treated as a throwaway. Overly saturated in the same effects as the A side, the song featured no vocals, as the band never got around to recording them. As was so often the case at that time, it was just something to stick onto the flip side. What stuck in De Jesus's mind about the songs was a cymbal Jerry owned. "Jerry had this huge cymbal." Joseph called it the "ocean" cymbal, "because . . . it was like "shhhhhhh, shhhhhhhhh." Laughing, he added, "That song had a lot of that cymbal."

Unable to garner any major-label interest, the record was issued on the independent Roaring Records label and went nowhere. Jerry was soon on his way, looking for bigger and better things. But there were no hard feelings. De Jesus recalled a smiling Jerry fondly: "A really happy-go-lucky guy that had the world totally in front of him."

And what was in front of him was his old friend, Buddy Bowzer, returning to New York, Buddy had played in bands touring army bases in Indonesia and Japan, making enough money to buy his own car. He was now getting lots of work in New York. "I used to play in Harlem, making steady money. . . . I was playing every day of the week." He had enough cash to treat Jerry to an occasional meal. "I'd go, 'Come on Jerry, let's have a steak,' and we'd go to Tad's steak house on Eighth Street." They'd discuss their plans to take over the music world, what they heard in the clubs and what lessons they derived from it. They were struck by an act they saw the previous year who were now back in town: the Jimi Hendrix Experience.

In the summer of 1967, the Experience played at the Scene and at the club Salvation in New York. In between, Hendrix had set his guitar on fire at the Monterey International Pop Festival and pretty much changed the world. The Experience were louder and wilder than anything Jerry and Buddy had seen before, certainly wilder than the Peepl, whose two guitars were tame in comparison to Jimi's one.

By early 1968, Jerry and Buddy were hanging out at the Scene. On any given night, they'd run into Janis Joplin, the Chambers Brothers, or Johnny Winter. One night, they bumped into Hendrix himself. Jimi had his girlfriend go over and get Jerry to come over and talk to him. He admired Jerry's red-on-red velvet suit. Jerry proudly told Jimi that he'd designed it himself.

The days of the greasy pompadour, Cuban heels, and Continental suits were gone. Not only did Jerry have the red suit Jimi loved so much, but he had long hair parted in the middle, black knee-high boots, and a Fu Manchu mustache. Times had changed, and Jerry changed with them. Corinne: "He used to call me his flower girl. It was back in the '60s, flower power. . . . We were hippies."

Jerry liked to stand out, or, as he called it, "profile." While Jimi liked his look, not everyone did. Corinne recalled, "There was such ignorance back then about long hair. He got hassled a lot." To Jerry, this was the life he chose. He didn't want to be like everyone else: A "civilian." Getting hassled was the price he had to pay to be someone special. He was tough, and anyway, all those people who hassled him would one day want to be him.

In March 1968, the Fillmore East opened on Second Avenue near East Sixth Street. Until it closed in June of 1971, it was the number one venue in New York to see concerts. Outside of the Beatles and the Stones, nearly every rock band of the day played the 2,700-seat theater. Most shows were triple bills, with two sets a night. Peter and Jerry would bring sleeping bags to get there early enough for up-front seats for groups like the Doors and the Who. It became one of their regular stomping grounds.

The Fillmore shows crammed Jerry and Buddy's heads with ideas of how they could make an impact with their own group. As they ate their steak and potatoes at Tad's, they devised a strategy. Jerry still had access to a house in upstate New York that the Peepl's management owned. Buddy recalled, "To take a bath we'd have to heat the hot water up off the stove. It was funky, but it was ours." Jerry and Buddy went there to devise a plan.

On their portable record player, they spun Albert King, the Beatles, the Rolling Stones, and Cream. These artists and Hendrix were the core of their new idea.

What they devised was a Hendrix/Cream–style power trio, but with Buddy in front as lead singer, making the band a quartet. They had a concept, but they also had a *profile*. Buddy and Jerry had the Hendrix look down pat: loud colors, long, wild hair, flowing bell bottoms, tall boots, and fringe vests.

After Jerry called in his contacts to get the house upstate, it was time for Buddy to see what he could do. He called someone he met playing at the Apollo Theater named Teddy Vann. Teddy had a long résumé in the music business as a writer and producer. Though he had been a performer himself, he was most well known as the producer and composer of the 1963 multimillion-selling hit "Loop De Loop" for Gil Hamilton, aka Johnny Thunder, not to be confused with Jerry's later musical partner, *the* Johnny Thunders. Almost thirty years later, Teddy won a Grammy for composing Luther Vandross's "The Power of Love." In between, he wrote and produced numerous sides, working with the Bobbettes, of "Mr. Lee" fame, and Estelle Bennett, who with her sister Ronnie formed two-thirds of the legendary girl group the Ronettes.

Teddy was a music business pro and could smell a new trend a mile away. Working for the legendary, mob-connected, music industry wheeler-dealer Morris Levy, he also knew something about making money in the record business. Intrigued enough by Jerry and Buddy's profile, at least, Teddy agreed to nurture the group, producing, managing, and financing them. His efforts paid off, as he acquired them a recording contract with ABC Paramount. Buddy and Jerry called their group Maximillian.

"It was me and Jerry," said Buddy. "The other two guys . . . I discovered them in Central Park." Guitarist Anthony Mojica, aka "Mojack," and seventeen-year-old bass player Moby Medina were recruited into the lineup.

Just like the Strangers back in Lawton, Maximillian were a racially integrated band. In fact, Jerry was the minority member, the rest being black or Hispanic.

The band hurriedly prepared to record. In retrospect, the rehearsals were perhaps too hurried. Their music was a mix of hard psychedelic rock and blues. The influences were apparent throughout; the multi-tempo "The Name of the Game" mimicked Hendrix's "Manic Depression"; "New Lover" aped Blue Cheer with a touch of Hendrix's "Foxy Lady"; "Kickin' 9 to 5" sounded like the Jefferson Airplane meets the Grateful Dead; "Little Amazon" alluded to Country Joe and the Fish; "Scar of My Memory" echoed Big Brother and the Holding Company; "New Lover" evoked Jethro Tull but without the flute; and "Road Rat" parroted Cream. Smatterings of Iron Butterfly and Steppenwolf could be recognized throughout the record. The difference, however, lay in the fact that all of the bands that had influenced them were successful. Maximillian were not.

The guitars, bass, and vocals blared throughout the Maximillian LP, and bore little of the craft, charm, or subtleties which the band's influences possessed. The drums stood out particularly in their dullness, especially when compared to Mitch Mitchell's sound with Hendrix. Where Mitchell's drums were tuned wide-open without dampening, in the jazz tradition, Jerry's drums were muffled and lifeless. It seemed as if no one on the session knew how to record a set of drums for the type of music Maximillian were attempting.

This failure lay at the feet of Teddy as producer. It was his job to get the best sound out of what the artist presented to him, especially young and inexperienced musicians such as Maximillian.

Teddy had little experience recording musicians playing "hard rock" like Maximillian—his previous records were purposefully light on drums while heavy on vocals, piano, and strings. The vocals and rhythm sections on those records are refined in a way that Maximillian's were not. They also displayed deep vocal harmonies, which are absent from Maximillian. Drums on his previous records were pushed way down in the mix and centered on the snare drum, which kept an almost constant two/four beat. There were almost no tom-tom flourishes or cymbal crashes. Any added backbeat was provided by handclaps, percussion, or the other members of the rhythm section.

To make matters worse, Jerry and Teddy did not get along.

Moby the bass player recalls Teddy "holding Jerry by his shirt against the wall. I'm not sure if it was racial or what, because Teddy Vann was funny about that sometimes, and Jerry wasn't having it."

While the issue of race being at the center of Jerry and Teddy's conflict was only Moby's suspicion, Teddy was involved in the black consciousness movement and described himself as "born-again African." In 1966 Teddy wrote and produced a series of radio plays called *The Adventures of Colored Man*, based on a fictional black superhero. He also released a soul/funk rewrite of "I Saw Mommy Kissing Santa Claus" called "Santa Claus Is a Black Man" in 1973. Just as Hendrix was pressured by members of the black community to have an all-black band, Jerry may have sensed the same pressures being placed on Buddy by Teddy.

But it's also possible that Teddy saw Jerry as the weak link in the band, or painted him as such, because he had no idea what to do with a hard-hitting post–Mitch Mitchell drummer.

Either way, the result was that Jerry was out of the band.

"We went to take pictures at ABC," said Moby, ". . . and Jerry was left out. It happened shortly before [the record] came out and they didn't even give him any credit."

When the record was finished, everyone got paid except Jerry. "Jerry was running around Greenwich Village without a pot to piss in, broke, living with his mom," said Buddy. The band attempted to continue without Jerry, but plans for a tour with Aretha Franklin never materialized. Maximillian were over.

After getting knocked down, Jerry planned to get back on the horse ASAP. Besides hitting the clubs looking for a gig, he put classified ads in two music papers in the spring of 1969. One was in the local *Village Voice*. The other ended up in the June 14 edition of *Rolling Stone* magazine. It read as follows: "HEAVY DRUMMER looking for original funky group. Travel. Jerry Nolan-MI 7-7523 (day), ST 4-3134 (night), 189 Pine St., Brooklyn."

While placing his own ad, Jerry checked out some of the others, coming upon one that caught his eye. He dialed the number. On the other end of the line was a young guitarist and songwriter named Tom Bakas. The two agreed to meet in Manhattan. "I met him on Eighth Street," said Tom. "And he was incredible looking because he had all these colors." Tom was three years younger than Jerry, who was now twenty-three. "When I saw him, Jerry was like a god to me. He had the look, and he was everything that I aspired to be. He had the cockiness. I was attracted to him because of his flair, not because of his drumming. His drumming came later."

Searching for additional musicians, Tom met lead guitarist Dave Halbert, who lived in Queens. Through Tommy, Dave was introduced to Jerry and bass player Gregor Laraque, a transplant from Port-au-Prince, Haiti, who'd been friends with Tom since they were kids.

Their band was called Ocean, not to be confused with the Canadian band of the same name, who had a gospel-tinged hit in 1971 called "Put

Your Hand in the Hand." "It was just pure rock 'n' roll," said Dave, "with a slight blues to it. Gregor wrote most of the tunes, and we collaborated on some."

Jerry's determination in acquiring fame and fortune was apparent to the others. Per David, "He had a far-reaching view of becoming famous. He was different than most drummers that would be in the back. He would always like to sit up in front. And Jerry was a very animated drummer."

Jerry passed along his knowledge to the others on how to dress and carry yourself like a rock star. Said Tom, "His term was 'profiling.' There is nothing more important in the world than profiling. Rain, winter, cold spell, whatever, you have to always look your best. Wear your colors and the tight pants and the whole nine yards. He was like our mentor."

In pursuit of success, Jerry took command of the band's look and style, even taking band members shopping. Said Tom, "He pretty much bought my clothes, because I didn't know anything about looking good for a rock-star look." Jerry even went so far as to teach the band members how to walk properly. "Like when they train girls how to walk like models, he would show me how to do that strut . . . like a rooster strut, just showing off his wings. He looked like he was in command of everything."

* * *

DAVID HAD AN APARTMENT ON WEST FORTY-SIXTH STREET AND Ninth Avenue, which the band used as their headquarters. The apartment was conveniently located near the famed comedy club the Improv, where comedians such as Richard Pryor, Lily Tomlin, and Jay Leno paid their dues on their way to stardom.

At the Improv, the band, under the name Gideon's Message, backed up a singer named Gideon Daniels. Said David, "We would just play blues music behind him as he did his act . . . and we'd do little 'stings' and stuff because part of his act was to run out to the crowd and take things from the audience's purses, say jokes and stuff."

Jerry, Tommy, and Gregor first met Daniels in Central Park, where he was singing gospel songs a cappella. Besides backing him at the Improv and other local clubs, they also backed him one Sunday when he appeared on the local ABC TV affiliate's *Like It Is* program.

Sometimes the Improv would also feature music, and as they did when performing as Gideon's Message, the band would stick around and help the comedians by adding aural punctuations to their jokes with sound effects, playing rim shots or "goosing" a joke with a well-timed musical turn of phrase.

One such night, supposedly on the same bill as comedians Robert Kline, Richard Belzer, and David Brenner, was a twenty-four-year-old redheaded singer. She was a buxom and bawdy Jewish girl, with a smile as big as her knockers. She'd just finished up a three-year stint on Broadway as Tzeitel in *Fiddler on the Roof* and was now trying to establish herself as a solo act.

While the band still worked under the name Ocean, they changed their name to the Rejects of Woodstock while backing up the bushy-haired vocalist. Jerry took a liking to her— they shared history. She was born in Hawaii, but being white and Jewish felt as if she was an outsider. He'd lived there as a young army brat, also feeling like a misfit; she'd lost her sister a year before in an auto accident; he felt a similar hurt losing his father, not once but twice. She was into 1930s and '40s swing music, the same music associated with Gene Krupa, his first musical idol.

The two of them hit it off and began dating. "I don't think Corinne knew about that," said Elvera, adding, "She didn't know about a lot of things."

Jerry's relationship with Bette Midler was a loose one—between his relationship with Corinne and each other's professional pursuits, they were fine having their occasional fling. But by the end of 1970, with the help of the Improv's founder, Budd Friedman, Bette had appeared on *The Tonight Show Starring Johnny Carson* four times. She also started appearing regularly at the Continental Baths, a gay bathhouse in the Ansonia Hotel, where she met piano player Barry Manilow, who became her musical collaborator. Her star was rising.

But Jerry kept hustling. "Jerry was a very determined person," said David, adding, "Our motto was 'Break on in and take on over.' We played all around town. Sometimes we'd just go into clubs and then convince the band to let us play, so we could take over."

Through shared contacts, they got a booking agent. Particularly fruitful were college engagements, which had large budgets for entertainment. Said David, "We'd be in these towns that we got a gig at. . . . Then we'd go around to the other clubs, put up posters for our band, and we'd get extra gigs that way."

Sometimes the audience would think they were the other Ocean—the one who had the big hit, which conveniently assisted the band in meeting girls. "A lot of girls confused us with the other band," said David. Still, when youthful libido exceeded the number of available young females, all tactics were fair game. "I would end up with some women that [Jerry] wanted and he would say to them, 'You don't actually want him, you actually want me. You actually think you don't want me, but actually you do.'" Tom Bakas concurred: "We got laid a lot."

Between gigging and girl chasing, the band felt they were on to something. "We always drew crowds," said David. They were confident and felt that a record deal was imminent. Jerry was the most experienced of the bunch; thus he took the lead in all business decisions. Per David, "A&M Records was interested in signing us. And Jerry . . . he was very business-oriented. On top of things, he was a wheeler-dealer." The agreement was for a development deal only, and Jerry talked everyone into passing on it.

Presumably, the band had no professional or legal assistance in assessing the A&M offer. It's also doubtful that Jerry had the wherewithal to assess the deal himself. It is not known whether this was an act of hubris or true faith in the band's abilities to get something better. What is known is that David's father was not happy. "We weren't really making a lot of money and I was holding down this apartment on Ninth Avenue and my father pressured me a lot." David had experience working as a studio engineer. When a job opened up in a professional studio, David leapt at the chance. "Jerry took me aside and said, 'David, if you leave this band, it'll be the biggest mistake you ever make in your life.' That's always stuck with me."

After David's departure, the others began to lose interest. Per David, "Gregor went off and had his own band, and Tommy did another thing. . . ."

Among the gigs Jerry found was at a Times Square strip joint. The piano player was named Billy John, who at times would be known as Billy Piano and Billy Balls. He and Jerry provided bump-and-grind music for the dancers. The place was on the sleazier side, with dancers well past their prime. Before each show, Jerry and Billy went out onto the street acting as "barkers," charged with convincing passerby to come into the club. Singer Lyn Todd remembers their street spiel as told to her by Billy and Jerry. "They'd say, 'Step right up gentlemen and see the sweetest pair of bazoombas in the Western Hemisphere!'"

4 STARMAN

BOTH MAXIMILLIAN AND OCEAN FOUND PERMANENT BAND members just by hanging around New York's Central Park. Among the park's attractions was the Bethesda Fountain, not far from the Seventy-Second Street entrance. Its glory days behind it, it had fallen victim to urban decay: By 1970 it was bone-dry, surrounded by an open-air drug market. Still atop the fountain was the eight-foot *Angel of the Waters* statue, referencing the biblical Gospel of John, which describes an angel blessing the ancient pool of Bethesda with healing powers.

This nonfunctioning fountain area became a hangout and meeting place for young people. Future New York Dolls bass player Arthur Kane described it as "the site of the true outdoor catwalk of street fashion."[1]

Arthur had been born in the Bronx. Tall, bookish, and shy, he was close with his mother, Erna, who died when he was seventeen. His father Harold's response was to find a girlfriend and give Arthur the heave-ho. Arthur gave up the books and turned to music. He started out playing guitar, but once he heard the distinctive tone of one of the other guitarists in a band he was playing in, he switched over to bass.

Arthur and his friend George Fedorcik, aka Rick Rivets, were wannabe musicians who hung out at the fountain to people-watch after acquiring their own unconventional fashions at thrift stores. Most noteworthy were a couple whose hair was as high as the heels on their boots. She looked like a Raggedy Ann doll, but he looked like a British rock star. Before even meeting him, Jerry told Corinne they would be in a band together one day. Her name was Janis Cafasso, and his name was Johnny Genzale. He would later change his last name to Volume and afterward stick with Thunders. Jerry recognized them both from shows at the Fillmore, as they always stood out.

Jerry kept reading the music classifieds and hit the clubs, using a personal touch to let people know he needed a gig.

In late 1970 Jimi Hendrix died from an overdose of barbiturates. His death stunned Jerry and Buddy particularly—Jimi and his Experience drummer, Mitch Mitchell, were touchstones for them, both musically and stylistically. For others, though, Jimi's death became just another opportunity to fill their pockets and further their careers. One such opportunist was Curtis Knight.

Curtis was an R&B singer who worked in a version of the Ink Spots, and later with his own band, the Squires. He and his manager, Ed Chalpin, took an interest in a guitarist named Jimmy James and signed him to a management agreement, recording several sides with him in 1965. After tiring of the chitlin' circuit, in 1966, James signed a new management agreement with a company belonging to Chas Chandler, the former bass player of the Animals, who was now a producer and manager. Disregarding his still-valid agreement with Chalpin and Knight, James and Chandler went to England, where James would put together a new band and change his name to Jimi Hendrix. Afterward, Knight and Chalpin proceeded to release the 1965 Jimmy James tracks, exploiting Hendrix's fame, starting a legal battle that would last for decades.

Knight further capitalized on Hendrix's death, writing a book on their time spent together, then recording and performing music that mimicked his sound. Jerry, Buddy, Moby, Tommy, and Gregor all did time playing in Curtis's traveling show.

By 1971, New York's newest hangout was called Nobody's Bar. "It was the kind of bar where you might run into . . . members of Jethro Tull," said photographer Eileen Polk. The new and notable trend of this Greenwich Village club was the Anglo stylings of those who entered through its doors. This look often featured satin pants, colorfully patterned shirts with wide lapels, and tall boots with stacked heels. Hair was still long, but not unkempt like that of hippies. New York Dolls lead singer David Johansen summed up Nobody's: "It was a pickup joint for young peacocks."

* * *

MEETING JERRY, BUDDY, AND GREGOR ONE NIGHT AT NOBODY'S, Curtis was impressed by all of them. He invited them over to his headquarters on Ninth Avenue. Recalled Gregor, "He had a studio. He had money. He had a shrine of Hendrix pictures all over."

There were also many young, scantily clad ladies around. With his straightened hair and Cadillac, everyone was convinced Curtis was a pimp. It was well understood by band members that they should avoid bringing their girlfriends around for fear that Curtis would pressure them into joining his stable.

Just as pimps are known to treat their women harshly, Curtis could also behave tyrannically toward his band, causing Tom to split and be replaced by Art Steinman.

Art was a blues-rock player, well versed in the music of Hendrix, Jimmy Page, Eric Clapton, and Jeff Beck. While still in high school, Art had been in the garage-rock combo the Jagged Edge, who morphed into the Off-Set, each releasing independent singles. Neither record charted, but Art caught the music bug. After two years of college he decided "to become a full-time starving artist."[2]

Art fit in fine with Curtis, although out of the gate the guitarist could sense that "Curtis wasn't that easy to work with." He refused to entertain the thought of allowing another band to outshine him. In one instance, Curtis was unhappy with Art's small Fender Twin amplifier. "That's not going to be loud enough," he told Art. "Go ask those guys and tell them you want to use their amp!" "He was really insistent on it. So I asked them and the guitarist . . . let me use his amp."

As expected, the band did a series of Hendrix tunes. During their rendition of "Fire," the crowd started going wild a few minutes into the song. "I was playing a solo at that point and going, 'Wow, I must be better than I think I am. They're going so crazy.'" In actuality, the borrowed amp had burst into flames.

Recalled Gregor, "Oh that was incredible. It's burning the speaker from within, burning through the mesh in front of the speaker. I grab a fire extinguisher . . . and it made this great mist all over the stage. . . . It's like a cloud. It just kind of hangs over the stage. It was fantastic . . . like our own fireworks." The crowd loved it, but the band who'd lent Art the amp wasn't digging it.

"We get offstage and these guys are now pissed off," Gregor recalls. "So Curtis is trying to tell them, 'Oh, yeah, we'll pay you,' and this and that." Meanwhile, he told his own band to "'just get everything in the truck.' Then we just screamed the hell out of there."

While Art had less dramatic postshow memories, recalling everyone passing the hat to pony up for the damaged amp, Gregor, Art, and Jerry all agreed it was time to find another gig. Jerry thought he had the solution: They would start their own band. They already had a name: Shaker, because their goal was to make your body shake.

"I remember him playing really, really hard. He'd beat the crap out of the drums," said Art. After years of playing small clubs with only vocalists going through the club's PA system, and guitarists adding stacks of speaker cabinets to their rigs to replicate the heavy sound of the day, Jerry found the only way to be heard was to play as hard as possible, with the heavier back end of the sticks. "There was no soft. It was just all-out. It was one level, and it was super-high energy playing."

Shaker began rehearsing steadily at Art's parents' house in Brooklyn, and at Gregor's in Queens. Art had a few originals, as did Gregor, but Shaker were primarily a cover band, playing power trio–style rock, including Cream and lots of Hendrix.

In May of 1971, Shaker got a weeklong gig in Wilkes-Barre, Pennsylvania, at a place Art recalls being named the Sportsman's Lounge. The band piled into Gregor's van for the trip, arriving at a local motel, where they split a single room with two beds and a pull-out couch.

Eschewing their usual stage makeup, because, as Art recalled, "we didn't want to get the crap beat out of us," Shaker did their usual set. The crowd was unlike those at the New York clubs they usually frequented. These were workingmen, who'd come out to down a few beers after a long day at the factory.

Afterwards, Jerry picked up a local girl, taking her back to the shared motel room. Art recalled, "I guess when women would see him, they'd resonate with that rock-star thing he had. Remember, he was playing with a band that nobody knew, that was doing mostly covers. But he had that rock-star way about him. I remember him bringing her into the hotel room . . . and they'd go at it right on the bed with us and Gregor sitting there."

Since all the gigs were in the evening, there was plenty of time to kill during the day. "He told me about profiling," said Art. "I didn't even know what profiling was, so he had to teach me."

Jerry started by taking Art to a Salvation Army, where they could acquire cheap used clothing. They immediately went to the women's clothing section, focusing on "old-fashioned ladies' shirts, the ones with the frilly jabots on the front. He said, 'Just try it on.' Then he said, 'Okay, that looks cool,' and he picked out some jacket. It didn't matter whether it was for a man or a woman." After Jerry helped Art choose a pair of high-heeled, white patent-leather shoes, the guitarist's outfit was complete.

Jerry made sure that Art understood he had to secure his own profile. Otherwise, he was just a "civilian." "He had a whole lexicon that other people didn't have."

Jerry was a keen observer of what musicians wore. "He'd take out albums . . . and say, 'Look at this guy,' and, 'You have to get that rock-star look.'" Like a style consultant, Jerry advised his associates. More than just a teacher, he was like a skilled politician working a crowd, making people feel as if he cared about them personally, taking them under his wing. "He wasn't pushy, but he was consistent in his support. He really helped me out. I think that's because he cared about me, [and] didn't want me to stand out like a sore thumb."

But Shaker were struggling, so Jerry pursued other gigs. Auditions were being held for a drummer in an all-girl band. But there was a twist. They didn't want a girl—they wanted a guy!

This Detroit-based band was called Cradle, and were the ultimate family affair, a five-piece combo consisting of four Quatro sisters—Suzi on bass, Patti on guitar, Arlene on piano, and Nancy on vocals—and drummer Nancy Rogers. Brother Mike Quatro and Arlene's husband, Leo Fenn, managed the group.

The earliest incarnation of Cradle dated back to 1964, when they were called the Pleasure Seekers, wearing matching outfits and going through choreographed dance steps. They evolved through garage rock and Motown, on through psychedelia, and into their present hard rock incarnation, assuming the name of Cradle in 1969. They'd had some success in their hometown of Detroit, appearing on local TV shows and even enjoying a short-lived deal with Mercury Records. After seven years in the music business, they were pros.

In early 1971, drummer Nancy Rogers left the group, who used it as an opportunity to reassess themselves. Per Nancy, "It was such a struggle . . . because you are not respected automatically like guy musicians are. So we went the other way. We tried to downplay our femininity to prove that we could do it. And we could. So then we kind of looked at it like, 'Why don't we try a guy?' It's not like it hasn't been a major battle being all girls anyway, and maybe that will just add enough spice to the band that we get a little more recognition."

They had a gig in New York and decided to stay and audition new drummers. Jerry was the first to audition, and he fit in immediately. "He seemed to have confidence," remembered Suzi. And "he looked like a girl. He had that sort of both-genders appeal."

Jerry was overjoyed. Unlike Shaker, here was a band with a following, playing original music. Being the only guy made him stand out. Plus, Jerry loved being around women. He trusted women and felt comfortable around them. According to Nancy Quatro, "Before he came into it, I think he loved it for the wrong reasons: going to score and all kind[s] of stuff." The Cradle girls were all about business. They would not date band members. They didn't allow drug use, and you had to be on time, or risk being fined.

Jerry gave assurances that he could follow their rules, particularly concerning drugs. Outside of a little marijuana now and then, drugs were something Jerry seemed to have little interest in. The music came first.

Jerry moved into the Quatro family home, living in their basement. Soon enough, Cradle were on the road, playing gigs in Canada and throughout New York State. Nancy recalled that the band by this time had become "a little harder and a little more precise." But the biggest change was in the group's presentation. "He was a showman up there. He was just wilder looking and had flair."

The band was excited by the possibilities of having Jerry in the group, but they also just plain liked him. Nancy in particular. "We did hit it off. He had a great personality. He was a typical dry New Yorker, the kind of sense of humor I adore. He kept me in stitches, all of us."

In the days before the Internet and smartphones, and even farther back, before the Sony Walkman, traveling bands were forced to talk to one another on the road. That, or sit in silence. Nancy and Jerry talked more than the others, having long, intimate conversations. "When you're a musician, a lot of your talks are about music, and being a musician is a real isolating and self-absorbed lifestyle. I think he wanted to get into a lot deeper conversation." Nancy sensed that Jerry had gone through a rough childhood and found it difficult to talk about, though he clearly wanted to. "You could tell it was a real vulnerable place for him to go."

Nancy was willing to listen, which was what he needed: a woman to understand him, to allow him to open up and be exposed. Someone he didn't have to be the tough guy around, and didn't have to profile for. Someone he could simply be himself around. For those reasons, the two of them got closer and closer, and soon enough it led to the inevitable. Suzi Quatro recalls, "When we were rehearsing one day in the garage he said, 'I'm in love with your sister.'"

This was a problem. As much as Nancy cared about Jerry, she did not want to have a relationship with him that was more intimate than that of friend, confidant, and bandmate. "I didn't want any part of that," she said. In retrospect, she sensed that she may have sent some conflicting signals. She wondered at times if she did like him as more than just a friend and confessed that she did flirt with him, but she chose not to allow the relationship to progress beyond that.

"It really . . . became a problem for him. That became a problem for the band. I think he just really wanted to connect. I don't even want to say it was with me. . . . I think if any of the other girls in the band would have shown him any kind of attention, I think he would have connected with them."

Nancy was now starting to feel uncomfortable. "He was going from one sister to another, whining about it." Jerry was now the outsider, alone, just like when his parents and siblings had left him, just like when he moved to Hawaii, and then to Lawton, and in Maximillian.

As the odd man out, Jerry found solace in that same place that many musicians have gone to when things weren't going their way. Earlier on, Nancy had sensed he was having some "substance problems." Outside of Ted Nugent, notorious for being the one straight musician during a very druggy epoch, "there wasn't anyone we didn't know, musician-wise, that didn't do that stuff." But Nancy was very clear with him that it wasn't allowed. Period. Just as importantly, she told him, "That doesn't have to be a part of your art."

There were signs that it was becoming an issue with Jerry, and thus the band. "There was one gig. We couldn't find him and even thought that he might not show up because of drugs." Arriving late, he confessed to Nancy that he'd been out scoring acid and smoking opium. It showed in his playing that night: He embarrassed the group by making them look bad. "When he started screwing up songs . . . that's where we decided to part ways and just tell him [to] go on back to New York. He didn't argue . . . and he really didn't say much of anything back. Even though it was humiliating, I think he was kind of ready for it to be over too, because he just wasn't handling anything. It was kind of sad, but it was very business to us."

Jerry never admitted to anyone the real reasons he left Cradle. Conveniently, Suzi was discovered by British music Svengali Mickie Most soon after Jerry left Detroit. Moving to England in 1972, she began a decades-long career of multiple hits, selling more than fifty million records and taking on a regular role in the late-'70s TV hit *Happy Days* as the character Leather Tuscadero. This gave Jerry an easy out, as he insinuated to everyone as the years passed that Suzi leaving Cradle was the reason behind his departure from the band. He never had to acknowledge his own shortcomings.

* * *

RETURNING TO NEW YORK, JERRY NEEDED A PLACE TO LIVE AND A gig. He reached out to Art and Gregor for both. Jerry's mom got married for a third time, to William Ballas: another veteran and, ironically, another Billy. The couple moved to Florida, leaving Jerry with one less place to stay. He would call his mother and have her wire him money, in exchange for listening to her ideas on how he should find gigs. One suggestion was for Buddy and him to "go to bars and grills to see if they could get work." Whether Jerry made up a few fibs or she hatched this idea in her elderly mind is unknown. Regardless, she insisted, "That's where Jerry worked for the Rolling Stones. Yeah, he played for them. What is his name, Jag, Mike, Magger? He and Jerry were friends. Jerry was in a bar on Eighth Avenue trying to get work and this Mike Jagger was at this bar. So you know how two people meet: 'Hey, have a drink on me,' and this and that. Jerry drank Coke. He never drank whiskey. So this fella said to Jerry, 'My drummer quit and I don't know what to do.' He says, 'I'm in and outta these places lookin' for a drummer.' 'Oh,' Jerry says. 'You got one here.' So they went to a studio and they practiced and he played with Mike. Is that his name? Mike? Oh, Mick. He played with him for about . . . oh . . . two or three weeks. But he played with him. And that's how he met Zeppelin."

Back in the reality-based world, Jerry knew he could live with Corinne in Queens, but all the action was in Manhattan-not just music, but also girls. Recalled Gregor, "Jerry was a womanizer. He said he had 'cockitus.'" Woman could satisfy not only his sexual desire but his deflated ego. Sometimes they could provide him with a place to live. But even that was fraught with problems. "What would happen was he'd end up with more than one girlfriend," said Art Steinman, "and they'd kick him out. I seem to remember him going from girlfriend to girlfriend."

When Jerry ran out of girls to take advantage of, he was forced to hit up his former bandmates. Art came through.

Life was cozy for Jerry in Mill Basin, Brooklyn, with Art's mom cooking his meals. Prodded by Art, she made Jerry some Jewish specialties he'd never eaten before, such as stuffed cabbage, matzo brei, and matzo-ball soup. He liked them all, except for one. "He did not go for the gefilte fish."

Living with Art had an added benefit. The guitarist explained, "I said to him, 'Now you're an honorary Jew. I've got to give you a Jewish name.' So I gave him the name of Murray and he called me Sid. So when we talked to each other it was Murray and Sid."

But "Sid" began to feel that "Murray" was taking advantage of him, turning into the guest who wouldn't leave. "He was polite but . . . we couldn't get him to move out." Art finally had to tell him to leave. "He couldn't just live there forever."

Jerry moved into Gregor's basement in Queens for a spell. But he also moved from one girlfriend's apartment to another, surviving off "chump change" gig money and the benevolence of others. Just as Corinne said, Jerry knew how to manipulate women.

Gregor recalled that "the only books that Jerry ever read" were by the celebrated pimp Iceberg Slim, whose most famous books were *Trick Baby: The Biography of a Con Man* and *Pimp: The Story of My Life*. Slim's work was lauded by gangsta rappers including Ice-T and Ice Cube, whose names alone were undeniable homages. "He got a lot of weird stuff from Iceberg Slim, ways of talking . . . and how he treated girls," recalled Gregor.

Taking a pimp as one's role model is not what most people would describe as "enlightened." But Jerry was committed to his lifestyle. "I always thought he had one goal, and that was to be a rock star," said Art. Others existed only to serve that purpose.

While this single-minded pursuit caused him to act selfishly, being around him made other's feel better about themselves. Jerry shone. This was why so many girlfriends and bandmates put up with his self-centeredness.

Another group Jerry met at Nobody's also shone. They turned out to be some of the people he recalled from the Bethesda Fountain in Central Park, and in the audience at shows at the Fillmore, who copped huge profiles. The bass player looked like a drugged-out Frankenstein with wild blond hair and giant sunglasses, wearing a ballet dancer's tutu. The singer looked like a cross between Mick Jagger and a member of the Little Rascals in ladies' pumps. Sometimes one of them would wear a leather motorcycle jacket over leopard-print tights. If they weren't wearing women's shoes, they would wear giant platform boots, the latest fad from England. They all wore makeup, jewelry, and various bits of women's wear, but they didn't look like any women Jerry had ever seen. To him, they looked like members of a rock 'n' roll street gang.

One of the guitarists stood out above the rest. He had hair that was teased up in the back like Rod Stewart or Keith Richards but exaggerated to the point where it looked as if it had exploded all over his face. It was that Johnny Genzale fellow. He now went by his new name: Johnny Thunders.

This gang of glammed-up misfits had a band they were calling the New York Dolls. After getting acquainted, Jerry and Gregor were invited to their rehearsal space on Amsterdam Avenue between Eighty-First and Eighty-Second Street. It was in a bicycle rental and repair establishment called Rusty Beanie's Bicycle Shop.

In their basement rehearsal space, the band assembled a bare-bones musical laboratory, working on R&B covers like Otis Redding's "Don't Mess with Cupid," and "(There's Gonna Be a) Showdown" by Archie Bell and the Drells, plus early versions of originals like "It's Too Late" and "That's Poison," which later morphed into "Subway Train."

Guitarist Rick Rivets recalled Jerry's visits to their rehearsals, saying, "Everybody liked when he'd stop by. He wasn't pushy." Dolls drummer Billy Murcia never seemed threatened by Jerry, letting him use his kit to sit in with the band when he took a cigarette break. Jerry would politely switch a few things around on Billy's right-handed kit, making it usable for him to play on Bo Diddley's "I Can Tell," and just as politely returning the kit to its proper state when he was through.

Jerry was an early adopter of the Dolls, attending some of their first shows in 1972. He continued to see the band's members socially, whether at Rusty Beanie's or at Nobody's. The latter was still a happening place, but as the English music scene evolved, so did Nobody's. By 1972 glam rock was starting to make its way over from England. In the States, more often than not, people called it "glitter rock."

Glam was louder, younger, simpler, and flashier than what had previously dominated the charts. Instead of jeans and army fatigues, bands wore glittery clothing, makeup, and stacked-heel platform boots. While the American charts were filled with the more adult, introspective singer-songwriter styles of Carole King and Cat Stevens, or the light pop of the Carpenters or Bread, glam was anything but adult, introspective, or light. It was youthful, celebratory, rebellious, and carnal. Glam was less about love than it was about sex, and the sex didn't necessarily need to be between a boy and a girl.

In early 1972 the glam leader of the pack was Marc Bolan, an elfin figure with corkscrew curls similar to Billy and Sylvain Sylvain's (né Sylvain Mizrahi), the Dolls' other guitarist, who took over from Rick Rivets at the start of 1972. Bolan was the leader of the English group T. Rex, whose 1971 album, *Electric Warrior,* gained attention in America with the tracks "Jeepster" and "Bang a Gong (Get It On)."

Bolan was a full-fledged star in England, where record companies started churning out glam records. Sweet, Gary Glitter, Slade, and Jerry's former bandmate Suzi Quatro all dominated the British charts over the next few years. Older bands, such as the Rolling Stones, the Kinks, or Rod Stewart and the Faces, were also wearing satin, glitter, and makeup while playing up their feminine sides.

Another glam star, David Bowie, was also gaining attention in England. Not only were his records rocketing up the charts, but a song he wrote and produced for the struggling Mott the Hoople called "All The Young Dudes" resurrected their career, hitting number three in the UK.

Like T. Rex's Marc Bolan, Bowie struggled for years in England before becoming a major star. Bowie's *The Rise and Fall of Ziggy Stardust and the*

Spiders from Mars was released in the summer of 1972. By the end of the year, Bowie was England's biggest homegrown star since . . . Marc Bolan.

With his stick-thin figure, unusual outfits, heavily made-up face, and short, mod hair, Bowie reveled in androgyny. He was enamored with Warhol, Lou Reed's Velvet Underground, and Iggy Pop's Stooges. Now that Bowie was taking his Ziggy show to America, he was looking forward to absorbing more of the American demimonde.

England wasn't the only breeding ground for glam. Alice Cooper used violent imagery along with shock makeup and gold lamé when he hit the US charts in April of '71 with a song about disaffected teenagers called "I'm Eighteen."

Despite their singer's name, the sexual ambiguity had begun to fade from the band by 1970, when they relocated to Detroit, home of proto-punks the MC5 and Iggy and the Stooges. With input and support from manager Shep Gordon, they came up with an over-the-top theatrical presentation that featured multiple executions, knife fights, and a live snake. With the addition of producer Bob Ezrin, they created a sound that was as dark as their stage show, yet comfortable to the teenage ear. Thanks in no small part to Gordon's marketing savvy, heavy airplay and legions of fans followed. By the end of the summer of 1972, the single "School's Out" was a worldwide smash. With it came increased parental outrage, press, and ticket sales.

Over the coming year, several New York groups variously influenced by glam, glitter, or shock rock, including Teenage Lust, the Harlots of 42nd Street, the Magic Tramps, and Wayne County's Queen Elizabeth would start playing local clubs. Jerry also pushed for Shaker, already wearing stage makeup, to profile as glam. He began sporting platform heels, and Gregor wore Indian war paint. Jerry was also keenly aware of the gender ambiguity apparent in the glam scene, but despite his former manager from the Peepl, Peter Glick, suggesting that Shaker call themselves the Fabulous Fags, Jerry was satisfied with the band's present name.

* * *

WHILE HANGING OUT AT NOBODY'S ONE NIGHT, JERRY RAN INTO bass player Danny McGary, an alumnus of Curtis Knight's bands. Danny mentioned that he and his friend were looking to start a new group. Norman Kaslinger, who lived above Nobody's, managed a group from Boston called Magic Terry and the Universe, who gravitated between their Massachusetts hometown and New York. After the group broke up in the early '70s, Kaslinger wanted to bring their lead singer, Billy Squier, to New York to start a new band

"In the spring of '72 I was living in Boston," said Squier. "I came back down to New York to play with [guitarist] Jerry Hawkins. We used a bass player from Queens, Danny McGary. Danny suggested Jerry to us." They called themselves Kicks.

After losing his gig with Cradle, Jerry was staying away from strong, mind-altering substances. "He had a cautious nature to him, so hanging out with me and Jerry Hawkins was probably somewhat terrifying to him in moments. We were pushing the envelope a lot more than he did, but he was a fun guy."

Recalled Danny, "He used to sew his own clothes . . . and was the first musician I ever worked with that wore makeup." Plus, just as Jerry had demonstrated to the members of Cradle, he knew how to perform. Billy: "Jerry was kind of the dandy of the band. He liked to put on a show. He was really a little rock star."

Kicks played sporadic gigs in and around New York, including a place called the Mercer Arts Center. Located at 240 Mercer Street, the Mercer was accessed off a side street through the University Hotel at 673 Broadway. The location's history was impressive: Theaters had been housed there since 1850, and stately hotels since 1870.

These theaters were off-Broadway, noted for productions that were more experimental and less financially viable than those at larger theaters uptown on the Great White Way. They were breeding grounds for new ideas and potential hits to come. Besides its five theaters, the facility housed a video production room, an actors' workshop, a bar, and a boutique.

Once a grand and majestic space, the site, like the Bethesda Fountain uptown, had fallen victim to urban decay. By 1970 it had become a $5-a-night welfare hotel that teemed with junkies, drunks, and prostitutes. New York State Attorney General Louis Lefkowitz called the hotel a "squalid den of vice and iniquity . . . an open and notorious public nuisance and a den of thieves."[3] In the first six months of 1971 there were twenty-two robberies, a homicide, three rapes, seven petty larcenies, five grand larcenies, six felonious assaults, eighteen drug-related crimes, forty-nine burglaries, and six miscellaneous offenses. Proprietor Seymour Kaback claimed he was "taking a run-down, rat-ridden pestilence and making it into an oasis."[4]

Despite these dangers, the Mercer's proximity to New York University and Washington Square Park placed in its vicinity thousands of young people who could potentially explore the multiple art forms offered there. But Kaback needed more of an attraction than avant-garde and experimental theater to turn them into paying customers. The answer: rock 'n' roll.

Those who flocked to the Mercer replicated Nobody's crowd: glitter rockers reminiscent of T. Rex and Alice Cooper, but with a decidedly artistic New York bent, drawing on Andy Warhol and his Factory "Superstars," John Vaccaro's experimental Theater of the Ridiculous, and drag queen culture for inspiration. Among the first bands to play there were the Magic Tramps, fronted by dancer and former Warhol superstar Eric Emerson. The all-male band wore makeup, feathers, and nail polish, while Emerson wasn't averse to covering himself with glitter. These were the first rumblings of original glitter rock in New York.

Appearing at the Mercer with Kicks were the Dolls. According to Billy Squier, this was where lead singer David Johansen, who also soaked up inspiration from the Theater of the Ridiculous, first saw what Jerry could do onstage.

* * *

DAVID JOHANSEN WAS FROM THE NEW YORK BOROUGH OF STATEN Island. His was a family that appreciated the arts: His insurance salesman father sang opera but also appreciated Harry Smith's *Anthology of American Folk Music*. His mother was a librarian. A self-proclaimed high school dropout, David studied art but was captivated by music: girl groups, Chicago blues, and Motown, as well as the Paul Butterfield Blues Band and Janis Joplin. He spent time as a member of Charles Ludlam's avant-garde Ridiculous Theatrical Company: This experience, combined with his love of art, R&B, and rock 'n' roll, brought elements of streetwise literateness and artful burlesque to the Dolls.

Jerry also watched the Dolls. He already knew they didn't look like anyone else—now he realized they didn't sound like anyone else, either. Though they were a blues-rock band in the tradition of the Rolling Stones, their music was crude but exciting. There were no long, complex solos or anything that smacked of indulgence. Their songs were short and made their point quickly, like classic pop tunes. The Dolls were thoroughly of their time but invoked the more feral rock of the '50s. Jerry found them electrifying.

Five weeks after their May 5 debut at the Mercer, the Dolls returned, beginning a fourteen-week residency in the complex's Oscar Wilde Room. But before this string of shows began, they played at the Palm Room of the Diplomat Hotel ballroom on May 29 with Shaker as an opening act.

Syl and Billy had met in high school, bonding over the fact that they were both immigrants, Syl from Egypt and Billy from Colombia. In the late '60s they joined together to start a clothing firm called Truth and Soul, selling their hippie sweaters first in Woodstock, New York, and then in trendy stores in New York City. After cashing out and spending time in Europe, they returned to the states, bringing a Jaguar automobile and three Marshall amps back with them. It was now all about rock 'n' roll for them.

Billy and Sylvain lived in Queens, as were Jerry and Gregor, leading them to Gregor's basement for jam sessions. However, the real party was at the Dolls' loft at 119 Chrystie Street, in Lower Manhattan. Syl, Billy, Arthur, and Johnny and his girlfriend Janis all lived there at one time or another. In fact, any band members, or friends who could contribute to the $200 monthly rent were welcome.

One block east of the sleazy Bowery, Chrystie Street was only a notch better. The upside was the cheap rents and large, bare spaces. The downside was the stares from the locals and the potential for violence after dark. It was an area where Chinese, Italians, older Jews of the Lower East Side, and Puerto Ricans mingled. It was right by Sara Delano Roosevelt Park, where children played alongside hookers and drug dealers hawking their wares.

Jerry and the rest of Shaker visited the Dolls' loft for jam sessions. Art recalled the surroundings: "It was up a few floors, and it was a huge loft. The guys made bedrooms for themselves by putting up [what] looked like Indian fabric. That's how they divided [it] up . . . into living space. There was a rehearsal area. We would jam till all hours of the night and morning. There were mental lubricants readily available for us."

Like Jerry, the group did whatever they could to avoid straight jobs. Arthur collected unemployment from a previous job repairing pay phones, and Johnny would get involved in the occasional pot deal. A roommate might have a job, but friends and family, mostly Johnny's, would send care packages of food. However, it was easier and more fun to throw rent parties.

Recalled Syl, "All the kids would come and we would charge $2 at the door. Of course, Jerry didn't have to pay. We would have jam sessions and practice . . . meet girls, and guys who had drugs would come . . . sell their shit. The girls that would be dancers would come up and try to pick up all the rock 'n' rollers."

Meanwhile, Jerry's home life was teetering on the edge. Jerry and Corinne had been living with each other on and off for ten years while he continued catting around, profiling, and seeing other women.

46

Corinne had become ill, entering a hospital to have surgery for an intestinal obstruction. Upon release, she never felt quite right. Years later she was diagnosed as bipolar, but at the time all she knew was that something was wrong. "I was in and out of the hospital. Then I went into this really bad depression." Jerry's lack of dependability only made her feel worse. "It wasn't helping. . . . He was just coming and going and so I just told him to leave. That's how I knew I was really depressed . . . because I didn't care about anything." Over forty years later, Corinne has never married. "He was the love of my life."

* * *

THE DOLLS' PARTIES WERE A GREAT PLACE TO HANG OUT, AS WAS Nobody's, but there was another joint that had become the in place to be.

Max's Kansas City was a club on Park Avenue South, just below Eighteenth Street. First opening in January of 1966, Max's wound up a favorite watering hole for artists. Founder Mickey Ruskin laid out a free buffet of chicken wings and chili from 5 to 7 p.m., but outside of those hours, artists could trade work for food. This encouraged them to stay and purchase alcohol, a win/win situation for everybody. A large group of regulars came from Andy Warhol's Factory headquarters, which, having moved in 1968, was three blocks south at 33 Union Square East. The backroom was the favorite private watering hole for Andy and his entourage.

The art world was not a place where Jerry was comfortable. He was a rock 'n' roller. But by 1972 rock 'n' roll was challenging art for dominance at Max's, with glam leading the way. The Dolls started hanging out and playing at Max's, their first shows there on July 24 and 25 interrupting their Tuesday-night residency at the Mercer. They played Max's five more times in 1972, including one night with Shaker opening.

Wayne County, later becoming Jayne, was a Max's regular who straddled both the Warhol and glam scenes. Originally Wayne Rogers, hailing from Dallas, Georgia, County came to New York at age twenty-one and embraced New York's gay and transgender scene, taking part in the Stonewall riots and befriending drag performer and Warhol Superstar Jackie Curtis. After appearing in Curtis's play *Femme Fatale*, also featuring a young Patti Smith, County wrote and performed in a series of underground plays, including *Pork*, which came to London in August 1971, captivating a barely known David Bowie.

County's love of '60s garage rock, theatrical flair, and general outrageousness led her to start her own band, called Queen Elizabeth. But though the music was important, Wayne wanted to put on a show

STRANDED IN THE JUNGLE

just as worthy. In an environment with bands named Harlots of 42nd Street and Teenage Lust, Wayne got to work.

County had writing partners in brothers James and Tom Wynbrandt, whom she had worked with on and off since *Femme Fatale*. Their college friend Dale Powers played bass, but they had trouble locking in a regular drummer. Jayne recalled seeing Jerry at the Mercer: "I had always noticed him, as he was always a really smart dresser."

Jerry came to a band audition and impressed everyone with his looks from the get-go. Recalled Dale, "He looked like a clone of Johnny Thunders. He had the high-heeled shoes and the Kamali pants and teasedup hair. That's the only reason we hired him."

Tom, however, was impressed by Jerry's skills. "Jerry was obviously good. He could keep a beat. He understood what we were doing, and he was into it."

Wayne voiced some concerns about Jerry to her friend photographer Leee Black Childers. "[Wayne] was worried a little about him getting a lot of attention, because he was so cute and dressed so cool in those days. We had a lot of telephone conversations . . . trying to figure out what Jerry was like personally, what his sexual orientation was, all that kind of stuff."

The band noticed right away that despite his flamboyant appearance, Jerry wasn't gay or the arty, theatrical type. "[Jerry] had that 'hitter' thing going on," said James. "It's from the way he talked, not necessarily the way he dressed, obviously, because he was a little more on the glam side. . . ." He reminded Tommy of Leo Gorcey of the Bowery Boys, but a "much more dapper, handsome version of Leo Gorcey."

James, Tommy, and Dale shared an apartment on East Twelfth Street. Tommy recalled that upon his first visit, Jerry called it a "dynamite dump." "He was a really colorful speaker."

During their rehearsals, Queen Elizabeth dressed down, or at least didn't dress up. Jerry had yet to see what the full Queen Elizabeth experience held in store. In fact, he chided them all, saying, "You guys got to cop a profile." Little did Jerry know what would hit him when the show began.

The band never fully revealed to Jerry what the show looked like until they hit the stage. By then, Jerry had no idea what was about to happen. Said Dale, "Half of the show was rock 'n' roll songs, and half of the show was theater." For the finale, Wayne brought out a toilet with dog food in it, masquerading as turd. He would sit on it as he sang, 'I've been shitting, baby. I like it. Because I'm a lowlife.' Dale continued: "Then he would reach into this commode and get the Alpo and rub it on himself. People would go crazy. I mean, you're looking at a guy who's wearing . . . a belt with a dick on it."

After getting offstage, Jerry told the band, "You guys are the greatest thing ever! I can't believe it!"

Before the show, Jerry looked at Queen Elizabeth as just another gig. Afterward, he saw things differently. Said Dale, "When the show went on, we were the stars. He was just the drummer. And then he got with the program right away, and that was that. He was no longer a Queens guy."

PART 2
BABYLON

SEVEN-DAY WEEKEND

5

JERRY WAS PLAYING WITH SHAKER, KICKS, AND QUEEN ELIZABETH, plus a drum and guitar duo called the Dynamic Duo, but he was still struggling. He also had no girlfriend or permanent place to live.

This same period was a whirlwind of activity for the nascent New York Dolls. Several key people came into their lives almost as if directed to them by otherworldly forces. First and foremost was Marty Thau.

Marty had an astonishing run in record promotions, with a wall of gold records earned for Question Mark and the Mysterians' "96 Tears," the Ohio Express's "Yummy, Yummy, Yummy" and "Chewy, Chewy," Melanie's "Lay Down (Candles in the Rain)," the Edwin Hawkins Singers' "Oh Happy Day," and Van Morrison's album *Moondance*. In early 1972 he became head of A&R at Paramount Records, but he quickly realized their only interest was in movie sound tracks, and Marty was interested in selling rock 'n' roll records.

He quit, but while there, he befriended a nineteen-year-old working in the publicity department, who told him about the Dolls, saying they were the best unsigned band around. Marty and his wife went to check them out at the Mercer Arts Center. The teenager was right. His name was Danny Goldberg and his instincts would prove right many times over throughout a long and successful career in the music business, handling public relations for Led Zeppelin; managing Nirvana; becoming president of Atlantic Records, chairman and CEO of Warner Brothers, and then of the Mercury Records Group.

Like many who saw the Dolls, Marty wasn't sure if he'd witnessed the greatest band in the world or the worst band ever. They were so jarring to the senses of anyone who had formed an opinion of what a rock 'n' roll band should be in 1972, they could leave you flummoxed as to what you'd just seen. Years later Marty recalled that night. He described their look as "remarkable. While everybody in America [was] wearing army coats and earth shoes, here were these guys decked out in leather and leopard skin with bouffant hairdos, black nail polish, lipstick, six-inch platform boots, chopped jeans, feather boas, armbands, and pantyhose. It was a style beyond femininity and thrown together in such a way as to appear natural."[1] Then he listened to their music, describing it as "loud and hard ghetto music about girls, sex, drugs, loneliness, heartbreak and the rites of teenage romance. In other words . . . real rock 'n' roll."[2]

Aware of his success at promoting singles, Marty had been approached by infamous industry mogul Morris Levy about starting a singles label. Despite his knowledge of Levy's ties to the mob and other nefarious business dealings, Marty agreed to give the idea some thought. He considered the Dolls as a possibility for the new imprint.

Meeting the band in the back room of Max's soon after the Mercer gig, Marty was impressed by their vision and intelligence, particularly David's. When David told Marty, "We're gonna conquer the world, and we're here for your sons and daughters,"[3] Marty was convinced: He had to manage this band. He was no longer interested in Levy's offer. He was backing the Dolls with everything he had.

Marty's expertise lay in promotion. He needed someone else to handle the business end and turned to a William Morris agency veteran who was striking out on his own. Steve Leber had booked the Rolling Stones and other major acts since 1965. With his partner, David Krebs, he had started Contemporary Communications Corporation, which everyone just called Leber-Krebs. Krebs's main responsibility was attending to another of their stable's bands. This band also had a Jaggeresque lead singer, and a post-Stones, blues-rock sound. Like the Dolls, this group also had an element of drug sleaze but less of an emphasis on style. They were from Boston and had just signed a record deal with Columbia Records, reportedly for $125,000 up front. Their name was Aerosmith.

With Marty's passion and promotions experience, he convinced Leber the Dolls could work. By the end of June, a contract was signed whereby the band was to be managed by the Thau/Leber-Krebs team. The young Dolls had no outside legal counsel when they signed their contract but they were over the moon just to have someone give a damn about them. Plus, they were now on salary: $75 per week, plus a onetime $100 clothing allowance.

Marty put them into Blue Rock Studio in Greenwich Village to record some demos so he could assess their songs. They recorded nine numbers, including six originals: "Bad Girl," "Looking for a Kiss," "Human Being," "Personality Crisis," "Jet Boy," and "Frankenstein." The recordings were raw, sloppy, and markedly slower than the versions that ended up on the Dolls' studio albums. Billy's drumming was particularly one-dimensional and rudimentary. But the essence was there. Marty knew he could do something with it.

Over the next few months, Marty and Leber-Krebs started booking the band at Max's in Long Island, and the outer boroughs. Press mentions started to pop up. One writer who was smitten by the Dolls was influential journalist Lillian Roxon. A regular in the back room at Max's, Roxon had a front-row seat to the new groups in New York's underground music scene. She also had her own acolytes, including a teenager named Kathy Miller, who would later write for *Creem*, *Fusion*, and *Crawdaddy*.

Kathy became friends with Laura Kaufman, publicist for Leber-Krebs. Laura told Kathy that in exchange for helping promote the Dolls, handing out flyers and building an audience, she and whoever assisted her would always be on the guest list. Kathy and five friends canvassed neighborhoods whenever there was a Dolls show, going to every single Dolls gig in the New York area.

The Dolls made another friend for life when photographer Bob Gruen saw them that summer. Bob described the Dolls as "very intelligent. Their lyrics [were] very intelligent and their jokes were very intelligent. And I found that very interesting. They didn't look like anybody else. People make a comment that the Dolls tended to dress like women. No women dressed like that. They were dressed up as guys who wanted to be beautiful."

* * *

ROY HOLLINGWORTH OF ENGLAND'S MELODY MAKER SAW THE band at the Mercer, raving about them in the British weekly's July 22 edition, saying, "They might just be the best rock 'n' roll band in the world."[4] Marty saw an opportunity. The Dolls were viewed as glam, which was exploding in England. He would use this to entice British promoters to book them and use that as bait to get American labels interested.

David Bowie invited the Dolls to see him perform at Carnegie Hall on September 28 and arranged to meet the group beforehand as well as see them perform at the Mercer on September 26. The impact of the Dolls would be apparent on his next record, 1973's *Aladdin Sane*, with the chugging "Watch That Man" supposedly written about his encounters with the band, and "Time" name-checking Billy and Syl.

Bowie was not the only star to see the Dolls. Alice Cooper, Lou Reed, John Cale, and even Truman Capote saw the band. Marty was succeeding in getting the band attention. Ever the epitome of New York cool, the Dolls acted like it was no big deal. Kathy Miller recalled a backstage encounter with David Johansen and her sister Dot at the Mercer when someone yelled, "David! John and Yoko are here to see you." His response? "Oh no, I'm talking to Dot."

Another key figure in the Dolls story was Paul Nelson, who heard the street buzz on the band and made a point of seeing them. Nelson was an A&R representative for Mercury Records and knew right then that he wanted to sign them.

A Minneapolis native, Nelson had helped launch a local folk music fanzine called *The Little Sandy Review*, leading to a friendship with a young Robert Zimmerman, who used Nelson's record collection to form the bedrock of his artistic self, eventually changing his name to Bob Dylan. Nelson later wrote for *Creem* and *Rolling Stone*, displaying a passion in his criticism like few others. In 1970 he worked for Mercury Records publicity department, zealously promoting the records of a pre-*Ziggy* David Bowie and pre-fame Rod Stewart, the latter remaining loyal to Paul for years to come.

Publicity was a somewhat unsuitable position for Nelson, as he was unable to do what anyone in publicity must do: As Danny Goldberg put it, "He was incapable of being insincere."[5]

Because he ardently talked up those he admired, Mercury felt that Nelson would be more effective working with artists as an A&R rep. Nelson took this as license to sign bands he was passionate about, assuming sales would follow. In that vein, he developed an unwavering commitment to getting the Dolls signed to Mercury. He was so convinced of their potential he was willing to gamble on them knowing full well that their failure could cost him his job.

Nelson brought Mercury's higher-ups to see them several times. Each time they passed.

Nelson persisted.

Bud Scoppa, who had assumed Nelson's position in promotions at Mercury, was equally as skeptical the first time he saw the Dolls. "I gave them a second chance, and somehow this original idea I had, that they were just this cartoon version of the Rolling Stones, changed into something a lot more nuanced. I fell in love with them pretty quickly after that."

The Rolling Stones comparison was common, much of it due to Johansen's Jagger-like pout and Thunders's role as his Keith Richards–like foil. Even locals like Wayne County noticed the resemblance but knew the Dolls were more than just a look. It was possible that, like that of the Stones, their music could transcend commonly known genres. "I remember standing there next to Danny Goldberg,"[6] said Wayne. "He watched the Dolls and he said, 'This is the most important band to come out of New York City since the Velvet Underground,' and I said, 'Yeah it is. They're the *real* Rolling Stones.'"[7]

* * *

MARTY'S IDEA OF BRINGING THE BAND TO BRITAIN WAS COMING to fruition. Steve Leber used his contacts to get the Dolls some English dates. The deal made was with British promoter Roy Fischer, who would book the shows in exchange for recording a few songs for a possible UK single. Thirteen shows were booked from October 19 through November 11, the highlight being a show on October 29, third on the bill to Rod Stewart and the Faces, in front of a crowd of twelve thousand people, an audience some forty times the size of any the Dolls had ever played for.

Before playing any gigs, the Dolls recorded four tracks at Escape Studios in Kent: "Personality Crisis," "Looking for a Kiss," "Bad Girl," and "Subway Train." Compared to the Blue Rock sessions, this was a positive step forward. Four additional months of gigs had solidified the arrangements and made the band a more cohesive musical unit. The sound was improved, with more snap to the snare drum, some double tracking of David's vocals, and Johnny's signature guitar sound close to fully formed. Back on the drums, Billy, though having advanced as a player since the sessions four months before, was still somewhat laid-back. It was almost as if the rest of the band was on speed while Billy was on Quaaludes.

There were gigs with Lou Reed at universities on October 19, 20, and 26, and headlining gigs in London on the twenty-second and twenty-fifth. Finally, on the twenty-ninth, came the twelve-thousand-seat Wembley Empire Pool show with Rod Stewart and the Faces.

In attendance were three teenage Faces fans: Paul Cook, Steve Jones, and Glen Matlock. Glen thought the Dolls were great: "This was like a real breath of fresh air." As much as Glen dug their music, he also loved their flippant, devil-may-care, non-rock-star attitude. He recalled that Johnny "broke a string and he didn't have a spare guitar." Everyone had to wait "while a roadie was going round begging a string off of Ron Wood or something. Got the string. Put it back on. Didn't even turn down. 'Yowng! Yowng! Gowng! Yowng!' Tuned up again. Start the song over. Got to exactly the same place in the song and broke the string again! They didn't care!"

Several more shows in early November led to a November 4 show at Liverpool Stadium, again with Lou Reed, who unceremoniously tossed the Dolls off the bill—presumably tiring of having to compete with them.

During the trip, Marty made overtures to several record labels, getting interest from Charisma, EMI, Virgin, Rolling Stone, Atlantic, and Track. Despite several labels making paltry offers or dropping out, Track Records were serious. Run by partners Kit Lambert and Chris Stamp, the Who's eccentric managers since 1964, Track was the home of not only the Who, but the late Jimi Hendrix. It was considered a boutique independent label.

After negotiations, both parties came to an agreement with an advance payment of $100,000. This was exactly what Marty had planned: an offer from a British label who could either license the record to an American company or put pressure on US labels to sign them. In less than a year, the Dolls, all barely into their twenties, were seeing their rock 'n' roll dreams come true. Little did anyone know that on this very same day, the band would suffer the first of many nightmares to come. On the night of November 6, while in final negotiations with Track, Marty received a phone call with news that made the record deal moot, and for that moment, irrelevant. Billy Murcia was dead.

After going to a party with a group of strangers, Billy combined alcohol with Mandrax—the British brand name for American Quaaludes. He either fell asleep or lost consciousness. The other party guests panicked, threw him into a bathtub, and force-fed him coffee to revive him. Inadvertently, they suffocated him.

Marty got the Dolls out of England on a 7 a.m. flight to New York, avoiding the press. Malcolm McLaren, who a few years later served a short stretch working with the Dolls before managing the Sex Pistols, later described Billy's death by saying, "I just know that it was a tragedy not spoken about thereafter. Ever."

Dolls folklore would have us believe the band considered packing it in, with Jerry, Kathy Miller, and Dale Powers all saying so. But more revealing is what Syl was quoted as saying in the November 16 *Village Voice*, less than ten days after Billy's death: "We're looking for another drummer, and we hope to come out strong by the New Year."[8]

They began auditions for a new drummer at Charles Lane Studios in Manhattan after placing an ad in the *Village Voice*. But it wasn't necessary, as word of mouth on the street was fierce. And of course, Jerry knew all about it and jumped at the opportunity, letting members of Queen

Elizabeth know ahead of time. They wished him the best. Tom Wynbrandt recalls, "The Dolls . . . In those days, you couldn't get bigger."

Few drummers could play to the band's particular standards *and* look right. In the end, it came down to two entrants: Jerry and Marc Bell, who a few years later became Marky Ramone, replacing original member Tommy in the Ramones. Previously he was the drummer in hard rock band Dust.

Dust released two albums in 1971 and '72, reminiscent of Led Zeppelin, Deep Purple, and Mountain. The band never took off, leaving Bell looking for a gig. Marc knew the Dolls from hanging out at Nobody's and Max's and had seen them perform at the Mercer. Dolls roadie Peter Jordan recalled Marc's audition: "He definitely had chops. But he was more . . . heavy metal, whereas Jerry could play a twist beat. The heavy metal sounds of the early '70s . . . seemed to have gone right past Jerry without affecting him. Jerry could play any type of soul styles or twist styles or anything like that."

Another element Jerry had going for him was his developing relationship with Johnny Thunders. Max Blatt, who was Jerry's drum roadie throughout most of his time with the Dolls, recalled that "Johnny suggested to the other guys, 'This drummer should get the gig.'"

Jerry had seen the Dolls numerous times, and knew their set backward and forward. He played a more varied style than Billy but still held back from overwhelming the music. He gave them something Billy never understood: drive. It's the ability of a drummer to propel a band, just like Gene Krupa and other big band drummers did. Jerry recalled the audition: "I was so on it was pathetic."[9]

According to Syl, another deciding factor was what Billy once told him: "'If anything happens to me, Jerry should be the guy.' So I took that into consideration, shared that with the rest of the boys and they said, 'Okay, let's get Jerry.' I called him up . . . and I said, 'Jerry, welcome to the New York Dolls.' I could tell his tits got hard."

LOOKING FOR
6 A KISS

AFTER GETTING THE DOLLS GIG, JERRY STILL MOVED FROM PLACE to place, with no permanent home. He was twenty-six years old, with no girlfriend and no apartment.

One couch he'd crash on when visiting Manhattan was at a studio apartment on Twelfth Street and Broadway. It was through its occupant that Jerry would meet his next girlfriend, Michelle Piza.

Michelle met Susan—who lived at the Twelfth Street apartment— while working part-time during Christmas season at Lord and Taylor, a luxury department store in midtown Manhattan. Michelle was a student at the Fashion Institute of Technology and mentioned to Susan how much she liked her boots. Susan had made them herself, and offered to make her a pair. Michelle went over to the apartment to get measured and then tagged along to a party. Jerry was there, "moving around through the crowd, being very touchy-feely with people. I remember not really getting a good vibe from him at all." The girls had a nickname for him: Supercock.

On another visit to the apartment, Michelle rang the bell and Jerry opened the door. It was raining and Michelle, carrying a new umbrella, had trouble closing it. Jerry, ever the gentlemen, helped her close it properly. "It was obvious that he was smitten with me. He kept flirting. I was like, 'Oh, God . . . please, don't bother me.'"

Michelle's parents had divorced a few years before, and she lived with her grandparents in Brooklyn. Told she would she need to move out when she turned eighteen, she was desperate to find a new place, but she was also desperate to get out of Brooklyn. She relayed this to Susan and her roommate, Jean, who were looking for a third roommate. Although Michelle liked the idea of moving in with them, she was concerned about living somewhere that Jerry frequented. Clearly he was trouble.

Jean and Susan tried to play matchmaker between Jerry and Michelle for several weeks, but Michelle was having none of it. "But I moved in." This was around the time Jerry auditioned for the Dolls.

After he got the Dolls gig, surprisingly, the band thought his appearance actually needed some work. While Jerry may have seemed feminine to Shaker, to the Dolls and their crowd, he seemed a bit too masculine.

Johnny and Syl were assigned the task of "Dollifying" Jerry. After meeting on Fourteenth Street, they took him to their favorite places to buy boots and scarves. After a few purchases and a little hairstyling, Jerry was Dollified to everyone's satisfaction. Afterward, Michelle took notice. "I was like, 'Hmm. He's not so bad. He's cute.'" She was now willing to go on a date with him. Their first date was set: New Year's Eve 1972, right after Jerry's gig with the Dolls at the Mercer.

This was Jerry's fourth gig with the Dolls. His first gig on December 19 was also at the Mercer, advertised as "The Return of the NY Dolls." Binky Philips, guitarist for opening band the Planets, remembers the first set as "a train wreck"[1] and the second set, which began at 2:30 a.m., as "astoundingly good."[2] Unfortunately, all the record company executives left after the first set.

Jerry's second and third shows were December 22 and 23 at the Village East Theater, formerly the site of the Fillmore East, where he and his old pal Peter had seen scores of bands. These were undoubtedly emotional shows for Jerry.

Kathy Miller and her friends waited for him at the stage door to tell him what a great job he'd done. "He was truly happy and flattered. Big smile. Not a cool rock 'n' roll star attitude. He was never stuck-up, just a real down-to-earth guy."

It was apparent, even three gigs into his tenure with the Dolls, that he was making an impact. "Billy Murcia was a nice guy. He wasn't much of a drummer," noted Kathy. "Jerry was a killer drummer and Arthur . . . wasn't a strong bass player. But when Jerry became the drummer . . . they had a rhythm section."

When Michelle finally got to the Mercer on New Year's Eve, it was a madhouse. Kathy recalled, "That gig was so crowded and sold out. The papier-mâché chandeliers . . . literally, from body heat condensation, turned upside down and melted." The audience was filled with critics and record company executives. Everybody had the same thought: This band is going to break through.

Michelle was extremely nervous at the show. "I was standing in the audience . . . and I was thinking, 'Oh, God, I have a date with this guy!'"

After the show, the two of them went to a party at the penthouse of the legendary Freddie Sessler. Rolling Stone Ronnie Wood described Freddie as "the drug pusher to the stars."[3] This was a long way from Michelle's bedroom in Brooklyn at her grandparents' house. From that night forward, she and Jerry were an item.

With Jerry earning a regular income for the first time in his life, the couple's first step was finding their own apartment, and they found one on the Upper East Side, at 1394 York Avenue, between Seventy-Fourth and Seventy-Fifth Streets. It had an elevator, and the door in their bedroom opened to a terrace. In comparison to their previous living situations, it seemed as if they had moved into the Taj Mahal.

* * *

THE NEW YEAR SAW MARTY AND LEBER-KREBS PUSHING THE Dolls full tilt toward a record deal, setting up weeklong stays at Max's, followed by a twelve-day run at Kenny's Castaways, with a couple of Tuesdays at the Mercer in between.

The run at Kenny's Castaways turned into more of a party than normal for the Dolls as Mike Gormley, Paul Nelson's boss at Mercury, attended the January 30 show and was ready to make an offer. Despite Paul's instructions from label head Irwin Steinberg never to mention the band in his presence again, he won over Gormley, and Mercury pulled the trigger. On March 20, the Dolls signed a two-album deal with Mercury for $25,000, one-tenth of Marty's original asking price. The band's reputation, first as drug addicts due to Billy's death, and second as "fags," had been a hindrance to getting them signed. Under the circumstances, Marty was satisfied with the offer. The band members didn't care. They were happy with any record deal, plus they got an equipment allowance and had their weekly take-home pay raised to $200 each.

David, in a self-deprecating but proud and insightful moment, summed up the deal with a perspective all his own: "We single-handedly lowered the standards of an entire industry."[4]

Jerry made the most of his new largesse. Michelle: "He ridiculously and impulsively decided to go out and buy Chinese-red paint, and proceeded to paint the whole apartment, except the bedroom, that color."

Now that the Dolls were signed, management could find Jerry an endorsement deal from a drum manufacturer. While two Slingerland sets were purchased for immediate use, one white and one lime green, he got his endorsement deal from the Ludwig drum company. Jerry didn't want just any old kit off the rack, though. What he chose made a statement to the band and their fans that he was not just a replacement for Billy. It was a stake in the ground that would put a stamp on his career forever, a statement to the world that he was a Doll and that his style was as singular and as valuable as that of any band member.

He chose pink drums. Oversize pink drums.

Tony Machine, a Leber-Krebs employee and a drummer himself, recalled: "He loved Elvis Presley's colors. That's why he got pink drums." But it was also a way for Jerry to both embrace the femininity the band had requested of him and stand out from the crowd. Most drummers are in the background, keeping the beat while the lead singer and guitarists work the audience up front. Jerry would now have a profile that could bore through anything placed in front of him. Visually, he was now as important as any band member.

Jerry meticulously put the kit together, choosing an extra-deep hanging tom and an old-style extra-large bass drum. He also selected two floor toms and, in another nod to the past, a canister-style drum throne. Not only could it be used to store hardware, it would match his kit, which standard thrones could not, as they were skeletal frames topped off by a padded seat. As always, looks were of utmost importance to Jerry.

While awaiting delivery of the new drum kit, the band gigged consistently, with a February 11 blowout at the Mercer billed as "An Endless Valentine's Day All-Night Party." In attendance was Barry Miles, observing for the British music weekly *New Music Express* (*NME*). He noticed what many others had: The audience was as wild as the band on the stage. Miles described the crowd as "wandering ghosts of a lost humanity."[5]

A young guitarist had the same epiphany after seeing the Dolls at the Diplomat Hotel. Richard Lloyd would later help form the band Television. "Here was a band . . . dressed up as 'glam.' The most amazing thing . . . was the packed audience were also all dolled up. And they spent most of their time looking at each other and themselves, and chatting about how great each and every one of them was. I'd never seen that before. Here was a group that were drawing people who were equally interesting. It's almost like the Dolls were a backdrop to a giant social event."

Such was the impact of the Dolls. Like Sinatra's bobby-soxers or Beatles fans who'd grown their hair to match that of the group, scores of Dolls fans sensed that to attend a Dolls show was more than just enjoying the band onstage. They felt an urge to be part of an experience, a rebellious experience, in which they cast aside their outsider identities and basked in being part of a community while simultaneously proclaiming their individuality. This, as much as the music and the bands' look, was a big part of Marty Thau's and Leber-Krebs's attraction to the band and a key element to what they saw as the potential of the Dolls. They felt it could spread exponentially.

Opening slots for Captain Beefheart and gigs in Boston were all secondary to preparing for their first album. The label wanted to hear what the band could do in the studio. After another gig at Kenny's Castaways, the Dolls entered Planet Studios with Paul Nelson to knock out some demos.

Despite two previous demo sessions, the Dolls' inexperience and lack of discipline was still apparent, as Johnny ignored David's count-off for "Personality Crisis." Still, the tracks showed the band had improved with Jerry behind the kit. "Frankenstein" was decidedly faster and more fully realized than the Blue Rock Studio demos. "Personality Crisis," despite the false start, was also improved with its faster tempo and Jerry kicking the accents in the repeated choruses near the end. "Bad Girl" had a more frenetic air with Jerry than with Billy. "Human Being" was now danceable. All of these songs would become classics in time.

After completing the demos there was still the issue of who would produce the record. It soon became apparent that the problem was not so much who the Dolls wanted, but who would "stoop so low" as to produce a band that still had a reputation for being more concerned about their makeup and the next party than playing their instruments.

Roy Wood, formerly of the British avant-pop band the Move and a founding member of the Electric Light Orchestra, was considered but then dropped, thought to be too eccentric. With a group as wild as the Dolls, the thinking was that their producer needed to be a more stable and disciplined presence.

As the Dolls had a penchant for girl groups like the Shangri-Las and the Ronettes, as well as teen idol pop stars like Dion and Ricky Nelson, several producers from the pre-Beatles era were considered. Phil Spector was discussed but never pursued. However, some of his mentors, the team of Jerry Leiber and Mike Stoller, were. Their songs and productions were among the band's favorites: singles by Elvis Presley ("Hound Dog" and "Jailhouse Rock"), the Coasters ("Searchin'" and "Yakety Yak"), and Ben E. King ("Stand by Me"). Despite the Dolls presenting themselves as markedly different than their usual clients, Leiber and Stoller possessed the experience, discipline, skill, humor, and taste that in theory could have given the Dolls hit records. Alas, they were out of the band's price range.

Shadow Morton, producer and songwriter of the Dolls' favorite group, the Shangri-Las, was unfortunately recuperating from a recent auto accident. A more modern consideration was their pal David Bowie. They thought he could do for them what he'd done for Mott the Hoople with "All the Young Dudes," or Lou Reed with "Transformer," but Bowie was busy working on *Aladdin Sane*, the follow-up to *Ziggy Stardust*.

David Johansen claimed over twenty producers were approached, all turning the Dolls down. The studio time was booked and the record company was pressuring the band into finalizing their choice. The solution, as it turned out, was no farther than Max's Kansas City—their drinking buddy Todd Rundgren.

By 1973, twenty-four-year-old Todd Rundgren was seen as a "boy wonder." He was a producer in high demand, with credits including the Band's 1970 Top Five album *Stage Fright*, and much of 1971's *Straight Up* by Badfinger, which included the Top 20 hit "Baby Blue."

From his days with the Nazz, whose 1968 single "Open My Eyes" was included on Lenny Kaye's highly influential 1972 collection of pre-punk garage rock *Nuggets*, to his solo albums like *Something/Anything*, there was a side of Todd that embraced a lack of virtuosity in favor of passion and creativity. Despite his finely tuned melodic composition skills, his garage-rock, autodidactic side made him seem like a good fit for the Dolls. Plus he was available and would do it for the money offered.

The rainbow-haired Rundgren first saw the Dolls at Max's at the behest of his girlfriend, model Bebe Buell. Unlike Bebe, he was not convinced of their greatness. Todd, like so many others, was confused by the Dolls. He found them to be an incompetent group of Rolling Stones imitators in drag, but he also saw them as funny and possessing a real rock 'n' roll attitude, which might overcome their lack of technical ability.

Todd had his concerns. "I was apprehensive about whether they'd be able to re-create their live excitement, and whether they would play with some degree of competence. A couple of them were . . . there because they were pals, particularly Arthur—but they improved quickly once they were in the studio."[6] Game for the challenge, Todd and the Dolls began sessions for the first New York Dolls album in April at New York's Record Plant studios.

While Todd's productions for Badfinger and the Band were chart successes, the process of making those records was anything but smooth. Todd was young and impatient, and used to making his own records and decisions. He was less adept at delicately negotiating relationships between other band members who had their own issues to muddle through before coming to any sort of consensus.

Producers are often looked at by a band as schoolmarms, wagging a disapproving finger in their direction at the behest of management or the label. Few, especially the Dolls, start rock 'n' roll bands to be told they must follow rules. If, however, as in the case of the Beatles and producer George Martin, the stars are aligned, trusted partnerships can form where artist and producer bond behind a shared vision. In the Band, Robbie Robertson was Rundgren's trusted partner. Bass player Rick Danko and drummer Levon Helm, who supposedly went after Rundgren with a drumstick after Rundgren referred to keyboard player Garth Hudson as an "old man," were less enamored with him. In Badfinger, sole surviving member Joey Molland remembered Todd as "rude and obnoxious. . . . It was really a horrible experience for me."[7] Todd would have the same issues with the Dolls.

Todd found both partners and adversaries in the Dolls. "The band was evenly split between troublemakers and go-along guys, with Arthur the Charlie Watts of the band, a quiet facilitator."[8] As for Todd's partner, that was David, who he described as "a sweet guy and a conciliator."[9] Sylvain was also commended as having "the most pleasant disposition."[10]

While Todd may have credited Syl for his willingness to make things work, there were still moments where things didn't sit right with him. Syl recalled Todd bringing his dog into the studio, where it "took a crap on top of the board. Todd's like, 'Aaah fuck it! That's only going to help these guys. . . .' I thought, 'this guy's a fucking dick.'"

Todd's adversaries were Johnny and Jerry. "Johnny Thunders . . . was snotty, always had a heavy attitude; so did Jerry," he said later.[11]

Marty Thau was aware of the issues, saying, "There was always some friction between him and the group. [Todd] was not as warm as he could have been. But then again, there were all kinds of people that were coming to those sessions . . . loads of writers, and friends of the Dolls, and it was kind of like a madhouse."

Singer/songwriter Elliott Murphy, also managed by Leber-Krebs, was recording his first album, *Aquashow*, at the Record Plant at the same time. "My recording sessions were like a church service. Theirs were like a party in decadent Rome!"

One bone of contention between Jerry and Todd was the drum sound. They both liked loosely tuned drums, which should have helped them bond. But the looser the drum, the less natural resonance it had, which didn't necessarily take advantage of what a studio like the Record Plant had to offer: terrific rooms where sound could take on its own character, to be captured by strategically placed microphones. Todd's hit "Hello It's Me" exhibits exactly this sort of deficit just before the second verse, when the tom-tom fill on the preceding beat sounds like it was recorded by a ham-fisted amateur. The record's beauty comes through despite this by all the other wonderful things it offers: a well-composed song, expertly arranged with great vocals and performances by the supporting band. But no drummer likes to hear his drums sound like they were recorded on a cheap cassette player in his bedroom.

Making this worse was Jerry's decision to play with the butt ends of his sticks. While useful during live shows where volume was needed to cut through the Marshall stacks, this could be grating on the ears when used on cymbals. Despite his inspired playing, the hi-hats on "Looking for a Kiss" sounded practically abrasive.

One of the writers visiting the studio was Ron Ross from *Cash Box* and *Circus* magazine. He remembered distinctly "being very turned off by Jerry. . . . He was absolutely correct that the drums were wrong, but Jerry was both arrogant and inarticulate. I think he made matters much worse with Todd."

Years later, Todd still had unkind words for Jerry, saying his bad attitude was "unjustified by the quality of his playing,"[12] adding, "It became apparent in the studio that Jerry's time was totally fluid."[13]

While it was somewhat ironic for Todd to say such a thing, based on his acceptance of his own erratic drumming, Syl also recalled some issues with Jerry's internal metronome. "There were a few times where Jerry just couldn't keep the beat."[14] Todd tried to guide Jerry by whacking a cowbell, miked into Jerry's headphones. "Sort of a live click track."[15]

While every drummer has his own sense of time, no drummer is a human metronome. Charlie Watts, famous for his steady hand, often played on the most straight-ahead songs with a tempo best described as fluid—"Honky Tonk Women," for example, is decidedly faster even by the end of the first chorus than it was when it started. To dismiss Jerry's playing because his time may not have been metronome perfect does not begin to do it justice. Even Sylvain qualified his previous statement, summing up his playing on the record by saying, "Jerry was incredible on that album."

The resultant tracks may not have been perfect, but they were *exciting*. An occasional turnaround or fill would come back a little early on the beat, adding to the looseness, but if there were any problems with tempo, the blame lies as much with the other Dolls, who were still novices at the art of ensemble playing. Arthur often lagged behind the beat, while Johnny was usually ahead of the beat.

In retrospect, Jerry did a remarkable job of holding things together against the chaos that was their default setting. But there was little Jerry could do about the intros to "Vietnamese Baby" and "Lonely Planet Boy," which are a mess. The stops in the latter after each chorus are imperfect, as they are in "Jet Boy" as well. But so are the stops in Led Zeppelin's "Moby Dick," some of Bob Dylan and Neil Young's most revered records, and scores of '60s garage-rock hits. Complaints regarding those records are universally dismissed because there's so much more to celebrate than the few flubs they contain. Perfection is of little concern in rock 'n' roll, and the exhilarating experience that is the Dolls' first record proves it.

After all the tracks were recorded, overdubs made, and vocals added, it was time for making sense of it all in the mixing room. Sadly, despite whatever miscues went down live, this is where the record suffered the most.

With everyone in a hurry to finish the record and get back on the road, several key mistakes were made. Due either to the speakers, the board, or the space itself, Todd thought the sound was off in the only room available to mix at the Record Plant. Then—generally considered a huge mistake—all members of the band were present during the mix. Todd: "They did what was typical for a band: Everyone only hears themselves, so everyone's standing over your shoulder saying they wanted to be louder, and at the end of a mix the faders are all at the top of the board."[16]

While Todd listed many good reasons for why the mix was wanting, the fact that his own history at mixing was checkered cannot be ignored. The Band's *Stage Fright* was given an alternative mix by British heavyweight Glyn Johns, which to this day is the preferred mix used on reissues. Badfinger's "Baby Blue" was also remixed by studio engineer Eddie Kramer, known for his work with Jimi Hendrix and for hit records by the Beatles and the Stones, with specific instructions to give the snare drum in the first verse and middle eight more impact.

Marty, the ever-dutiful manager, heard Jerry's displeasure at the way his drums sounded and asked Todd why they were so low in the mix. "His comment was something like, 'I've been producing records for years now, and that's my drum sound.' As soon as I heard that, I just figured, well, he's the producer, maybe I should just back off on that. I was trying to be very gentle . . . because that's sensitive to criticize anyone who's creating something. So I gently backed off, but I didn't think that his response was very friendly."

Syl, like Jerry, felt underappreciated by Todd. But he also understood that after two months of babysitting the Dolls, "I think he was just sick and tired and he wanted his money and wanted to get the hell out of there." Todd did have somewhere else to be: Criteria Studios in Miami Beach, to record with Grand Funk Railroad, for which he supposedly received what was then a record $50,000 advance payment.

Marty saw past the flaws of the record and heard something unique. "The first album, probably its only criticism was that it didn't quite capture their live power. But still, the bottom line was . . . it was a classic, and Todd Rundgren did a very good job. Jerry felt that it didn't capture the raw power as well, but eventually, I think he was pretty pleased with the way it turned out."

But the truth is that Jerry was never pleased with the way it turned out, blaming the results on Todd's shortcomings as a producer and mixer, and on David's disregard for the value of a more painstaking basic track process. Whatever the reasons, once the record was finished, Jerry's feelings persisted: he thought the record, and particularly his drumming, was recorded badly. Jerry's whole being hinged on being a star drummer, profiling in sound as well as in fashion. Todd was an impediment to that. Todd's treatment of Jerry never seemed like the act of a mentor, but that of someone judging and dismissing him, like the band director at Lawton Central Junior High. Marty never lost confidence in Jerry, though. "I never had any question about his drumming."

Contrasted with the demos Billy played on, and despite lingering questions about the sound, Jerry's abilities and performances were spectacular. Jerry understood that in this type of music, the song was king, and a good band member never forgets that by obstructing the listener's opportunity to hear the hooks. And he drove the band like a locomotive.

Examples of where he took the band that Billy couldn't abound: The way Jerry differentiates sections of each verse and chorus of "Personality Crisis" and "Looking for a Kiss"; the extended rolls and buildups in "Vietnamese Baby" and "Frankenstein"; the drive and explosiveness of "Pills" and "Bad Girl"; the controlled, multidimensional, tension-and-release, dramatic playing on "Jet Boy."

"Trash," especially, is a standout, with Jerry playing like a rocked-out Gene Krupa right from the top. Sylvain is still so awestruck by Jerry's performance on this song, he becomes tongue-tied when trying to articulate what he brought to it. "He really . . . I mean, he wrote that line, you know, which fucking made my song like . . . you know . . . catapulted it into stardom . . . you know . . . forever!"

Throughout the record, Jerry shows that minimalism, simplicity, and economy can coexist with inventiveness, swing, and drive. Sylvain was right: Jerry was incredible on the album. But so was everyone. By the end of the record, you feel as if you've spent a night club-hopping in New York, high and wired, listening to the best party band since the Rolling Stones first took off. It's a one-of-a-kind rock 'n' roll statement that still stands up over forty years later.

* * *

THE FINAL ELEMENT REQUIRED BEFORE THE ALBUM COULD BE considered finished was the artwork. The band was happy with the back-cover photo, posing on the southwest corner of St. Marks Place and Second Avenue in front of Gem Spa, an East Village twenty-four-hour newsstand, known for making a New York fountain specialty called an egg cream. The front cover turned out to be more of an issue.

The original plan placed the Dolls in an antique shop, posed among old clocks, furniture, and moose heads. After reviewing the photos, the band were unanimous in their response: They hated them. Given a two-day reprieve and a $900 budget by Mercury, the Dolls set out to create a cover that was worthy of their name. What they ended up unleashing on the world was as controversial as anything they'd ever do.

After contacting some of his old friends in the *schmatte* business, Syl connected with *Vogue* photographer Toshi, who brought along a crew of hair and makeup artists. Meanwhile, the band found an old couch in the street, dragged it inside, and tacked a piece of white satin over it. The stage was now set.

The Dolls appeared with their makeup painted thick and hair dialed up to ten. They all wore platform heels except Syl, who inexplicably wore roller skates. There was a beer can with a straw in it, a champagne glass, a can of hair spray, and a pack of Lucky Strikes in the shot. Arthur let a cigarette dangle loosely from his lips, while David preened into a compact mirror. They looked tough, but also feminine in a twisted sort of way. And the energy, despite the decadence, was of children playing. And Jerry? Bud Scoppa thought he "looked the most ridiculous, because he was the most sort of normal, regular dude."

In the period between completion of the Dolls' album—now officially titled *The New York Dolls*—and its release, Todd's work with Grand Funk Railroad at Criteria oozed with potential. Criteria was the same studio where the great Tom Dowd recorded Derek and the Dominos' "Layla" and James Brown recorded "I Feel Good." It seemed like the $50,000 advance Todd received was money well spent when Grand Funk Railroad recorded and mixed a single that everyone agreed was so hot it was released before the album was even finished. It was called "We're an American Band." On September 29, 1973, it hit number one. Maybe Todd had the magic touch after all. Maybe some of it would rub off on the Dolls.

 **JET BOY**

AFTER A FOUR-DAY RUN AT KENNY'S CASTAWAYS, ON JULY 27 THE Dolls went back to Coventry, a small club in Queens that the band always packed to the gills, to celebrate the release of the album and the single "Trash," backed with "Personality Crisis."

In the middle of their three-day stretch at Coventry, they played their first US show away from their northeastern base, at the nineteen-thousand-seat Tiger Stadium in Massillon, Ohio. They were third on a four-band bill, scheduled before Dr. Hook and the Medicine Show, and headliner Mott the Hoople. It would be the first of fourteen shows they'd play with Mott through the fall.

Rock critic Lester Bangs was there reviewing it for *Phonograph Record*. Seemingly writing in an all-night blaze, Bangs described the crowd as "fatboy yokels"[1] wearing "those goofy Hillbilly Bear hats."[2] As the Dolls walked through the audience in "purple leotards and platforms,"[3] the crowd took note, muttering, "Ooogh! Faaaggits!"[4] But then "the Dolls hit the stage and it's the selfsame faggots they was just about to beat up! And what's more they're good! In fact they're GREAT!"[5]

Bangs raved about the show. But in a public-put down of the Dolls, Dr. Hook's lead singer exclaimed, "Hi folks, we're faggots . . . bigger faggots than the makeup faggots,"[6] presumably referring to the Dolls. Successfully taking their show out of New York City was not going to be an easy task.

* * *

ON AUGUST 3, THE DOLLS PLAYED THEIR SECOND SHOW WITH Mott at the prestigious Felt Forum, a five-thousand-seat hall that was part of the Madison Square Garden complex in midtown Manhattan. There was much to be remembered about this show; the sight backstage of Wayne County in full drag and a giant wig adorned with a Dave Clark Five sign; Todd Rundgren introducing the band, wearing a gold lamé suit to go with his rainbow-colored hair; and legendary radio DJ Wolfman Jack, most famous as a relic of the '50s and a champion of early rock 'n' roll, egging the crowd on to welcome the Dolls. What's more, Jerry's pink Ludwig kit had arrived, and tonight was its debut.

As hoped, the drums were a standout, an unforgettable statement.

Roadie Desmond Sullivan recalled what it was like when Jerry used his pink kit: "Coast to coast, all over the world, people used to flip the fuck out. Nobody else had pink drums. Just taking those drums out and setting them up, was like, 'Holy fuck, the guy's got pink drums!'"

Marty and the Leber-Krebs team were ready to send the Dolls across America to convert the masses. After a one-off show in Pittsburgh opening for Mott and Blue Öyster Cult, followed by several shows at My Father's Place in Long Island and Max's, the band were ready to fly out to Los Angeles on August 29.

Before leaving to spread the gospel, Arthur's girlfriend, Connie Gripp, became upset that she couldn't join him on the road. Her response, probably drug- and/or alcohol-fueled, was to attempt to cut his thumb off as he slept.

Connie was an ex–Frank Zappa hanger-on and a friend of the LA-based band the GTOs (Girls Together Outrageously) who'd come to New York and latched onto the Dolls' bass player with a technique she later used on Ramones bass player Dee Dee Ramone: Possess at all times your chosen prey's drug of choice. With Dee Dee, it was heroin. With Arthur, it was blackberry brandy.

Recalled Arthur's post-Connie girlfriend Eileen Polk, "Arthur told me she'd been sexually abused as a child, and she'd run away from home at fourteen. She was already a hard-core stripper, prostitute, hooker when I first saw her. I remember seeing Connie at one party with the Dolls. She was wearing six-inch platform shoes, a gold lamé and black lace merry widow corset with garters, fishnets, and a black feather boa, no skirt. She was very outrageous and very big. She was like six-foot-four in heels."

Per Eileen, Connie would hang around until her target "would get weak and get high with her. . . . But she wouldn't leave you alone. She was just a stalker."

Arthur's thumb would not heal sufficiently enough to allow him to play dependably for over a month. Luckily for the band, roadie Peter Jordan was an excellent bass player and subbed for Arthur, who continued to travel with the band, ready to resume his position as soon as possible.

The band flew to Los Angeles with photographer Bob Gruen and his wife Nadya Beck in tow, taking still photos and capturing them on videotape using an early portable video camera package.

The first shows in LA were at the Whisky a Go Go, where they performed for five consecutive nights through September 2, two sets a night, all sold out. Upon arrival, the band were met by the cream of the LA teenage groupie contingent, including fifteen-year-old Lori Mattix[†] and sixteen-year-old Sable Starr.

Johnny and Sable locked eyes before the band ever set foot in the Whisky, and began a torrid love affair. After a pre-show blow job, Johnny wanted to marry her. In no time at all the pair were appearing in photos together and making a name for themselves as the "it" couple of the moment.

Syl quickly caught the "Hong Kong clap" and, according to Peter Jordan, "[Arthur] had the ability of finding the most fucked-up girls all over the world . . . [with] torn stockings and a broken pair of highheeled shoes. I had to room with him with all these nut cases."

As for the rest of them, David "was not into groupies or anything like that," recalled Peter. And Jerry, according to Sylvain, was just happy being a Doll. "If he got a girl, forget it, to him that was a peach."[7] Peter had a different recollection. "He was quite a womanizer. He was very outgoing, but Jerry always would tend to go off, because he was always with girls."

As for his taste in ladies, Max noted, "Jerry always wanted the youngest girls. [It] wasn't a degenerate kind of thing. . . . He always kept to himself after the shows. He didn't smoke grass. He used to just take a girl and go in his room and you'd see him the next day."

Next stop for the Dolls was San Francisco for three shows at the Matrix. Jerry was met there by Michelle, the only girlfriend to make it out to the West Coast. She'd been invited by a friend of hers to meet in San Francisco, see the band, and then make the trip with them back down to LA for two television appearances.

"There had been all the talk about the groupies waiting for them." Jerry can be seen in video from backstage at the Whisky with his arm around a slender, long-haired brunette who is not Michelle. When Michelle brought up joining him in San Francisco, he was less than welcoming. "I remember him saying, 'Yeah, well, if you want to come it's

---

† Lori Mattix caused a mini furor when she admitted a few days after the death of David Bowie, in 2016, that she had lost her virginity to him when she was fifteen.

up to you, but I don't know how you are gonna get home . . . because we can't afford the airfare.' I risked it and I went to San Francisco."

Desmond recalled that in San Francisco, "everybody thought they'd go over incredibly well," being that it was, "the big fag town of the world. It didn't." There was nowhere near the press or groupie attention that existed in LA.

When they returned to LA, Michelle got wind of what Jerry had been up to. "One of the groupies was all over Jerry . . . rubbing his legs, and I'm sitting right there! She wanted to know who I was. Obviously, he had been hanging out with her. So it was a real wrench in his game when I showed up."

Michelle left before the band did their television spots, a September 8 lip-synching appearance on the local *Real Don Steele Show*, and a live performance on *The Midnight Special*, taped September 11, and broadcast nationally September 13.

On the day of the *Midnight Special* taping, Syl recalled running into a guest who was scheduled to be on the Johnny Carson show, a woman they knew from New York. "We're walking down the hallway, somebody's lying down . . . and yelling, 'Jerry! Jerry Nolan! Jerry!' And she's laying there, this little petite, kind of chunky chick, with all the hair. Of course, we knew who she was, because we had seen her at the Bathhouse. It's Bette Midler. 'I heard you were in town!' and 'Hi Guys.' I said to him, 'Bette Midler?' 'Oh yeah, I used to go out with her.' Now, he was proud."

Jerry was gratified to be associated with someone like Bette. In July, her single "Boogie Woogie Bugle Boy" hit number eight on the *Billboard* charts after her debut album, *The Divine Miss M*, peaked at number nine in March. Bette was going places, and he "knew her when." He had a history now of rubbing shoulders and sleeping with stars. This made him somebody. It was just another step to his own, fully earned stardom.

The band played live on *The Midnight Special*, with Peter standing almost out of camera range, playing, as Arthur merely posed with his bass. David is hoarse from all of their shows, and Johnny is more concerned with his appearance in front of untold millions as he hits a bevy of notes barely on the fringe of the correct key throughout the performance. Still, singing or playing out of tune could never damage a classic Dolls performance. They look great in leather, satin, spangles, platform heels, studded shirts, exposed nipples, high-piled hair, makeup, and cowboy gear from their trip to Nudie's the week before. And of course, the pink drums!

After the show aired on September 13, the band were anxious to see if album sales had risen. While most bands would see an upsurge in sales after national exposure, the Dolls album actually dropped in the *Billboard* chart from the week before, when it hit 116. The single "Trash" still has not charted.

* * *

IT WAS TIME TO TAKE THE SHOW ON THE ROAD, ACROSS THE country to the heartland, hoping for better days, and sales, ahead. It was here that Marty and Leber-Krebs knew the Dolls had to make serious inroads if they were to become a profitable band. With Arthur still along only for the ride, the band played in Houston and Dallas, all without incident until September 21 in Memphis, where David spent the night in jail after mouthing off from the stage at the rough handling of the crowd by security.

After springing David from the pokey, the band played their way through Detroit, Milwaukee, Atlanta, and Chicago, where Arthur finally began playing again. Chicago was Mercury's hometown, and the band felt they needed to put their best face on for this gig. No one had forgotten how David had gone up to their offices a few months back and fallen asleep in the middle of a meeting with the brass.

The band played on bills with Aerosmith and Mott the Hoople until October 13 in St. Louis, where they were on a bill with Lynyrd Skynyrd. As incompatible as this pairing may have seemed, they actually got along well. Opening for the Dolls, Skynyrd had one bottle of hard liquor compared to the Dolls' twelve.

"Ronnie Van Zant and the bass player [Leon Wilkeson] came to see what the hoopla was all about," recalled Desmond. "I remember Ronnie Van Zant backstage . . . basically saying, we saw you guys, and we thought you were a bunch of fags, and seeing how much you can drink and how much pussy you're getting, you guys must be cool. They became good buddies."

While the band continued working their way back home for a big Halloween show in New York, there was an early version of a Halloween celebration in Buffalo on October 17 that foreshadowed problems to come. Johnny and David had argued about Johnny's increased speed use as well as David nixing Johnny's desire to sing lead on some songs. Johnny sulked throughout the show, playing with his back to the audience, and tossed around some of the decorative pumpkins the promoter had placed on the stage, one landing on David's head during a dramatic portion of

"Frankenstein." A monster, built on drugs, frustration, and lack of success, was beginning to be unleashed.

The Dolls' American tour continued through Rhode Island, upstate New York, Pittsburgh, Philadelphia, and St. Louis before they canceled a show in Minneapolis on October 22 due to low ticket sales. The same week, *Billboard* magazine announced that Jerry's old flame Bette Midler had set the year's box office record during a seven-day run at the Universal Amphitheatre in LA in September. The total take was over $250,000.

Another one of Jerry's past acquaintances was kicking up some fuss around the same time. His childhood pal Peter Criscuola's band Wicked Lester had toyed with different looks before settling on full face paint. Each band member adopted a new persona and name. Peter's persona was of a cat, and his new name was Peter Criss. After changing the band's name to Kiss, they gigged around New York, recorded a demo, acquired a manager, and became the first act on Casablanca Records, run by Neil Bogart, an old business partner of Marty Thau's. Among Jerry's friends who had seen them, they were a joke. Jerry's career may have paled in comparison to Bette's, but not to Peter's.

After opening for Mott again at New York's prestigious Radio City Music Hall, the band made its first foray into Canada, headlining over a local band named Rush. Despite not yet having a record on the market, their years of playing on the local circuit had gained them a reputation worthy of an opening slot for the visiting Dolls.

A review of the show in the Toronto Star called the Dolls "unremarkably dull."[8] Amongst all the negativity volleyed the Dolls' way was a mention of Jerry as "knocking himself and everyone else senseless with his pounding."[9] Rush were mentioned in a single sentence at the end of the review: "The opening group, a rock trio called Rush, had been bad enough, but the Dolls only seemed worse because they had promised so much more."[10]

The Dolls flew from Toronto into Rhode Island for another visit to the Ram's Den in Kingston, where they had been two weeks before. At the airport, Johnny was acting particularly odd. He'd been taking speed by the truckload. Peter Jordan: "Johnny got to the point where he was seeing phantoms outside of a window; plus, he was staying up for like five days and getting really obnoxious." Added roadie Max Blatt: "He got real paranoid. He thought the FBI was following him through the airport. We really had to calm him down before we got on the plane."

Back then, a band could hustle their gear onto a plane as excess baggage. Desmond: "Start throwing twenties around, and we could get the whole fucking band on a plane." The Dolls had their gear on the tarmac and noticed another load nearby of what looked like musical instruments. As cool as cucumbers, Max and Desmond wheeled a stray cart in with their own gear. "It was Neil Young's stuff," recalled Max. "A Dobro guitar and some other acoustic. Johnny said, 'Wow. This one's mine. Syl, you get this one.' We come back to New York, Johnny sold his for fuckin' dope." While in LA, Johnny didn't only hook up with Sable. Her sister Corel Shields was dating Iggy Pop, who introduced Johnny to the wonders of injecting heroin.

* * *

DESPITE THEIR ALBUM DROPPING FROM THE CHARTS, THE DOLLS were welcomed as conquering heroes back in New York—but not before Jerry gave Johnny what everyone had wanted to for weeks: a knuckle sandwich. Jerry: "We got into a big fist fight in the back of the limousine and I kicked the shit out of him. Ever since that day Johnny was like my son."[11]

Johnny's father had left him before he was even born, leaving a hole in his life ready to be filled by his mother, sisters, rock 'n' roll, and drugs. Jerry, who'd endured similar abandonments, was six years older than the twenty-one-year-old lead guitarist and began to take a larger role in Johnny's life. They became a tight pair.

The big return celebration was scheduled for Halloween at the famed Waldorf Astoria. Years later, Marty Thau called this "the most memorable Dolls show." The art deco Grand Ballroom was the site of a rock 'n' roll party the hotel management never expected. The crowd was beyond even a Dolls crowd, with concertgoers dressed as pregnant nuns, and nudes in feathers and gold paint. Even Marty Thau got into the mood of the festivities by dressing as the pope. Recalled Kathy Miller, "There were people . . . staying at the Waldorf who were the typical customers. . . . Their jaws were dropping."

As for the Dolls, David was in white tails, Arthur was a football player with shoulder pads on the outside, Syl was Charlie Chaplin, Johnny sported a swastika armband, and Jerry, in an act filled with Freudian overtones, dressed as Bette Midler.

The show was oversold and, per usual, the Dolls were late for everything: the sound check and the gig. While they sound-checked, the impatient crowd waiting outside heard them and thought the show had started, lunging forward in a panic, breaking the glass doors.

Thousands of fans couldn't get in that night, and several news stations covered the event, focusing on the outrageous attendees and the equally wild band. While the Dolls had their problems in mid-America, they were hotter than ever in New York.

After recuperating from the Waldorf blowout for a few days, the Dolls played sporadic gigs and rehearsed for an upcoming trip to Europe, their first since Billy's death the year before. The tour was planned to capitalize on the European release of their first album, and of "Jet Boy" as a single.

Hopes were high that the record would receive new life in Europe. Nick Kent of *NME* praised them even before the album was out in the UK, reviewing the record on import in August. Kent proclaimed the album a masterpiece, stating, "They've just released a record that can proudly stand beside Iggy and the Stooges' stupendous *Raw Power* as the only album so far to fully define just exactly where 1970s rock should be coming from."[12] Kent also mentioned the band's lack of professionalism and being "barely competent."[13] But to him it mattered not: "This is exactly the brand of music I've been crying out to hear amidst the junk-pile of flatulent technique and lifeless professionalism that has hung like an albatross around the neck of high-energy rock."[14]

British audiences seemed to accept rock 'n' roll by artists similar to the Dolls: bands that were loud, shining, and thumbing their noses at the establishment. In the states, they were "cult artists," but in the UK, Bowie, Mott, T. Rex, Slade, and Suzi Quatro were stars selling loads of records. Marty and Leber-Krebs were hoping the same would be true for the Dolls.

The band played five shows in England, four in France, one in Germany, three in Holland, and three in Belgium, with various TV and radio appearances intertwined.

The trip to Britain was highlighted by an appearance on BBC2's *Old Grey Whistle Test*, a weekly UK TV program that differentiated itself from BBC1's *Top of the Pops* just as FM radio did from AM radio: It played "serious" music by "serious" artists. While AM radio had a history of loud DJs like Wolfman Jack or Murray the K, FM had quieter DJs, like New York's Alison Steele, aka the Nightbird. *The Old Grey Whistle Test* met this need by supplying the soft-spoken, laid-back "Whispering" Bob Harris.

The Dolls mimed to "Looking for a Kiss" and "Jet Boy" on the show. They are leather-clad, with A-bomb hair, and platform shoes. Not surprisingly, they could not convince Bob to take them seriously. After their performance, Bob laughed and dismissed them as "mock rock." The show was watched by scores of young people, many of whom seemingly agreed with Bob, as the Dolls' record made no dent in the charts. But to John Mellor, who later became the Clash's Joe Strummer, and Steven Morrissey, who as lead singer of the Smiths would be known as Morrissey, the Dolls were like a flash of lightning coming off the TV screen. Years later, Morrissey would write that catching the Dolls on *The Old Grey Whistle Test* made him see the rest of the world differently, saying, "In comparison, everyone else suddenly seemed like a traveling salesman."[15]

Afterward, Morrissey bought the 45 of "Jet Boy." When a store assistant mockingly said to another, "See . . . I told you someone would buy it,"[16] he rejoiced, saying, "At last I am someone!"[17] Next he purchased the LP. Upon viewing the front cover, he wrote, "Jerry Nolan on the front of the Dolls' debut album is the first woman I ever fell in love with . . ."[18] Morrissey's life was changed forever.

Next up were two gigs at the trendy department store Biba, where the newly opened Rainbow Room was christened for live music by the Dolls. Years later, author Kris Needs recalled the gig: "There was something magical here. A spontaneous combustion and attitude, which could've taken on the world, especially a few years later. Having been to hundreds of gigs since, I realize how great the New York Dolls were."[19] As for Jerry and Arthur, he said, "Forget the crap about not being able to play—the Nolan-Kane rhythm section was a powerhouse."[20]

Upon arrival at Orly Airport in Paris, in front of the waiting press, Johnny threw up. Though it could have been because of a bug, or too much alcohol, Peter Jordan thought differently. "I noticed that Johnny and Jerry were acting a bit funny. That was the first time I became aware of their abuse of narcotics." Jerry acknowledged in the *Village Voice* in 1991 that he had used heroin before this at Max's Kansas City, but hadn't touched it again until the Dolls went to Brussels: "Me and Johnny somehow got a bundle of pure Chinese rocks. We crushed it up and snorted it, and got fucked up. Me and Johnny took a real liking to it."[21]

Jerry claimed this was in 1974 or 75 after the second Dolls album was released, but records show the only time the Dolls were in Brussels was December 10 and 11, 1973. All members of the band, save Arthur, had dabbled with heroin at some point, but it is unclear as to Jerry's level of use at the time. He told others that he occasionally snorted it when he flew, as it calmed his nerves. Most reports show heroin was not a problem at this time in Jerry's life. Most probably, it was just like his glue-sniffing as a teenager: an adventure, and a regrettably poor decision, but not necessarily a permanent or eternally damning one, not yet. As many heroin users would say, Jerry wasn't an addict—he was "dabbling."

On December 4, the Dolls performed live on the German TV show *Musikladen*. Six songs were taped ("Pills," "Trash," "Looking for a Kiss," "Bad Girl," "Personality Crisis," and "Stranded in the Jungle"), but only "Looking for a Kiss" was broadcast on December 5.

Jerry is more animated than he was on *The Midnight Special*, gesticulating, waving his arms, shaking his head, and mouthing the words. While not straying far from the recorded versions of the songs, he's both driving the band forward and holding the group together. With Arthur's alcoholism, Johnny's speed ingestion, David's drunken theatrics, and Syl's own onstage antics, Jerry more than ably does his job.

The other songs have trickled out through the years, and it's understandable why they were held back from the original broadcast. The playing is often suspect: out-of-tune guitars and background vocals, with bum notes throughout. "Bad Girl" is a treat, though, with Jerry, particularly on the last verse, playing like a caged beast.

The Dolls certainly left their mark in Europe. They caused riots at the Bataclan in Paris, battled with homophobic crowds in Amsterdam, and came close to getting arrested in London. They ran out on bills in restaurants, left their record company with an $8,000 bar tab at a press meet-and-greet, and turned up late for everything. The band did radio and TV shows and reaped loads of press, sparring with journalists by insulting their clothing, culture, and even making Nazi jokes in Germany.

Johnny and David continued arguing about their respective roles in the band, as well as Johnny's speed intake. David had assumed the role of band spokesman, providing the press with verbal one-liners that made for choice copy. When asked whether the band were gay, he said they were "tri-sexual," because they'd "try" anything. When asked if the band was glam, he claimed that glitter "probably gives you cancer." But he bristled whenever anyone else spoke up. Recalled Sylvain, "His ego had gone completely overboard."[22] Arthur, like David, was also drinking too much, but unlike David, he would become as quiet as a mouse when drunk. And despite all the press attention, the record didn't dent the charts.

Mercury, in the face of all the mayhem (and disinterest), still green-lit another Dolls album. Though the label was disappointed that the first album had sold only 110,000, it was still the norm in the '70s to nurture an act that might be able to pay off in time. Bob Seger, Van Morrison, Steve Miller, and Bruce Springsteen are all examples of acts that flowered artistically and financially even after their first efforts lagged.

Nonetheless, there aren't a lot of second acts in politics or showbiz. The Dolls had to step it up and make the record that would catapult them from cult status to stars.

PUSS 'N'
8 BOOTS

BEFORE GETTING DOWN TO THE BUSINESS OF RECORDING A
second album, the Dolls played a handful of December gigs, including a
New Year's Eve show in Detroit with a $14,000 payday. This much-
bootlegged show sounds close to what punk rock would sound like a few
years later: a steamroller of exuberant, take-no-prisoners rock 'n' roll,
teetering on the edge of collapse. As they toured the states and Europe
over the previous four months, there were times when the Dolls might
have been at each other's throats, but on a good night, the throat was
exactly where they could grab an audience, bum notes be damned.

As for a second album, the Dolls would not only have to come up with
new songs and top-notch performances to match their first effort, but
they would have to find a simpatico producer, a David Bowie–like
individual who could turn a "Jet Boy" into a "Suffragette City," or a
"Subway Train" into an "All the Young Dudes." Unfortunately, in January
and February of 1974, Bowie was busy recording his own *Diamond Dogs*
album, whose riff-bashing "Rebel Rebel" could have been a template for
the New York Dolls version 2.0.

Before selecting a producer, the Dolls recorded demos at New York's
Media Sound, again with Paul Nelson. Included in the recordings are a
nondescript original blues-harmonica number called "Lone Star Queen,"
along with a cover of Otis Redding's "Don't Mess with Cupid." But with
so much time and effort put into touring (and partying) after the release
of their first album, the Dolls had few new songs. Recalled Sylvain, "The
truth is, we only wrote like two songs for that album. Everything else was
songs that were not put on the first album. The leftovers, like "Human
Being," were raided from the first album. So the only new songs were
"'Puss 'n' Boots,' . . . 'Babylon,' . . . and . . . the Johnny one ['Chatterbox']."

It might have helped the band in finding a producer that no less than *Creem* magazine declared them best new band of 1973. Of course, in typical Dolls fashion, they were also named worst new band of the year.

The producer chosen for the next album was George Francis Morton, aka Shadow Morton, producer of '60s girl-group and band favorite the Shangri-Las.

Morton had recorded the Shangri-Las' dramatic yet streetwise anthems "(Remember) Walking in the Sand" and "Leader of the Pack," plus "(Give Him) A Great Big Kiss," which the Dolls covered in their set and nicked a few words from for "Looking for a Kiss." Shadow, who'd also produced hits by Vanilla Fudge and Janis Ian, was chosen after the band looked at possibly bringing back Todd Rundgren, an idea that brought waves of revulsion from Johnny and Jerry. Leiber and Stoller were once again considered, as was Alice Cooper's expert producer Bob Ezrin. Both turned out to be too expensive. Shadow was available and could be had for $10,000. Jerry confirmed this was David's idea—and, in his opinion, a big mistake. Shadow hadn't made a decent record in years and was rumored to have been more interested in seeing the bottom of a glass than making great music.

Shadow sensed a spark of something special with the Dolls. "The Dolls had energy, sort of a disciplined weirdness. I took them into the room as a challenge. I was bored with the music and the business. The Dolls can certainly snap you out of boredom."[1]

But Shadow had been in an auto accident a few years before and was drinking heavily. Said David, "It was great working with him—he was funny but you had to keep the booze away from him."[2] During the recording sessions, he often just wasn't there.

The bulk of the work was left to head engineer Dixon Van Winkle and assistant engineer Dennis Drake. Dennis was working at New York's A&R Recording at the time and saw an upcoming booking for the Dolls, recalling, "We heard rumors about them . . . that they were kind of out there."

The band was booked into studio R1 at A&R on West Forty-Eighth Street. Dixon liked the room, having worked there a few years earlier on Van Morrison's *His Band and the Street Choir*, which contained the hit "Domino." Dixon: "It had a couple of nice booths and a stage for the drummer." The open space made for "good communication with the players."

Dennis had recently worked on a T-Bone Walker album produced by Leiber and Stoller, with A-list players including Jim Gordon, Paul

Humphrey, and Joe Osborn, plus jazz legends Gerry Mulligan, Zoot Sims, and Dizzy Gillespie. And then "these guys came in."

Dennis and Dixon were both struck by the Dolls' appearance. "They were in costume most of the time in some stage or another," said Dennis, adding, "They were the real deal."

The band got down to business, exhibiting a cohesiveness that the engineers didn't expect. "They were focused," said Dennis. "They knew what they were doing and it was our job as engineers just to capture the magic." Still, the band weren't averse to getting in the mood for making music. "They had a little bar set up at one end of the studio, and they really wanted to have a good time and enjoy the experience."

The band played the basic tracks as a unit. Dennis: "We used some baffles to get a little bit of isolation on the amps. But to a certain extent we wanted a live sound, a live feel. We didn't want this to be a layer upon layer of an overdubbed album. It was just fullthrottle rock 'n' roll."

Dixon: "Jerry was pretty much into making sure that time was kept, and I'm not sure that Sylvain or Thunders had quite the same idea what time was. A couple of times . . . they were really, really unhappy with each other."

Dixon sensed that Jerry was "a little more serious about the whole thing. Some of that stuff, you could hear some pretty loose playing around there." Jerry showed a professionalism the others were not capable of.

In fact, Dixon recalled, "a lot of loose playing." But David "was really indeed the catalyst." And as far as the other Dolls were concerned, that was the problem. "I always considered that album more of a David Johansen solo record," said Sylvain. "[Shadow] only really listened to him." Syl had another song that was totally ignored. It was called "Too Much Too Soon," and Johnny recorded it a few years later, minus two verses. "[Shadow] said to me, 'Well, you know, I gotta work with David and I've got this Johnny thing to fill up and . . . budget-wise, we won't have time to do that song.' I got so fucking sad. I said to all of them right there, 'Good night and goodbye.' I took my girlfriend . . . and I left the whole damned thing."

Even without Syl, the record continued its course. Shadow, who had a history in radio dramas, loved adding sound effects, as evidenced by the motorcycles in "Leader of the Pack" and the seagulls in "(Remember) Walking in the Sand." He was determined to do the same with the Dolls, adding gunshots to "Puss 'n' Boots" and jungle noises to the Cadets' old novelty number "Stranded in the Jungle."

He also had ideas about overdubs, adding bass marimbas and background singers to "Stranded in the Jungle." This particularly stuck in Sylvain's craw. "When we used to do the cover of 'Stranded in the Jungle,' we did it the way the New York Dolls did it. When we came to the studio, with Shadow Morton, he brought in black chicks. They were gorgeous to look at, to hear, and everything else. But it wasn't the New York Dolls. They did it perfect. And it took away the whole punch of what the New York Dolls was about."

Compared to the first album, Jerry's playing is now moved more to the forefront. "Babylon," with its Mitch Mitchell "I Don't Live Today" pattern, the multiple styles of "Stranded in the Jungle," or the call and response with Johansen on "(There's Gonna Be a) Showdown" put the drums at the center of each track. Still, Jerry's playing is creative but always appropriate. And there's still plenty of opportunity for Jerry to drive the band in hard-charging numbers like "Don't You Start Me Talkin'," "Human Being," "Who Are the Mystery Girls?" or Johnny's solo turn, "Chatterbox."

The album helped reestablish some of the same territory that the first one did: The Dolls were a band who weren't about instrumental chops but rather primal, raw, youthful excitement. Their influences came from girl groups, and rhythm and blues, yet they still seemed as current as T. Rex. "Babylon," "Chatterbox," "Human Being," "Puss 'n' Boots," and "Who are the Mystery Girls?" are all as driving and sexy as anything that came out that year. Plus, their raw simplicity and urgency are two years ahead of the punk rock revolution to come.

But what the record doesn't have is a song that has the hooks or pathos that come anywhere near the street-glamour quality of "Looking for a Kiss," "Trash," or "Personality Crisis." Despite all of Shadow's efforts to "tart" up the Dolls' sound, nothing was strong enough to get played on the radio.

Before the release of the record, the Dolls still had a few tricks up their sleeve to gain attention. The band remained a big draw in New York, and a Dolls gig was looked at as an event.

They scheduled their first headline show at the Academy of Music on East Fourteenth Street for February 15. The three-thousand-seat hall was the premiere theater-size venue for rock 'n' roll in New York following the demise, in June of 1971, of Bill Graham's Fillmore East. Headlining there was a big step forward for the Dolls.

As the show was close to Valentine's Day, the Dolls saw this as a promotional opportunity. In a twist on the St. Valentine's Day Massacre, the team of the Dolls and Bob Gruen created a film to precede the concert. It stands as one of their most memorable stunts. The film showed the band dressed as '20s-style gangsters, primping for the camera before heading off into Bob's Volkswagen Beetle, up to the theater to burst through the doors as the film ends. Then in a living continuation of the film, the real-life Dolls enter the theater, run down the aisle toy guns a-blazing, and onto the stage. It worked like gangbusters.

In the film, the Dolls called themselves the Lipstick Killers. Jerry appeared as "Pretty Boy Nolan, alias Scarface," with an appropriately placed fake scar on his right cheek. All the while, the strains of the Dolls' version of the *Courageous Cat and Minute Mouse* cartoon theme plays.

A few days after the Dolls show, the first Kiss record was released. Jerry and his pals in New York had never paid much attention to the band. Jerry and Peter hadn't seen each other much since Jerry was best man at Peter and Lydia's wedding in January of 1970, each pursuing their own separate careers. Still, Jerry felt a certain competitive spirit with his old friend, and took note of the album with the four made-up faces on the cover. Michelle recalled the band checking it out at Leber-Krebs' office. "They were all listening to it in a room with headphones and I remember Jerry said, 'Michelle, listen to this and tell me what you think.'" She thought it sounded pretty good. "Not what they really wanted to hear."

* * *

ANOTHER OLD FRIEND OF JERRY'S MADE A GIANT SPLASH AROUND the same time. On March 2, Bette Midler won the Grammy Award for Best New Artist. It seemed as if Peter's career was moving forward, as was Bette's. Jerry could only hope his hadn't stalled.

After a few weeks of sporadic shows before the record's release in May, the Dolls doubled up on their holiday marketing strategy with a series of shows around New York. On April 17, they began their so-called Easter Parade, with a show at Club 82 on East Fourth Street. The shows over the next week—at Coventry, the swanky Bottom Line (with Suzi Quatro), and Kenny's Castaways—would be all but forgotten in comparison to the show at Club 82.

Club 82 was rumored to have been a mob-run bar, allegedly used as part of the Genovese crime family's heroin operations. During the '50s, despite its drag queen entertainers, the club catered mostly to a straight crowd. Judy Garland was a frequent patron, as was Errol Flynn, who was supposed to have regularly played the club's piano with his penis. Such was the reputation of Club 82 before the Dolls even set foot on its stage.

The Dolls were regulars at Club 82 and, as a lark, chose to play there as part of their Easter Parade. To honor the club's history and goof on their own reputation, they elected to play in full drag, not just the glammed-up regalia that made up their day-to-day couture. Everyone wore a dress, though Johnny chickened out and changed into cutoffs before going onstage.

Johansen, who wore a dress with a leather motorcycle jacket over it, got completely immersed in the festivities, exhorting the band, saying, "Come on, girls!" or "Okay, Janis, let's do this thing." Arthur was also quite spiffy in his little dress with a swastika armband. Jerry, besides wearing a white polka-dot dress, made an impact in other ways, hanging a little doll from the old-school muffle on the front of his kick drum.

Attending this show was future Blondie bass player Gary Valentine. "I went up pretty much to the front to get my eardrums completely shattered." Also in attendance was future CBGB door person and photographer Roberta Bayley. This would be the first time she ever saw the Dolls, leaving her with the impression that they always performed in drag. The Dolls never seemed to run out of ways of confounding people.

Left to right: Mother, Charlotte, brother
Billy, Jerry, 1954. (Photo courtesy of
Billy and Frank Nolan)

Eighth-grade photo,
Central Junior High
School, Lawton,
Oklahoma, 1961. (Photo
Courtesy Cyndy Villano)

Lawton, Oklahoma, 1962.
(Photo courtesy
of Charlotte Lotten)

Lawton, Oklahoma, 1962. (Photo courtesy of Charlotte Lotten)

Playing guitar, Lawton, Oklahoma, 1962. (Photo courtesy of Billy and Frank Nolan)

Jerry and Gene Krupa, Metropole Club, New York, 1963. (Photo courtesy of Billy and Frank Nolan)

The Peepl, Jerry, second from left, 1967. (Photo Courtesy of Joseph De Jesus)

The New York Dolls,
1973. *From top,
clockwise*: Arthur
Kane, Sylvain Sylvain,
Jerry, David Johansen,
Johnny Thunders.
(Photo by Bob Gruen)

The Heartbreakers,
1975, *left to right*, Jerry,
Richard Hell, Johnny
Thunders, Walter Lure.
(Photo by Roberta
Bayley)

At SBS Studios, Yonkers,
New York, January 1976.
(Photo by Roberta Bayley)

Jerry and sister, Rose, 1976.
(Photo courtesy of Charlotte Lotten)

At CBGB 1976. (Photo by Eileen Polk)

Roxy Club, London, December 1976. (Photo by Ray Stevenson)

Roxy Club, London, Johnny Thunders and Jerry Nolan, December 1976.
(Photo by Ray Stevenson)

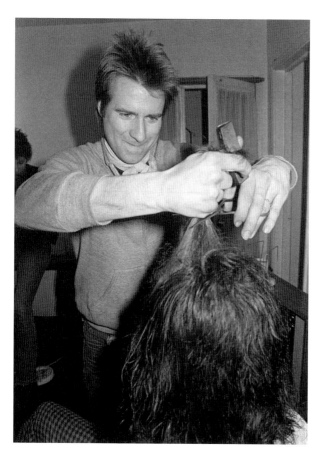

Cutting Keeth Paul's
hair, Pimlico Flat,
London, 1977. (Photo
by Ray Stevenson)

With Esther Herskovits
at Paddington Station,
1977. (Photo by Ray
Stevenson)

'L.A.M.F.' cover sessions. *Left to right*: Billy Rath, Walter Lure, Jerry, Johnny Thunders, August 1977. (Photo by Roberta Bayley)

Dolls "reunion" at Gem Spa, *left to right*, Johnny Thunders, Sylvain Sylvain, Jerry, Arthur Kane, David Johansen, August 1977. (Photo by Roberta Bayley)

Jerry and Esther, backstage at Max's Kansas City, New York, September 1978. (Photo by Eileen Polk)

Max's Kansas City, New York, *left to right*, Sid Vicious, (back to camera) Steve Dior, Jerry, Arthur Kane, September 1978. (Photo by Eileen Polk)

9 FRANKENSTEIN

THE NEW YORK DOLLS' SECOND ALBUM, *TOO MUCH TOO SOON*, was released on May 10, 1974. With a few minor exceptions, most notably *NME*'s Nick Kent, the same members of the press who liked the first LP liked the second. But it turned out to be even less radio-friendly than the first, which was anything but. As for the public, they responded to the record with a universal yawn. It was in cutout bins within a year.

David seemed to be the only member of the band who liked the record. The others felt the record had been hijacked by producer Shadow Morton and the management team to feature David. Syl was disgusted by the whole experience. Johnny at least got his shot with his lead vocal on "Chatterbox," but always thought, as did Jerry, that not enough time and effort were put into any of the basic tracks. Arthur, similarly out of his mind on inebriants, was also unhappy about the record. And Jerry? Just as he was disappointed by the sound of the first LP, he was even more disappointed by the second. He didn't like the choice of Shadow Morton as producer, favoring first album engineer Jack Douglas, who went on to produce most of Aerosmith's classic hits from the '70s as well as John Lennon's final album, *Double Fantasy*. But Jerry's protestations were ignored. Said Michelle, "He kinda felt like it was futile. He really didn't have a lot of a voice up against David. He was disappointed . . . because the same thing had happened all over again. It was almost like he had given up at that point."

Jerry's sense of "hip" was always a few steps ahead of everyone else's. Recalled Blondie drummer Clem Burke, "He cut his hair. He had that teddy boy quiff and everyone else had the long hair. That was a pretty extreme move." Be it clothes or music, he was usually onto something way before everyone else. He withstood bullying from teachers and classmates in Lawton, Oklahoma, and from squares on the streets of

Brooklyn, all because of the way he looked, only to see these same people worship celebrities with the same appearance soon afterward. Likewise, Jerry knew the Dolls were onto something new long before he was a band member. But with two albums rejected by American radio, Jerry was afraid his train was leaving the station and he'd never flag another ride on the road to stardom. He was now twenty-eight years old, ancient in a young man's game, and perhaps getting too old to have another shot at the brass ring.

The Dolls set out on a promotional tour to support the record on May 9. The first scheduled stop was the Harvard Square Performance Center in Cambridge, Massachusetts. Portending things to come, the Dolls pulled out of the show as Arthur twisted his ankle, tripping over his platforms. One can assume that his growing alcohol intake was a contributing factor. Said Peter Jordan, "I'd wake up in the morning, and Arthur would be sitting . . . having a fucking brandy for breakfast, old Mr. Boston blackberry brandy. And we'd literally have beer for breakfast, and go on from there."

Even more foreboding was the fact that the reputation of Leber-Krebs was saved by stablemates and local heroes Aerosmith, who stepped in to sub for the no-show Dolls. Aerosmith's second album, *Get Your Wings*, had been released two months prior and was making serious radio inroads, the likes of which the Dolls would never see. Produced by Jack Douglas, the album, featuring radio staples "Same Old Song and Dance" and "Train Kept a-Rollin'," would be certified gold by the spring of 1975 and would ultimately go triple platinum. At the same time, an edited version of "Dream On," from their first album, was still getting heavy radio play. Its continued success on album-oriented FM radio would push the unedited version to be rereleased as a single in 1976, hitting number nine. Leber-Krebs could see where their future success lay: with Aerosmith, not the Dolls.

On May 17, the Dolls began crisscrossing the country, appearing on bills with Nazareth, 10cc, Blue Öyster Cult, Leon Russell, War, Rare Earth, Quicksilver Messenger Service, Ike and Tina Turner, and the Electric Light Orchestra. On their first tour, bands like ZZ Top and Lynyrd Skynyrd had wanted to hang with the Dolls, being the wild, partying chick magnets they were. On this tour, 10cc wouldn't even share the same dressing room with them.

Included on the tour were several shows with Kiss, with Jerry's boyhood pal Peter Criss on drums. In Jerry's mind, as well as the minds of many New Yorkers familiar with both bands, Jerry was always the better drummer. Plus, the Dolls had been the toast of the town, while the locals laughed at Kiss, some calling them a "clown band."

But outside the insular crowd of downtown New York hipsters, Kiss were entering the hearts and minds of mainstream Middle America rock fans. While their first LP was selling poorly, even less than the Dolls' first LP, Kiss were proving to be a formidable live act. Besides their immediately identifiable face paint, Kiss shows featured blood spitting, dry ice, smoke bombs, and fire breathing. Kiss' pyrotechnic-laden concerts were winning over America in ways the campier Dolls' show never could. Kiss were onto something.

On June 14, the Dolls played at the Allen Theatre in Cleveland, the second of three consecutive shows with Kiss as the opening act. After being forced to use a bathroom as a dressing room, Peter's band felt slighted and were now ready to pull out all the stops to show the Dolls just who the real rising stars were. Reviews of the show described Kiss satisfying the crowd with their "fireworks, sirens, lights, and acrobatics."[1] The writer summed up the show by saying Kiss played "damn good music; fast, loud, and raunchy."[2] The Dolls show was the inverse of Kiss's set; the show ended with only "twenty or thirty people applauding after each song. . . . It was embarrassing."[3] The reviewer noted that the Dolls were "the best answer to all the glittery glam rock that's been coming from overseas"[4] and deserved better from their audience. But maybe this was all they'd get?

Throughout the continuing tour, halls were partially filled. It would be generous to say the reviews were mixed. Phrases like "indifferent reception," "small crowd," and "applause dwindled" described audience reactions. As for the music, one review went so far as to describe the Dolls as a "badly oiled thrashing machine." Another noted their "borderline competence." Once they reached Los Angeles on July 24, the downward slide seemed unstoppable.

Unlike their 1973 visit, where they sold out ten shows at the Whisky a Go Go and were met by groupies galore, this LA trip was different. When they taped their appearance on the nationally televised *Don Kirshner's Rock Concert*, the utter unresponsiveness of the audience was so pronounced that applause was dubbed into the final edit. For viewers at home who saw the Dolls' set on November 9, it seemed as if the audience were truly enjoying themselves. In actuality, the crowd followed most songs with boos and indifference.

Besides the disappointed crowd at the *Don Kirshner's* taping, their scheduled four-day stint at the Roxy Theatre was reduced to a single night after the band and crew destroyed props for *The Rocky Horror Picture*

Show, which was appearing at the same venue. In the past, shows were canceled by headliners throwing the Dolls off their bill out of fear of being blown off the stage. Now it was the Dolls' childishness getting in the way.

The lack of success, Arthur's alcoholism, and Johnny's love of methamphetamines were affecting the Dolls, not only professionally but emotionally. The once-tight unit were getting on each other's nerves even more than the previous year. Said Peter Jordan, "Syl and Johnny for a long time roomed together . . . until Johnny's antics got too much for Syl to put up with. Jerry sometimes roomed with David. Then [band 'valet'] Frenchy had to wind up staying with Johnny because we had to keep an eye on him to make sure that Johnny didn't decide to jump out the window to make sure that a flying saucer hadn't landed in the parking lot. The erratic behavior was driving everyone kind of nuts. David wound up staying by himself."

This all fed into Jerry's natural tendencies toward depression and lack of self-esteem as a response to rejection, going all the way back to his abandonment by his mother's first husband. Jerry found it hard to fit in. Playing the drums and looking like a rock star—or, as Jerry would say, "profiling"—were only a facade covering up his self-doubts. There was still the lingering feeling that everything would go sideways. As the Dolls disintegrated, Jerry experienced even more negative feelings, dating back to his entry into the band after the death of much-beloved original drummer Billy Murcia. Per Michelle, "He confided in me . . . that he always felt . . . that he was never really a Doll. He always felt like the fill-in for the real Doll, Billy. He never really felt like he was a part of the band wholly."

Jerry's dreams of stardom were fading as the blows to his ego were mounting. If there was anyone who'd worked at becoming a star, it was Jerry. It had happened for Bette Midler and Suzi Quatro, and it was happening for Peter Criss. Why wasn't it happening for him? He had no backup plan and was panicking.

But there was one Doll he still connected with: Johnny. Two of the things they shared were the lack of a dependable father figure growing up, and the sense that David was getting too big for his britches. Now there was a third thing to share: heroin.

Bob Gruen recalled a change in the band's behavior soon after the release of *Too Much Too Soon*. "One day everybody was kind of sitting there by themselves nodding off, facing in different directions. And I remember . . . just wondering what was up with everybody, and then realizing pretty soon that Johnny and Jerry had gotten into the drugs.

Arthur was pretty deep into the booze. David and Syl were not into those kind of drugs, and so there was kind of a drifting apart."

Another friend who noticed a change was Peter Criss. At that same June 14 show where Kiss left the Dolls in the dust, Jerry got together with Peter after the show for old times' sake. Peter pulled out a gram of coke to celebrate, but Jerry wanted another high. He convinced Peter to let him trade the coke for some heroin. All Peter had to do was give it to him and Jerry would go off, make the trade, and be back in a jiffy. Peter begrudgingly went along with Jerry's idea. In the end, he didn't see Jerry until the plane ride back the next morning. When he confronted Jerry, he realized the boy he'd grown up with was a different person. He would never speak with Jerry again.

Marty Thau assumed Jerry was using because Johnny was: "They were a tight duo." In time, Jerry told his mother about his introduction to heroin. Her version of the story was one that would leave most informed listeners skeptical at best: "One time the group was playing . . . and after that, some of them went to bed, like Jerry. He was tired. During the night, he was awoken when one of the members in the band had put a needle in his arm. That's how it started. He didn't know about it. And they wanted him to do it and he wouldn't do it. But they got him when he was asleep. They put it in his arm, ya know, and squeezed the needle and it went into the system."

After hearing this story, future Heartbreakers (Johnny Thunders's and Jerry's post-Dolls band) manager Leee Black Childers howled: "Oh, give me a break! He told that to his mom? [Mothers]' first fault [is that they] will believe anything. The rigmarole that is involved with the shooting of heroin . . . it's unlikely you'd sleep through it unless you're already on heroin. That's such a typical, easy Jerry lie. He wouldn't have dared told us that."

Questions persist as to who introduced who to heroin first, Johnny or Jerry. Syl insisted that it was Iggy Pop who introduced it to Johnny first in 1973, though Leee Childers disagreed. He felt strongly that Jerry introduced it to Johnny. "I do not think it was Iggy. I lived with Iggy a long time and he was a junkie, but he was another kind of junkie. He didn't bring people in like Jerry did. He wasn't ashamed of being a junkie, but he also didn't really want to make other people junkies. I never even saw him pass a joint, frankly."

According to Arthur's wife, Babs, Arthur blamed Jerry for turning Johnny into a heroin addict. "Arthur felt that Jerry stole John away from the Dolls. Johnny wasn't a junkie when the Dolls started up. He was a pothead. He drank and liked his blow, but never did heroin."

Peter Jordan reiterated what others said. "I think that [Jerry] had at least been involved in heroin use prior to that, but when he joined the Dolls, he wasn't even smoking cigarettes or drinking. But of course when you're on the road and traveling and you're in a hotel every day, you get to drinking. By the time we finished, he was smoking Marlboros, drinking, and everything else."

Dolls and Thunders biographer Nina Antonia suspected Vietnam War veteran Frenchy was the culprit. "It would make sense because of the Vietnam connection." Unlike Nina Antonia, Babs was confident it wasn't Frenchy. "Frenchy liked his speed, always, and pot. He was an up head. He wasn't a down head. If it was anybody, it would have been Max Blatt."

Max didn't doubt it: "Might have been me. I don't even remember. We used to get high together. I was the only roadie that was using it. I was shooting up for just about as long as Jerry was. I remember we started snorting it before we shot it."

Like the rest of the Dolls and their crew, Max and Jerry got paid every Friday at Leber-Krebs's office. By the fall of 1974 it became a ritual of another sort. After cashing their checks, they'd catch a cab down to the East Village to see a friend of Max's. "He had an apartment on East Ninth Street between First and A. He got high all the time. We'd give him money and he'd go cop for us, because he knew where to go, because he bought shit every day. That was pretty much how he got his stuff, by copping for other folks. We'd turn him on or he'd take a little before he gave it to you back . . . and he would inject us. We weren't shooting ourselves at that point. That was kinda the beginning of the whole thing."

One of the sad ironies of addiction is that the shame and stigma of addiction further degrade one's self-esteem, which is often one of the causes of addiction, making it a self-perpetuating cycle. Said Babs, "A lot of rock 'n' roll dudes are rather insecure people. Like most artists, they're very creative, but they have to find a source that protects them, because they are so creative, but then so insecure too, and they don't fit into the, quote, 'real world.' So their source of protection either comes from deep within, a spiritual path, or it comes from a substance."

About this time, Michelle got a call from a friend telling her Jerry was using heroin and if she looked around their apartment, she'd find the evidence. "I remember saying, 'I really doubt it, but okay, I'll look.' And I went and looked in his drum kit and I found it. It was a shock to me. Absolute shock, I had no idea. I had never seen him with a needle, near a needle; I had never seen him high."

This made Michelle reassess her trip to Europe in late 1973, on tour with the Dolls. Jerry behaved erratically several times, throwing a fit in a

London restaurant and walking several feet behind her while in France. "We were walking around the streets and . . . he was in his own world. . . . I always seemed to be walking ten feet ahead for some reason. There was definitely a disconnect there."

She also noticed him vomiting more than once during the trip. She initially dismissed it as a bug he picked up while traveling. "I never saw him sick like that before, but when I look back on it, I realize he must have been snorting heroin during that trip. Why else would he be vomiting? I don't think he was shooting up at that point. I didn't see any signs of that. But his demeanor, definitely, he was depressed."

Jerry kept in touch with Nancy Quatro from Cradle. Though she'd spurned his advances, she still cared about his well-being. He phoned her. "He was pretty screwed up. He had said something to me about [how] he had tried heroin, and because drug addicts lie a lot I really didn't know if he had even been doing it when he was in our band, or if he had just discovered it like he said he had. I actually told him, 'This is now the love of your life,' because he was talking about it like it was a love affair, like he met a new chick that was his soul mate. I really tried to stress to him that this is the worst drug you could have picked. His personality type would have just taken him quick . . . to addiction. Depressed and always looking for answers, looking to be filled internally by the external, not knowing that he can only fill the internal by the internal." She tried to warn him: "'It's not like you'll have good friends, because your good friends will be people that do drugs with you. Those aren't good friends. You've got to know all that.'"

Despite midnight calls to Nancy Quatro, he continued his relationship with Michelle, although, much like the Dolls, it was fraying at the seams. The drugs only made it worse. Said Michelle, "One time, he called me at my job, and he had a bone crush." Also known as "cotton fever," a "bone crush" is described in the White House Office of National Drug Control Policy's street drug glossary as "critically high temperature associated with accidentally injecting cotton fibers into the blood stream."

"It's extremely painful. . . . He was like, 'Michelle, Michelle, I need an ambulance!' You know, I'm sitting at my job!"

Said Sylvain, "Most people know Jerry . . . as a junkie. I'm here to tell you . . . his whole life was not being a junkie. Just like Johnny. They were really, really sweet . . . but once he became a junkie . . . a lot of that sweetness dissipated."

After a final show in Cleveland in late July, the band ambled back to New York with their tails between their legs. The August 1974 edition of *Circus* magazine was now on the newsstands. Earlier that year, the magazine selected the Dolls as the best new band of 1973. This edition featured Uriah Heep's lead singer, David Byron, on the cover, part of Warner Brothers' promotional efforts to move the band's new album, *Wonderworld*, up the charts. The magazine came with a free poster of up-and-comers Queen, featuring lead singer Freddie Mercury and guitarist Brian May, in all their velvet-and-flash resplendence. There were also articles on the Eagles, Mott the Hoople, Bad Company, and Suzi Quatro, and an interview with Kinks leader Ray Davies. All were positive and respectful.

And on the cover, across the top right, was a white, diagonal banner that read, "The N. Y. Dolls: 'Too Much Too Soon' or Too Little Too Late"? The article was on page six with a beautiful color photo of David, Syl, and Jerry playing live, with Jerry's pink drum kit at center stage. The Dolls were perfect for *Circus*. The magazine thrived on bold colors and loud bands. For the second month in a row, they appeared in the magazine's Top 20 list. They were at number sixteen, up from eighteen.

As for the article, it was based on an interview with David, who waxed rhapsodic on the new LP. Outside of his own ringing endorsement, the article never let up on the controversy surrounding the band as undeserving of so much attention. One section was headlined "Flash in the Pan." Another followed David's comment about the Dolls being "artistic"[5] by saying, "What the Dolls were doing could hardly be called artistic."[6] Another mentioned a talent scout refusing to sign them because "they just weren't talented."[7] In reference to the track "Stranded in the Jungle" the writer asked, "Is there any song on the Dolls album that is *real* music and *not* a novelty cut?"[8] In one of the final paragraphs, it said, "If the rest of the press is behind the Dolls, the reason is not easily apparent. The new LP is another wall of noise, cut after cut of annoying screeching, with David's feeble voice drowned out of each cut."[9]

It's rare for feature articles in rock magazines to be filled with so many negatives. While it would be reasonable for a feature to examine any controversy surrounding an artist, rarely would there be such a harsh, subjective opinion on the quality of their art. That's saved for the review section. But the Dolls acted like rock stars out of the gate and thumbed their noses at the industry. Though David may have once joked that the Dolls "single-handedly lowered the standards of an entire industry,"[10] the industry grew tired of being made fun of and struck back.

This same edition contained a lead review of *Too Much Too Soon*. No surprises would be found there. The very first sentence read: "Not wanting to be snotty or self-opinionated, I still think the New York Dolls are the most overrated, dreadful band I have ever heard."[11] And the last sentence? "Get your cotton ready and dive in . . . but don't say I didn't warn you."[12]

As if things couldn't get any worse for Jerry, after the tour ended in late July, he returned to the New York apartment that he shared with Michelle. A friend of his had seen her at an Eric Clapton concert with another man and phoned Jerry to tell him. "I met someone where I was working," said Michelle. "It was like an affair, I guess, but it was very short. It wasn't like I fell in love with this person. But I did go out with them. [Jerry] found out about it and he went crazy." Referring to the groupies she knew Jerry slept with, Michelle continued, "He had been doing a lot of things . . . that were a betrayal to me. It was almost like I had worked up some kind of resentment too and [was] maybe looking for a way out."

At first Michelle denied the affair, but Jerry found an Eric Clapton record that had been given to Michelle by her illicit paramour, hidden in their closet. He now put two and two together. Jerry set his sharp tongue to the side and instead used his fists. "He was slapping me all around to get the truth out because I tried to not divulge it. But he kept slapping me in the head. I was crying and he kept asking. I wish I wouldn't have confessed it—but hey, part of me was like, 'Yeah, hello, aren't you doing the same thing?'"

In retrospect, Michelle probably should have left Jerry right then and there. They had cheated on one another and he had now beaten her. This was indefensible. But, like too many victims of domestic violence, she did not. As for Jerry, perhaps he got his just deserts for his constant philandering, but it still hurt to know Michelle had cheated on him. Throughout his life, he'd seen the results of infidelity, betrayal, and abandonment. He offered an insight to Michelle. "After the affair . . . he said, 'I'm not your father, I'm not gonna leave you.' My father and mother got divorced when I was thirteen, but when I was eighteen, my father pretty much cut me off and it was pretty brutal. I was still reeling from that. So I remember when he said that to me . . . I was thinking to myself, 'Why would he say that to me?' I couldn't believe those words were coming out of his mouth, because I hadn't really thought about that. Maybe he had some insight? What he knew was that I suffered sort of a similar loneliness. . . . He knew more about me than I knew about myself at that time."

Michelle and Jerry decided to give their relationship another go. Jerry did have one more insight to pass along, though: "He said to me, 'Just be careful, because after a while you won't feel anything anymore.'"

* * *

AFTER A SHORT BREAK AT THE END OF JULY, THE DOLLS BEGAN gigging again. With *Too Much Too Soon* going nowhere, their shows became less eventful, with fewer paying customers. The Dolls' devil-may-care attitude didn't help either. On September 1, they played the unlikeliest of gigs: the Minneapolis State Fair. In attendance was a young college student named Andy Schwartz, who a few years later would helm the influential music periodical the *New York Rocker*. Said Andy, "They were like forty-five minutes late getting onstage. They came out . . . and Johansen goes, 'What I want to know is who won the pie-eating contest?'"

Their New York–area dates didn't have the cachet of the Felt Forum show after the first album came out, the previous Halloween's blowout at the Waldorf Astoria, or the Valentine's Day performance at the Academy of Music. They were back to playing little bars like Coventry in Queens and Mr. D's in Elmwood Park, New Jersey. Farther out of town, the Dolls were still playing in dance halls and theaters, but they were not filling up the seats.

Early fan Kathy Miller summed it up: "It was almost like everybody in New York forgot who they were. Aerosmith are going up the charts and getting Top 10 records. And Kiss, who we all thought were a laughingstock—well, we all know what happened with them. And the Dolls were playing Kenny's Castaways."

David and Johnny were at loggerheads and a communication breakdown occurred. Drunken David could be mouthy, but a junked-out or tweaked Johnny was uncommunicative and uncooperative. Peter Jordan: "As Johnny developed more and more material, it cut into David's space. David did not feel like playing tambourine while Johnny sang five songs. That was another point of friction." All the while, Jerry was egging his drug buddy on.

The infighting continued through an aborted demo session with Jerry's dream producer, Jack Douglas. Johnny didn't show, Arthur was too out of it to play, and Jerry went off to cop. To make matters worse, the infighting was no longer the sole reserve of the band. Leber-Krebs were fighting with Marty about the band's future, and decided to shut off the money spigot. Marty was just worn down by the band's behavior and was fighting with his business partner. Marty Thau: "Mercury Records did want to do another album with them, but only if they cleaned up their act. And . . . it fell on deaf ears. Then I resigned. I said to my partner, 'Steve, you take care of it. If you can do a better job, let's see what you can do.' But I knew at that time it was destined to fail."

Attempts were made to reconcile. Leber offered a tour of Japan if the band would sober up. There was also the offer of a third album from Mercury on the table as a motivator. Johnny even pledged he'd straighten up if David would keep his drinking, and his ego, in check. But according to Peter Jordan, "The real pain in the ass was David wouldn't work with Jerry if you gave him a million dollars."[13] Jerry's drug-fueled delusions of grandeur were even upsetting the more stable Sylvain: "Jerry used to brag to me . . . 'Oh man, when you're on heroin, you never get sick.'"[14]

It seemed as if no one, not even the Dolls themselves, wanted the Dolls as they were. Not Middle America, not Marty Thau or Leber-Krebs, nor the radio or even their hometown of New York City. However, there were smatterings of old fans who were inspired by what the Dolls had accomplished—people who didn't look the way rock stars were expected to look, who didn't kowtow to industry expectations, and who didn't exhibit virtuosic abilities. Clem Burke, the drummer from Blondie, recalled, "Everyone cut their hair and took their platform shoes off, walked up to the Bowery and put on leather jackets. That's when so-called punk rock started."

A spiky-haired transplant from Louisville, Kentucky, named Richard Meyers rechristened himself Richard Hell. After realizing his dreams of becoming a poet were fraught with difficulties, he decided to pick up a bass guitar and start a band with torn clothes and short hair, playing angular yet raw rock. "I had been impressed by the way it had worked for the Dolls, that they had been associated with the Mercer Arts Center. I thought that we should find a venue that was doing badly enough that they'd accept these terms we had in mind, that we'd play there one night a week or something like that, regularly on a given night."[15] Such a place existed on the Bowery, New York's skid row. It had a strange name: CBGB.

Since the collapse of the Mercer Arts Center in August of 1973, several of the bands most associated with the venue—the Magic Tramps, Suicide, and Wayne County—were looking for a new place to perform their original music, and had found this place on the Bowery. As most clubs only allowed original music to be played by bands with record contracts and radio play, there were few places these artists could perform in public. These were the first bands to play at a Hells Angels bar once called Hilly's on the Bowery, for owner Hilly Kristal, who renamed it CBGB & OMFUG, short for "Country, Bluegrass, Blues and Other Music for Uplifting Gormandizers." Most people just called it CBGB or CB's. It wasn't until Hell's band Television began a residency there in

March of 1974 that the first stirrings of what would soon be known as punk rock took hold.

Another Dolls fan was Thomas Erdelyi, aka drummer Tommy Ramone: "The Ramones was basically a concept that developed in my head after seeing the New York Dolls and saw how entertaining they were. Even though they weren't virtuoso musicians they were still very exciting. At this time everybody was a virtuoso musician. Everybody was just noodling away . . . and I thought, 'It's time for a change.' We wanted to go back to the two-minute song, which to us was more like a minute and a quarter."[16]

Future Heartbreaker Walter Lure summed it up: "The Dolls were really the mother of punk rock in a sense because they were the first band to show that kids could pick up a guitar and not know how to play it like Jimmy Page or fuckin' Yes and could start a band and get popular and have people enjoy the music."

Something new was happening on the Bowery. Jerry was the first Doll to recognize it and told Marty. "[Jerry] called me up specifically to tell me that there was a scene developing down in the Bowery at a club called CBGB's and that I should check it out, because there's probably a whole bunch of groups down there that I'd like. He felt that . . . with what I knew and what my connections were, I was the perfect person to come in and get involved with it. I don't think he mentioned any particular band as much as it being the scene that was developing." Jerry was right: In time, Marty would produce the first demos by early CBGB artists Blondie and the Ramones, work with Richard Hell, and manage minimalist synth duo Suicide.

Someone else was noticing what was happening at CBGB: Malcolm McLaren, an old friend of the Dolls from London who owned a youth-oriented clothing shop there. He was in New York on another fashion adventure when he ran into Sylvain. Recalled Syl, "I was walking on Twenty-Third Street and I saw Malcolm come out of the Chelsea Hotel. He recognized me and I was kind of down, and he asked me, 'How're the Dolls doing?' And I said, 'Fuckin' we're about to break up.' And that's when there were very ugly things, junk and alcohol. All that stuff was really . . . fucking up the whole thing. It was fucked up, and our management fucked us up and the kids had left us. We'd seen the top and . . . now we're at the bottom. We were poor again, playing little clubs, and I told Malcolm. That night I asked him to help us. And he said, 'I love the Dolls. I'll do anything.'"

# 10 SHOWDOWN

AS 1974 CLOSED OUT, TIMES WERE TOUGH FOR THE DOLLS.
Leber-Krebs were no longer bankrolling them. Gigs were their only source of revenue. Peter Jordan was on bass once again, as Arthur was back in rehab. Jerry and Johnny were both using heroin, and David was fed up with them both, as were they with him. Syl, despite his displeasure with David and the second album, reached a détente with him, collaborating on new songs. Ever the pragmatic mediator, Syl held out hope he could get Johnny and Jerry back into the fold.

And now, the New York Dolls, the band people said couldn't play, were about to be managed by Malcolm McLaren, someone who at the time knew nothing about the music business. He was the first one to admit it. His experience lay in designing and selling clothing.

Malcolm had discovered the Dolls in August of '73 while in New York for the National Boutique Fair, with his wife and business partner Vivienne Westwood. The pair were attempting to hawk their new line, but not one American buyer was interested. "The only people that came to see our particular room, with all our wares, were the New York Dolls, and . . . Alice Cooper and a few other people, and we suddenly realized all these other people harbored around a café called Max's Kansas City."

Malcolm and Vivienne took to Max's like fish to water. "It was where all this demimonde of New York hung out at that time. Sort of Warhol-like creatures . . . They were video-makers and would-be stylists. They were stars or thought they were stars. Certainly . . . anyone who was in there was virtually a star. And this is where me and Vivienne hung out, and we got to know the Dolls."

Malcolm loved their music, seeing them as masters of the art of being bad. He loved their record cover, loved that they would play at Biba, and loved following them to Paris like a groupie. It was all so inspiring to him, that despite knowing nothing about the music business, he wanted to try his hand at it. He figured if the Dolls could make music, he could be a manager. It was also more exciting than returning to his shop.

Malcolm knew the Dolls needed serious help, not only as a band but as individuals. But how could he assist a band in such a dysfunctional state? Malcolm: "I could dress them up. Yes, I could inspire and help them, but manage them?" He addressed Arthur's drinking, Johnny and Jerry's heroin use, and David's displeasure that he "wasn't the star he was supposed to be and was pissed off because of it." He told them in no uncertain terms, "We need a complete reassessment of the entire band, its image, and its songs. We've got to change everything. Not just your drug habits, not you, Arthur, and your drinking habits, but we've got to change the songs themselves. We've got to change the way you look as well. I mean, let's face it: You're all a bit out-of-date.'"

The group were taken aback by Malcolm's comments, but at the same time were willing to follow the only person enthusiastic enough to make an emotional and financial investment in them. Malcolm felt the Dolls could capitalize on the scene developing at CBGB, which was, in a sense, their offspring. While small, it had potential. "This all sort of seemed to me to be revealing something new," observed Malcolm. "But the Dolls were . . . slightly old-school . . . and all these guys like Television were sort of new-school. So the Dolls were caught between being garage and what was later to become known as punk rock." Still, he felt that the Dolls could use the new scene around CBGB as a base to reinvent themselves. "This group always had the ability to strike a light."

Malcolm was right: Compared to the new breed, the Dolls did look out-of-date. Except for Jerry, they still had long hair. Platform shoes, satin jackets, and Norma Kamali pants were disappearing. Recalled Eileen Polk, "CBGB's was not the right environment for those kinds of extreme fashion statements. The floor was all crooked, for one thing. You could easily fall, even if you weren't wearing platforms. You wanted something you could run in. You didn't want to be wearing feather boas and seethrough dresses while you're in the Bowery. It was almost like a nouveau beatnik kind of fashion world where people were wearing peglegged pants, and pointy Beatle boots. Jerry fit in as well in that as he did when he was wearing hair spray and lipstick."

Malcolm digested the New York scene of Patti Smith, Television, and the Ramones, his lessons from Situationist politics, his British clothing shops, and observations of youth culture. He had an idea: "I'm just going to turn them into Chinese red guards." He gave the band instructions: "What I want you to do is . . . write songs and you've got to use the word *red* at least six times. And I want you to hold the Chinese Maoist book when you come out onstage." He would send patterns back to Vivienne to create red patent-leather clothing for each of them. With the help of David's girlfriend Cyrinda Foxe, Malcolm sewed a large hammer-and-sickle flag to hang behind them onstage, in front of which they would perform in their new brilliant red outfits.

Looking back years later, David summed up Malcolm as "a haberdasher to us."[1] But beyond that, he "liked him because for an Englishman he was full of revolution."[2] David insisted that the song "Red Patent Leather" already existed beforehand, as did the idea of wearing red patent-leather clothing. Still, there's no denying Malcolm had a larger vision and was willing to take it as far as it could go, encouraging the band to come along with him.

After moving into a rehearsal space paid for by Malcolm, the Dolls worked up six new original songs: David and Syl's "Red Patent Leather," "On Fire," and "Girls"; Syl's "Teenage News"; Johnny's "Pirate Love"; and a Johnny/David collaboration called "Downtown." For his part, Malcolm found the Little Hippodrome, a two-thousand-capacity theater at 227 East Fifty-Sixth Street. It was here the Dolls would premiere their new songs and look and show the world that they were back.

In keeping with the theme of the event, Malcolm decorated each table with red cloth and wrote a press release, headlined "FOR IMMEDIATE RELEASE FROM THE PEOPLE WHO BROUGHT YOU 'TOO MUCH TOO SOON.'" The release read as follows:

WHAT ARE THE POLITICS OF BOREDOM?
BETTER RED THAN DEAD.

Contrary to the vicious lies from the office of Leber, Krebs and Thau, our former "paper tiger" management, the New York Dolls have not disbanded, and having completed the first Red, 3-D Rock N' Roll movie entitled "Trash" have, in fact assumed the role of the "Peoples' Information Collective" in direct association with the Red Guard.

This incarnation entitled "Red Patent Leather" will commence on Friday, February 28th at 10 p.m. continuing on Saturday at 9 and 11 p.m. followed by a Sunday matinee at 5 p.m. for our high school friends at the Little Hippodrome—227 E. 56th Street between 2nd and 3rd.

This show is in coordination with The Dolls' very special "entente cordiale" with the Peoples Republic of China.

Malcolm wanted to shock New York with an updated New York Dolls for the new age. What he didn't realize was that New York, much less the United States, wouldn't respond to communism like Europeans would. In 1975, fresh from the Vietnam War, and still in the midst of the Cold War, New Yorkers just wouldn't go for this. Plus, the coordinated outfits were another hard pill to swallow. They made the Dolls seem desperate.

Just before Malcolm arrived, the production team of Jerry Kasenetz and Jeff Katz, creators of bubblegum hits by the 1910 Fruitgum Company and the Ohio Express, got in touch with their old PR man, Marty Thau, about working with the Dolls. When it was revealed that all they wanted was for David to sing over previously prepared music, the idea was dismissed outright. But the band's new color-coordinated clothing was similarly dismissed by many fans. With the added communist trappings, it was just too much for their old fans to accept.

Peter Jordan was on bass again for the Hippodrome shows, as Arthur "virtually had a nervous breakdown." Although he no longer worked with the band, Desmond saw one of the shows, reporting, "It was pretty stupid." Gary Valentine of Blondie said, "I remember it happening, and just thinking that it just sounded so absurd." Television's Richard Lloyd recalled, "It looked ridiculous. It was like Elvis in his worst days. They were kind of coughing out their last cough."

There were, however, those who saw something else in those shows. Blondie's Chris Stein said, "It was the tightest and the most organized they ever were as a band." *Soho News* writer Alan Platt had just moved to New York from England. Perhaps his British upbringing and the LSD he'd ingested gave him a different perspective, but he was astonished by the shows. "I've never seen anything so exciting. Johnny was on fire. They were . . . just unbelievably great. Never saw such energy. A whirlwind. Never been so impressed by a band in my life."

And Jerry? He too thought the band was at its best. As for his playing, it's some of his tightest and most creative ever. The first song, "Red Patent Leather," has an opening descending riff that Jerry plays in a hard rock Humble Pie/Bad Company style with quarter notes on the hi-hat rather than the usual stream of eighth notes. In the verse, after playing along on the ride cymbal to a Chuck Berry–like riff, he switches about halfway through to a more soulful Stax/Volt four-on-the-floor style. Switching back and forth between these three styles is not something most drummers would even have thought of, but Jerry pulls it off flawlessly.

Even the covers in the show are played with gusto. On the band's version of Eddie Cochran's "Something Else," during the signature opening riff as well as the intro, Jerry plays a floor tom–based backbeat that is truly astonishing: The snare is partially a surf beat, with a snare hit on the beat after the two—but also the beat after the four. However, on every other bar he plays the note before the two as well, and in the verses, he drives it like a train. Credit goes to Peter Jordan for some truly pulsating bass playing in the third verse, but it's clear that while Jerry could have coasted on an old standard, which most of the crowd would have never noticed, he put a lot of thought into what he was doing.

A second run of shows the next weekend were marred by Jerry missing the March 7 show due to hepatitis, assumedly caught from a hypodermic needle. He was replaced by Michael Sanders, aka Spider, from the all-black punk band Pure Hell. Michelle remembered hearing about Jerry's illness from Malcolm, saying, "'He's in Metropolitan Hospital,' which is this real skanky hospital in Spanish Harlem . . . a city hospital. . . . Malcolm just said to me, 'You know what he's doing, right?' And I said, 'Yeah, I know.'" Michelle recalled Jerry trying to get clean, even discussing entering rehab. "I would try and get him to stay home, and he just wouldn't. He'd be like, 'No, no, no. I'm going downtown.' And he would just get high again. It was heartbreaking . . . whenever I would see him high."

While the Dolls never really bought into Malcolm's vision, he still felt they were salvageable and had a plan. Peter Jordan: "Malcolm's scheme was to take the band on the road, which is where everything really went downhill."

* * *

SYL AND MALCOLM BOOKED THE BAND FOR A SERIES OF SHOWS IN Florida, starting March 31. While the money wouldn't be very good, it would get them out of New York, where the temptations were too great. On the road, they could develop a new esprit de corps. Peter recalled that the plan was for the band to "work our way to California, playing like every possible fucking club we could, and by the time we got to California, we would still . . . be able to wrangle our first show at some decent club in Los Angeles. We would have been rehearsed for two months, so by the time we hit Los Angeles, we'd be pretty tight. And Malcolm had a few bucks. He wasn't rolling in money, but the thing would have been selfsufficient enough to get us from point A to point B."

The band saved money in Florida by staying at a trailer park in Zephyr Hills, owned by Jerry's mother's most recent husband named Billy. He hated the band. Jerry's mom recalled: "We had three trailers and two cabins on the property." Peter Jordan recalled that there were "little mobile homes that looked like crickets, little green things. We were . . . in three of them."

Initially, to save money, Peter didn't go on the Florida trip. However, everyone quickly realized that Arthur was still detoxing and in no condition to play, so they bought a plane ticket for Peter to come join them. "The other reason . . . is that somebody fucking realized they had to carry all their amps around."

Adding to the strain of little money coming in was the fact that not only was there no air-conditioning at the trailer park, but Johnny and Jerry were, according to Peter, "completely bitching, endlessly, about everything."

They particularly didn't go for any of Malcolm's ideas. Soundman Bobby Belfiore recalled Jerry saying, "He's a bigger conniver than I am." Besides David and Syl, no one else took to Malcolm. Peter: "He was like this real English fruitcake. He'd have his nose completely covered with white cream. A brilliant guy, but he was such a little fucking wimpy guy in some ways." Max Blatt had another view: "I just thought he was a twerp."

Malcolm was full of ideas but found little enthusiasm from the Dolls. The heat didn't help, so they all decided to ditch the red leather gear and bought army-surplus fatigues.

A young Dolls fan named Jim Marshall, who later became a DJ nicknamed the Hound and the owner of New York's celebrated dive bar the Lakeside Lounge, lived in the area and found himself in the band's inner circle. Jim had seen the band in October 1973 at the five-thousand-seat West Palm Beach Auditorium, with Mott the Hoople and Aerosmith. Things were different in April of 1975. "They were playing in a little horrible club called the Flying Machine in Ft. Lauderdale. They were doing two sets a night in this horrible little bar."

Jim sensed the band were having internal struggles, with David, Syl, and Malcolm on one side and Johnny and Jerry on the other. And soon it became obvious what Johnny and Jerry were doing on their side. Becoming more desperate to cop, they turned to Jim for help. Jim had sold cocaine "before the Colombians took over the business, so I was the designated guy to find them some smack."

Unaccustomed to buying heroin, Jim found it difficult. "Dope really wasn't a thing in Florida. You saw Percodans. . . . Every once in a while, someone had some morphine, sulfate tablets or something. . . . It was pretty obvious that they were in need." He knew of two places to buy dope: Overtown and Liberty City.

Jim found it even more difficult than expected. "It was a major fucking pain in the ass. More trouble than it was worth." But with persistence, he came through. The second time, though, was a different story. Jim had a partner try and help him. "The cops . . . they didn't arrest him, they just took him for a ride and kind of scared him. And I think the second time we didn't come back with any dope, so those guys were pretty bummed out."

This started the ball rolling. According to Jerry's mom, "They had a fight, an argument. They threw the television out in the pool. And they threw the table and chairs downstairs out in the garden. They wrecked that place."

Per Malcolm: "Sitting around this campfire . . . we sat plotting to take over the world. And of course, arguments ideologically spewed forth, particularly from David Johansen, who said, 'I've had enough of this. I don't want to sit around here. I don't want to be with you guys . . . blah blah blah. . . . And Jerry and Johnny, who was persuaded by Jerry . . . 'This is too fucking crazy. McLaren's completely mad,' and blah blah blah."

According to David, "It was a drag being on the road and [John and Jerry] couldn't cope. As long as they had stuff, everything was okay. It wasn't as if we had a medicine crew with us to take care of that. It was every man for himself, so John and Jerry would have to go back to New York and score. It got kind of ridiculous. By the end, in some redneck outpost in Florida, it was, like, 'This is impossible. Let's not do this anymore.'"[3]

Jerry had his own version:

"David said, 'Anyone in this band can be replaced.' That did it."[4]

Malcolm: "And that's where it all broke up."

Syl, David, and Peter found some locals—among them a young Blackie Lawless, later of the glam-metal band W.A.S.P.—to do the remaining gigs, while Johnny and Jerry returned to New York. And Arthur? Eileen Polk recalled he feared the return of his off-kilter, knife-wielding girlfriend Connie Gripp. "Connie had followed them down to Florida. She was doing things like turning tricks along the way and trying to buy heroin everywhere, and she was making a spectacle of herself. Florida isn't the kind of place where you can do that kind of stuff easily. So Arthur just decided, 'The hell with it, I'll just go to California.'"

The New York Dolls—the new Rolling Stones, the band that was going to take over the world—were over. Word filtered back to New York to Kathy Miller, who had started putting together a newsletter, buttons, and eight-by-ten glossies for their fan club. Kathy and her pal Linda Dana went up to see Leber-Krebs's Laura Kaufman, and fill her in on their progress. "Laura took us aside and said, 'The fan club is not going to happen because the band just broke up . . . but you can start the Aerosmith fan club. Here, meet Joe Perry.' I didn't like Aerosmith. In fact, Aerosmith once went to one of the Dolls gigs at Kenny's Castaways uptown and Aerosmith lined up at the first row of tables and Steven Tyler was flicking lit cigarettes at David Johansen. So theirs was not exactly a marriage made in heaven."

A few years later, Steven Tyler would marry Cyrinda Foxe, David's ex. She maintained that Steven pilfered more than just women from the Dolls. "There is one Aerosmith album cover that shows Steven Tyler in a glitter outfit that is a complete knock-off of David Johansen."[5]

Paul Nelson soon left Mercury, knowing his days there were numbered. In the May 26, 1975, edition of the *Village Voice*, he wrote a sprawling and emotional piece on the life and death of the Dolls. Noting their struggles and victories, successes and failures, indulgences and sacrifices, he quoted internal Mercury memos, his personal dealings with the label, band members, and management. The reader could all but see tears and blood on the page. At times it read like an epitaph, at other times like a suicide note. With pride, though, and not a hint of sentimentality, Nelson wrote that the Dolls were "not altogether devoid of nobility. I will cherish always the friendship of each of them."[6] Painfully but proudly, more figuratively than literally, he wrote simply: "The Dolls were alive."[7]

The article closed with the following declarative statement: "I do not claim they were the best, but the New York Dolls are still my favorite rock & roll group, although I will understand if you do not like them. I will understand, but deep down, I will not want to know you."

He quoted something Jerry said that, for all its sadness, now seems prescient: "I suppose everyone will be like the Dolls in a few years."[8]

Jerry's instincts would turn out to be right on the money. While '60s garage rock, the Velvet Underground, the MC5, the Stooges, Bowie, and Boston's Modern Lovers all played a part in creating what would become punk, practically every band associated with it, whether from Cleveland, Ohio, or Manchester, England, listened to the two Dolls albums and saw the band as a lodestar. Each group, filled with their own misfits and nonconformists, would find strength in knowing they didn't have to play music that sounded like the records they heard on the radio, or look like the groups on *American Bandstand.* They could find their own voice, even if they only knew a handful of chords or had just started playing their instruments a few weeks before. It was okay to learn how to play in public. The passion and excitement came first. The learning could follow.

But for now, the Dolls were finished. This group, this *gang*, had disintegrated due to a public that wasn't ready for them, and to battles both with each other as well as their own personal demons. David reflected on it years later: "Pre-band we were all outsiders creating from solitude and from pure and authentic creative impulses, so when we got together, though we were then a 'gang,' we all still retained that outsider feeling as individuals. If you try to imagine what it's like to want to create an art that was outside of official music biz culture, you'll find that you had to be an outsider. We couldn't avoid the feeling that in relation to it, status quo cultural art in its entirety appeared to be the game of a futile society, a fallacious parade. Yet the fact remained even after a certain familiarity with the flourishings of an exalted feverishness, lived so fully and so intensely by the band, we all felt still as if it were our own self who was the outsider in the band."

PART 3

TOO MUCH
JUNKIE
BUSINESS

CHINESE

11 ROCKS

AS THE DOLLS WERE DISINTEGRATING, RICHARD HELL FOUND HIS position in his band Television untenable. Fellow band member, and childhood friend, Tom Verlaine chafed at Richard's drug use and lack of interest in learning his new songs. Losing patience with Hell, Verlaine minimized Hell's role. Recalls Hell: "First it was, 'Don't jump around when I'm singing,' then it was, 'We're dropping this song of yours'."[1] The band recorded a six-song, Brian Eno–produced demo for Island Records. "Tom would play only one song of mine, 'Blank Generation,' and he performed it like a novelty song."[2] In March of 1975 Richard left Television.

Within days, Johnny phoned Richard saying he wanted to start a new band with Jerry and him. "I didn't hesitate,"[3] said Richard. As far as he could see, they both wanted to make "tough, frantic music"[4] and Johnny was the most exciting guitarist around. Jerry wanted to make a break from the Dolls' look and sound, and saw Richard, with his short, spiked hair, and torn, safety-pinned clothing, as the way to do it. Richard was a driving force of this small but growing scene, writing the song that defined it as much as any, 'Blank Generation,' combining a detached, beatnik cool with streetwise poetry. Hell's songs and profile could connect them to the new bands coming out of CBGB.

The name of the new band would be the Heartbreakers. Sylvain insists he came up with the name. Others claim Jerry came up with it when the band were in Florida and saw flyers for Tom Petty's band of the same name. Thinking Petty's bunch would never get out of Florida, they figured it was ripe for the taking. It sounded street, like the name of a gang of gigolo thugs.

Johnny didn't want another situation like he'd had in the Dolls, where he could only sing one song per show. Jerry felt the same. No one would be designated as lead singer. It was agreed: Richard would sing his songs, and Johnny would sing his.

Before even playing a gig, they did a photo session with Bob Gruen by a burnt-out van on New York's waterfront. Each band member had a distinctive look: Johnny was still long-haired but looked like a street urchin in dungarees, a dog collar, and black Converse sneakers; Richard had tight black jeans and a jacket with a turned-up collar, dark glasses, and shorter hair; Jerry was now wearing an early-'60s-style, slim-lapel Continental suit, with '50s two-tone loafers and a shorter shag. The group still hadn't coalesced behind a look, but they definitely weren't glam.

They rehearsed at the Dolls' old space on Twenty-Third Street, sharing it with another band called the Demons. Although some claim they played an informal set on April 30 opening for Wayne County at Club 82, their first real show was May 30 in Queens back at the Coventry, with the Ramones. The seven-song set contained Johnny's "Pirate Love" and "I Wanna Be Loved," Richard's "Blank Generation," and Jerry's first publicly played composition, "Can't Keep My Eyes on You," written about his shyness around Debbie Harry. They opened with a song they only played once more, at their next show at Coventry on June 6, called "57 Chevy." Also played that night was a Richard/Johnny collaboration called "Hurt Me," and a Dee Dee Ramone/Hell piece titled "Chinese Rocks," a paean to all things heroin, reflecting an avocation all involved pursued enthusiastically.

The band were rawer than raw, with only seven songs. Most bands would have waited until they had at least ten or more songs before playing a gig, but, according to photographer Roberta Bayley, they "needed the money." Coventry always did well when the Dolls played there: Thus two Dolls playing for only a half hour was fine. The club management knew the band would draw enough to make it worth their while.

Bootlegs of the June 6 show reveal the Heartbreakers playing at grindingly slow tempos. Walter Lure, then playing with opening act the Demons, credited it to the fact that "they were all on downs or some other weird drug."

The Heartbreakers felt they needed a second guitarist to fill out their sound. One of the first people they contacted was Boston-based John Felice, who'd previously played with Jonathan Richman's Modern Lovers, later forming the Real Kids.

Felice received a call from Thunders just before Memorial Day. "I left on a Friday after work, went down, took my guitar and the clothes on my back."[5] The band spent their time "shootin' dope, shootin' speed, rehearsing for three or four days straight. It was hard stuff. We'd rehearse for a few hours, get high, go out, go to a bar and get fucked up and come home."[6] John knew this wasn't a sustainable lifestyle. "I figured if I stayed in New York I'd end up dead within a year."[7] Felice returned home to Boston.

Another guitarist who auditioned was Rob Duprey of the Mumps, featuring Lance Loud of *An American Family*, the Public Broadcasting Service series credited with being the first true reality show. "Apparently, Richard admired my playing, because he started asking me to come and join." At the audition, "Johnny had that super-loud yellow Les Paul Junior. He played so loud that I had to kneel in front of my amp to hear my own guitar." Despite Richard's persistence, Rob decided to stay with the Mumps.

Blondie's Chris Stein also stopped in at the Twenty-Third Street loft with his guitar. "It was sort of an audition and just curiosity to see what they were up to. I don't know if I was actually dead set on wanting to be in the Heartbreakers. I certainly didn't try to impress them. I remember sitting down through the whole thing."

A more serious contender was Jonathan Paley, a Boston transplant formerly of the band Mong. "The first time was kind of an audition. I remember that Chris Stein was leaving as I came in. Johnny really liked the way I played. He'd say, 'Yeah, do more of that kinda stuff,' in places where he wanted leads. Hell asked me if I could think of any background vocals for 'Blank Generation,' so off the cuff I came up with the descending 'ooo ooo ooo ooo' with the extra 'wee-oo' at the end."

Attending multiple rehearsals, Paley got the sense he was in the band. When Bob Gruen came by to take some photos, he suggested the band get out on the fire escape. "Johnny, Richard, and Jerry got out there and as I was coming through the window Jerry pushed me back and said, 'No, not you.'" At the band's next gig, "Richard told me . . . Jerry didn't want me in the band. Later on I heard from a couple of people that he just really disliked me." While Paley suspected Jerry's aversion to him had something to do with pursuit of the same woman, drugs might have been the deciding factor. "All those guys knew I wasn't into heroin."

The fire escape photos show Richard in a torn shirt; short, unkempt hair; and dark glasses, looking cool and wasted. Jerry is sitting down with a can of soda pop in his hand wearing a two-tone motorcycle jacket with metal studs on the belt and epaulettes, staring at the camera, challenging the viewer. He's still wearing New York Dolls–style, ladies' stacked heels, but with Johnny looking frighteningly deranged holding a guitar, they all look like nothing less than a badass rock 'n' roll street gang ready to cut you for being on their turf, which was probably their intention.

The search for a fourth member finally hit pay dirt when Demons guitarist Walter Lure caught Johnny's eye at a Club 82 gig. The band's singer, Eliot Kidd, was already a drug buddy of Johnny's and Jerry's when Thunders showed up. After the gig, Johnny spoke to Walter. "He says, 'You want to join the band?' So I said, 'Yeah, sure.'"

The band still went through the formality of auditioning Walter, which was where he first met Jerry. Afterwards, Walter heard nothing from them for several weeks and assumed they'd changed their minds. But then the Heartbreakers and the Demons shared the bill at Coventry on June 6. "That night at the show, Jerry pulled me over. He said, 'Did you see anything that you liked in that audition with us?' And I'm going, 'Yeah, I loved the fucking songs. I thought it was great.' Then he starting going, 'We were thinking we wanted you to join the band.'" Walter joined without hesitation.

After another show as a three-piece at CBGB on June 25, the new four-piece Heartbreakers made their debut on July 4, also at CBGB, headlining over both the Ramones and Blondie. But first Walter had one more show to play with the Demons, coincidentally the night before at CBGB. On July 3, he played to what seemed like twenty people. The next night, with the Heartbreakers, he played to a packed house. In one day, Walter had moved to the head of the class. "Debbie Harry and Chris Stein used to call me the 'Rookie of the Year' because I came from nowhere into one of the biggest bands in New York," said Walter. "It was a big change in lifestyle."

Unlike the rest of the band, Walter was educated, but he wasn't as "cultured" as Richard, the band's self-styled poet. The most levelheaded of the bunch, Walter had spent several years as a trained pharmacist, which was also an attraction to Johnny, who got a large quantity of powdered Quaaludes from Walter early on in Lure's tenure as a Heartbreaker. The tall and gangly Walter stood out onstage but meshed well with Johnny's guitar style. He was also happy just to be there for the ride, and not a threat to the other three.

From the get-go, Walter got a sense of the three different personalities he was dealing with. "Jerry was different than John even though they were birds of a feather. Jerry was more down-to-earth. John was like a whack job. They both were whack jobs in a sense, but Jerry was more levelheaded even though as I got to know him later on, he would flip between hot and cold too. John could be real charming and nice . . . when he wasn't stoned or high on something. Then he would . . . go running after someone or get high and he'd be oblivious to the rest of the world. Hell was probably . . . more standoffish even though he wasn't nasty or anything like that. He was just involved with his beatnik poetry and stuff like that. But Jerry was a little different. Jerry was more 'chummy,' getting 'buddy-buddy.'"

After taking him under his wing, Jerry introduced Walter to the world of heroin, saying, 'Let's go cop.'

Walter: "As soon as I got into the band . . . I found out they're all into junk. I was a relative novice. I never stuck a needle in my arm. I tried heroin a couple of times in the '60s during the whole drug era . . . and I didn't like it. It made me sick. But eventually . . . they sort of weaned me into it. There wasn't any pressure, but you sort of wanted to find out what it was all about."

Walter lived in Brooklyn Heights, just over the Brooklyn Bridge from Manhattan. Johnny lived in Chelsea, just north of the West Village, and Jerry lived on the Upper East Side, still with Michelle. Conveniently, Richard lived in the East Village, a half block from scores of drug dealers in Alphabet City. Joining them in their revelry was Dee Dee Ramone. They called Richard's apartment Hell's Kitchen.

The July 4 show was quickly followed by another on July 7, also at CBGB. Bootlegs of this show present a band with more confidence than they had just six weeks before. Jerry, who plays with a touch of big-band swing, sounds especially assured compared to the rest of the band, who seem hopped-up and unfocused. Still, they jell. Jerry's now added a train rhythm to his part in the chorus of "I Wanna Be Loved"—one part Sun Records rockabilly and one part northeastern R&B, reminiscent of the Coasters. "You Gotta Lose" also contains a remarkable lightness of touch not generally apparent in other CBGB bands.

But while Jerry's playing is thoughtful, make no mistake: The Heartbreakers were a musical steamrolling force of nature. Hell's former bandmate Richard Lloyd described them as "a fucking freight train . . . they were wickedly, unbelievably powerful." As both Hell and Thunders were somewhat limited in Lloyd's eyes, he attributed much of it to Jerry, adding, "I loved it."

Speaking of Hell and Thunders, Gary Valentine of Blondie remarked: "They were great. . . . They're both very different, both very striking icons. Hell was this electrified beat poet, and Thunders was this pirate rock god . . . so there was friction and tension between them onstage. Some of my favorite shows in the early CBGB days were seeing those guys."

Gary's partner in Blondie, drummer Clem Burke, was equally smitten: "The Heartbreakers were a really great band. They really had three, four front men. I don't want to sound clichéd [but] you could call them the punk rock Beatles. Each person really stood out."

After a July 23 show at Max's they headed back to CB's on July 25 and 26 as part of the club's festival of unsigned talent. "That's kind of when people starting taking notice," recalled Eileen Polk.

Bands had been coming to New York for months, as the CBGB scene held out hope for a new breed of underground groups. Many still saw the New York Dolls as the beacon that had brought them to New York. Talking Heads, a quirky art-school band who sounded nothing like the Dolls, were a prime example. Talking Heads bass player Tina Weymouth was very explicit about the strength they received just from knowing a band like the Dolls existed. First seeing them in *Creem* magazine while in college, Tina thought, "They were so raw but because of them I knew New York was the place for us. I told David [Byrne] that if we went there we could do our band."

Talking Heads were just one of the bands who played at what was awkwardly billed as the "CBGB Rock Festival Top 40 New York Unrecorded Rock TALENT." The partial listing of bands in the *Village Voice* ad that week included future major label artists Blondy [*sic*], Mink DeVille, Ramones, the Shirts, Talking Heads, Television, and Tough Darts [*sic*]. The Heartbreakers were one of the largest draws of the weekend.

But the Heartbreakers did rub some people wrong. Some saw them as arrogant, including would-be Dolls savior Malcolm McLaren, and *NME*'s Charles Shaar Murray, who noted that Thunders felt he had a "right to demand to use the back door at CBGB so he doesn't have to walk through the audience."[8] Some thought Johnny and Jerry were capitalizing on the work of others, usurping the territory earned on the backs of original CBGB bands like Television and the Ramones, who both played at CBGB a full year before the Heartbreakers. Jerry sensed it: "I felt a lotta hostility from a lotta bands toward the Heartbreakers. It was like, 'Well, you guys had your chance in the Dolls and you blew it, now stay away.' What, they got rules and regulations, you only allowed a certain number of chances"?[9]

The Heartbreakers' biggest problem was their reputation. Going back to Johnny and Jerry's days with the Dolls, and also owing to new songs like "Chinese Rocks," everyone, particularly record companies, knew they were junkies. Johnny Ramone, even though he felt the Heartbreakers were the only band as good as the Ramones, said, "They were a bunch of junkies so I don't have to worry about them. Their career is going to be short."[10]

Jerry always claimed no matter how high he was, he always came through onstage. Clem Burke recalled an early CBGB show: "The

Heartbreakers were playing and Jerry just took his head to the side . . . and started throwing up while he was playing." In fact, Debbie Harry claimed there was a time Jerry sat in for Billy O'Connor, Blondie's first drummer, when he had ingested too many downs to play.

As the Heartbreakers were trying to make a name for themselves in New York, David and Sylvain put together a new version of the Dolls with Peter Jordan on bass and Tony Machine on drums, doing a ten-date tour of Japan in August. Known somewhat derisively on the scene as the Dollettes, they were a more refined but relatively well-received version of the original band.

The money for the Japanese tour was plentiful enough that David and Syl could ride out the rest of the year with only the occasional gig. The Heartbreakers, even as one of the top-drawing acts on the New York underground scene, were still struggling to make ends meet. They played at CBGB August 15 and 16 with Talking Heads and Blondie, and then again September 5 and 6 with Tuff Darts. They were clearing about $500 a night, nothing close to what David and Sylvain were making with the reformed Dolls.

The Dollettes invariably got under Jerry's skin. Jerry didn't let on that he'd taken the fall of the Dolls as hard as he had, keeping up his tough demeanor at all costs. His response was to openly hold a grudge against David for misdirecting the Dolls. "Jerry hated David with a passion," said Walter Lure. "John sort of didn't like him after the Dolls either, but Jerry just blamed everything in the Dolls on David."

While Jerry still lived with Michelle, in many ways they led separate lives, as she worked in the daytime and Jerry "worked" at night. Their relationship hadn't recovered since he'd discovered her affair and slapped her around. "We shouldn't have been living under one roof, but I had nowhere else to go," said Michelle. "I'm sure he was using me at that point."

Jerry now pursued other women, the object of his immediate desires being a young brunette from Brooklyn named Donna Destri, sister of Blondie's keyboard player, Jimmy.

"I wouldn't even call it going out on dates. We would meet at a club; we'd go sit and make out in the corner. He was always well dressed, and he always looked great."

Jerry filled her in as to who he was now taking style tips from. "He idolized Willy DeVille." Willy and his band, Mink DeVille, played a style of R&B that evoked Phil Spector, Doc Pomus, and the urban, street-corner romance of both the Drifters and Lou Reed. Jerry told Donna, 'You got to see this guy! This guy is so cool, even his girlfriend is cool!' Willy and his sweetheart, Toots, who, like Jerry, were also junkies, were the epitome of a new style of retro-hip, evoking the Puerto Rican gangs of Spanish Harlem. Willy had skinny ties and pointed shoes, and Toots had a nose ring, a tattoo, and a beehive hairdo almost thirty years before Amy Winehouse. "She was a tough customer. If you *looked* at him, she'd be right there ready to rip your face off. I think that's why he was attracted to me, because I was that Brooklyn tough girl."

Donna was also dating the drummer from the Fast. "[Jerry] said, 'Get rid of that guy. He's a jerk.' And I didn't."

That same night, Jerry was with Donna at Max's after ingesting some barbiturates. He could function well on smack, leaving most people unaware that he was high. But on downs, he was much different. "He was very weird that night. Very pushy and arrogant and not like himself. He just got foul . . . very evil. He was not the type of person that could do barbiturates and be nice. And he pushed me; he pulled my hair, which was something that he never, ever did. He was always a gentleman. And he went downstairs and started a barroom brawl."

That's when Jerry got stabbed, or so the legend goes.

There were many witnesses that night at Max's, including Chris Stein and Clem Burke of Blondie, photographer Eileen Polk, Eliot Kidd from the Demons, Philippe Marcadé of the Senders, and Johnny and Walter at a nearby table. Most people agree that Jerry inadvertently bumped into someone, spilling their drink. Philippe insists that the fellow who lost his drink called Jerry a "motherfucker,'" resulting in a six-punch combination to the head. After Jerry told Philippe, "The motherfucker shouldn't have fucked with me,"[11] the not-quite-unconscious victim picked up some broken glass and slashed Jerry's upper thigh, just missing his testicles. Everyone agrees with Chris Stein's assessment that "the little foyer at Max's was thick with gore." Philippe described it as "like a shower, blood was just pouring onto his shoes."[12]

Eileen recalled that Jerry was "drunk . . . stumbled," knocked over the guy's drink, laughed, and got stabbed. Chris Stein insisted that Jerry never got stabbed. "He was fighting with a guy. He rolled over onto broken glass and it cut his femoral artery." Nonetheless, people were yelling 'Get an ambulance!' Max's owner Tommy Dean pressed some cloth napkins onto the wound and put him in a taxi. Wayne County's manager Peter Crowley said that Tommy "handed the cabbie a twenty and said, 'Get him to St. Vincent's as fast as you can.'"

Some say Philippe rode in the cab with Jerry to the hospital; others say it was Michael Sticca, Blondie's roadie. Peter added, "In order to save Max's liquor license, the authorities were told the action went down out on the sidewalk. Because the perp was connected, his name was withheld from investigators." Tommy strongly suggested to Jerry that he not press charges.

Donna and Gail Higgins, cousin of Johnny's old girlfriend Janis Cafasso, visited Jerry in the hospital. "He was on this welfare ward," said Donna, "and he was really embarrassed about that. There were like twenty beds to a room." One person who never visited or contacted him was Peter Criss. Despite their estrangement, Jerry felt he should have at least received a get-well card from Peter. Jerry never let go of this slight.

Once Jerry was out of the hospital, his heroin use became more brazen. He openly shot up at Donna's house, putting the nail in the coffin of their relationship. It seemed like smack was the only thing, more than music or the loving touch of a woman, that could suppress his pain.

Instead of confiding in Michelle, he reached out to his old crush Nancy Quatro, who'd heard stories of Jerry's heroin use. "Jerry would do the very happy act, try to be encouraged and positive and [say], 'I think my life is going in a better direction.' Then I would throw in the fatal question: 'But are you still doing heroin?' He wouldn't lie, he would say yes. I would say, 'Then it's not going in that direction yet.'"

Jerry was proud of his song "Can't Keep My Eyes on You" and told Nancy he needed drugs to keep writing. "It was just an extreme lack of belief in himself. The drugs gave him the false sense of 'It's okay.' He got peace from heroin, because that's what heroin does—until it doesn't do that anymore."

He said he saw a therapist and felt encouraged. "I thought it was really a great idea just because it may be an objective viewpoint. But therapists . . . are only as good as the story you are telling them." Nancy added, "When I heard he had gotten so badly into heroin, I remember thinking, 'He found his girlfriend.' That became the love of his life. He didn't call ever again."

By the end of 1975, Michelle was sleeping with her money in her socks, to hide it from Jerry before he could steal it. She was unsuccessful: He purloined some of her Christmas bonus.

* * *

THE HEARTBREAKERS, DESPITE BEING A TOP DRAW ON THE NEW underground rock scene, had no record deal and played no gigs outside of Manhattan besides the Coventry in Queens. In the fall, they played at a new club called Mothers, started by Peter Crowley, across from the Chelsea Hotel. Despite two gigs there in November and December, they were still primarily a struggling local rock 'n' roll group with no record deal.

New Year's Eve is always a big payday, with fees often double what an act could normally demand. To ring in the New Year, the Dolls were playing the 2,800-seat Beacon Theatre on the Upper West Side.

Unlike the Dolls—or what was left of them—who were now trying to appear more mainstream while searching for a major-label deal, the Heartbreakers embraced a more threatening image. As part of the band's effort to seem "dangerous," Richard had the idea to create a special poster for their New Year's Eve show with the Ramones, and called on his former girlfriend and CBGB door person Roberta Bayley to help. She photographed the band as urban zombies from a black-and-white '40s noir film, with bloody shirts signifying they were at death's door. With the caption "Catch 'em while they're still alive," the poster was one of the most enduring images of the early New York punk rock era. The implied message was one of urgency: Go see this band, they aren't going to be around much longer.

The Dolls' New Year's Eve show was well received, but in-the-know locals favored the Heartbreakers. Clem Burke: "The Heartbreakers were really carrying on the tradition of the Dolls for me a lot more than David and Sylvain. . . . It was a watered-down version. . . . The Heartbreakers were doing something that was more focused and the songs were great and they were wild. Jerry and Johnny Thunders together was dynamite."

On New Year's Eve, Gary Valentine recalled, "Everybody got to know both the Ramones and the Heartbreakers, because they just did pretty much exactly the same set over and over three times. But it was great."

Under pressure from Jerry and Richard, Johnny finally cut his hair. Like the other three Heartbreakers—and unlike David and Syl—he now looked like something from the newly spawned punk era.

Unlike the Dollettes, who would hang out but never play CBGB, the Heartbreakers fully integrated into the scene, regularly sharing bills with the Ramones, Blondie, Talking Heads, and Mink DeVille. Those bands had their own respective traditional pop sensibilities and commercial potential. The Ramones became the blueprint for three-chord, leather-clad punk but could write a memorable pop tune within those limitations. Blondie were an art-pop experiment, with the emphasis on "pop" as well as a stunning visual focal point for a lead singer. Talking Heads were quirky but still retained a melodic and rhythmic danceability while holding true to their art-school ethos. Mink DeVille were straight urban R&B meets Phil Spector with a charismatic lead singer right off the set of *West Side Story*. They were all courting managers and record labels. But the Heartbreakers were still stymied, suffering from lack of discipline and their lingering drug reputation.

In the New Year, to go along with their new look, the Heartbreakers hoped to change their luck by recording demos at SBS Studios in Yonkers, recording ten songs: Richard's "Love Comes in Spurts," "Blank Generation," and "You Gotta Lose"; Johnny's "I Wanna Be Loved," "Pirate Love," and "Goin' Steady"; Jerry's "Can't Keep My Eye on You," sung by Richard, as was Richard and Dee Dee's "Chinese Rocks"; the Johnny/Richard collaboration "Hurt Me"; and Walter's first band contribution, "Flight." It was essentially a refined version of their live show done in a studio, with few, if any, overdubs.

The whole demo delivers touches of rockabilly, girl groups, Stones swagger, Dylan disdain, blues-rock, surf, and R&B. With a little guidance from a trusted, mentoring producer, and some discipline, the Heartbreakers had the potential to make a record of serious substance.

Still, no managers, producers, or record companies came out of the woodwork. The recordings were still too undisciplined for the music industry at large, and the band's reputation as unrepentant junkies hadn't changed. For now, they would play CBGB and Max's, with Peter Crowley moving there as booker from Mothers. Until they played Boston's Rathskeller on May 14, the band were stuck playing these two venues only.

In the March 27, 1976, edition of *NME*, Nick Kent relayed his conversation with Richard, who was "glumly resigned to a further six months in limbo before a half-way decent offer comes the way of his band."[13] As it turned out, Richard wouldn't wait six months. He was tiring of the direction the rest of the band favored, one where songs like "Goin' Steady" and "I Wanna Be Loved" summarized the height of their intellectual curiosity. Richard had a background in the poetry of Rimbaud and Lautréamont. The rest of them had a background in Dion DiMucci and the Yardbirds. Richard enjoyed, "stomping noise and violence and confrontation,"[14] but he also wanted to create music that had broader possibilities. The Heartbreakers did not offer those possibilities.

Richard denies there was ever any sort of rivalry between Johnny and him or any attempt on his part to take over. The rest of the band viewed it differently. Walter: "It was Richard versus Johnny, with Jerry being the key guy in between. They liked Hell because he was funny, and he had these beatnik ideas, and he had a couple of cool songs." But there was a difference. "Johnny and Jerry were basically rockers." Walter thought the four of them "were pretty good together until Hell turned into the megalomaniac that he was all along. We didn't see it in the beginning. He wanted to run the whole band, and that just was out of the question for Johnny."

Walter insists Richard wanted to limit the amount of songs the others could sing, and to approve Walter's lyrics. "At that point John just said, 'Fuck this, I'm not going to play with you if I can only sing two songs a set,' or something like that." Johnny left their rehearsal. After the remaining three finished up without him, Jerry and Walter went over to Johnny's place. Walter, having the least influence of any band member, was undecided about what to do, but ultimately followed Jerry. "Jerry probably had decided ahead of time: 'I'm gonna stick with Johnny.'" The die was cast: Richard was the odd man out. "We weren't really into this whole beatnik routine. We were rock 'n' rollers. We started looking for a bass player."

Jerry gave his version to the *Village Voice* in 1991: "Richard actually had the nerve and really thought that we would get rid of Johnny. I just fuckin' laughed. I said, 'Richard, I'm sorry, buddy, but do you think I would leave Johnny for you? You must be fuckin' nuts. You're the one who will have to leave.'"[15]

To this day, Richard insists he left by his own volition and that any utterance by Johnny and Jerry to the contrary was just macho posturing. Regardless of which version of the story was accurate, Richard was out. He played the few previously booked shows, giving them time to find another bass player.

Desperate for help in his stagnating career, Johnny approached former Bowie and Warhol protégé Leee Black Childers about managing the band.

Born in Kentucky, Leee had come to New York in 1969, first having spent time in San Francisco looking for Timothy Leary after reading about LSD and the Summer of Love in *Life* magazine. Leee quickly entrenched himself in Warhol's sexually uninhibited Factory scene after making friends with three curious characters he'd met within days of moving to New York: drag queens Wayne County, Jackie Curtis, and Holly Woodlawn.

Leee photographed the characters he'd meet while traveling through New York's underbelly, parlaying his talents into gigs as stage manager for Jackie Curtis's play *Femme Fatale*, Wayne County's musical *World—Birth of a Nation*, and Warhol's *Pork*. It was during *Pork*'s London run that he met David Bowie, who was so enamored by the experience, he hired several of the show's staff to be part of his management firm MainMan. Leee soon became executive vice president, traveling with Bowie and assisting with other acts in the Bowie/MainMan stable: Iggy Pop and Mott the Hoople.

Leee continued his pursuits as a photographer, capturing images of stars like Rod Stewart for popular magazines, and less popular acts like the New York Dolls for *Rock Scene*. Leee was drawn to the city's dark side, and its tragic, doomed creatures of the night, making him a regular at CBGB and Max's. A natural raconteur with an engaging smile, Leee loved to meet and gossip with anyone and everyone. It was under these circumstances that Johnny asked Leee about managing the Heartbreakers.

Leee considered the offer and asked his partner at MainMan, Tony Zanetta, to join him. A fan of the Heartbreakers, "Z" contemplated the offer but in the end realized that traveling with "a bunch of junkies and no money did not thrill me. I also underestimated my ability to do much for them as a manager. I guess I still thought that to be an effective manager one had to be very DeFries-like, which I certainly was not." Tony declined.[†]

Everyone told Leee not to do it, but he loved Johnny and had gained experience with junkies working with Iggy. His philosophy was, "You can't cure 'em. You can only keep them alive and keep them working."

Leee's feelings about Jerry were the opposite of his feelings about Johnny. "Jerry was very famous for being the manager slayer." Leee asked Johnny what Jerry thought about him becoming manager. "Johnny probably lied and said, 'Oh, Jerry's really anxious for you to do it." But Leee understood the reality of the situation. "Frankly, what it came down to was it was me or nobody."

Jerry made Leee's life difficult from the get-go. He criticized the way Leee dressed, where he went, and who his friends were. "You had to be really strong to be able to see things your way around him. He challenged [opinions] and made my life very difficult in what I was trying to do as far as the business of the Heartbreakers."

Jerry quickly tried scamming Leee into giving him money, telling him that his grandmother, who had been dead for years, had just died and he needed to fly to another state for the funeral. Leee saw it as a test and refused. From then on, "He knew that I was actually going to manage. I wasn't going to be a fountain of money."

Leee had plenty to worry about without having to also battle Jerry and his junkie lies. The band needed a bass player. He could sense that Richard's leaving had thrown them for a loop. In the eyes of many, Richard was their leader, and no one knew if any of the three remaining members could step into the breach.

---

† Tony DeFries' MainMan management company managed David Bowie from 1970–1975 and played a role in the careers of Iggy and the Stooges during their "Raw Power" period, and Mott the Hopple during "All the Young Dudes."

He toyed with trying to convince Richard to stay but decided against it. "He wouldn't have stayed," Leee posited. "All the bands Richard left, Richard was better off for leaving them, and the bands were better off for him having gone. Richard's not a joiner. All the stories were about the conflict between him and Johnny, but heaven knows what it was like between him and Jerry." Johnny could sulk or threaten to take his ball and go home. "He wouldn't defend himself. He certainly wouldn't defend himself against Jerry. He wouldn't defend himself against me. So Johnny wouldn't defend himself against Richard, because Richard's weapon is 'I'm smarter than you.' And he is smarter than everybody, but it's not necessarily good to use that as a weapon. And so I'm sure Johnny just caved, but Jerry wouldn't. Jerry wouldn't cave under anyone."

By the end of June, Richard Hell had an offer in hand from Instant Records, a production company created by Richard Gottehrer and his partner, former New York Dolls manager Marty Thau. Gottehrer had a long history in the music business as a writer, producer, performer, and businessman. Between Thau and Gottehrer, it looked like Hell had found for himself exactly what the Heartbreakers needed: experienced and well-connected musical mentors that could get him on an ascending career path.

While Jerry publicly belittled Hell, Richard had a point about Jerry's macho posturing. Hell signing a solo deal, especially with Jerry's ex-manager, undoubtedly made the drummer bristle. Hell was now just another person to add to the list of ex-pals who were doing better than Jerry was. Jerry also turned thirty on May 7. Deep down, he was worried that he was washed up. His painkiller was heroin.

Still, there was the issue of finding a new bass player. Despite the band's drug rep, the position of bass player in the Heartbreakers was a coveted one. The band adopted a search approach similar to the one they'd used to find Walter the year before. "They were having people from other bands come and play with them," said Leee, "which is kind of a sneaky thing to do."

The band auditioned bass players in an East Village loft during a spring heat wave. Included was a friend of Walter's, college buddy Albert Sce; Steve Shevlin, who later played with the Senders; and possibly Keith (also known as Keeth) Paul, who'd done sound for the Dolls. The person who finally got the gig came to them through a recommendation from Lyn Todd, a recent transplant from Boston and a singer with her own band, Peroxide. His name was Billy Rath.

After receiving a convincing call from Jerry, Billy flew into New York for the audition and was asked to join the band that night. "The audition was the first rehearsal. We were like a hand in the glove."

Billy wrote down some chords and played the same bass lines he'd used for years. "I knew I was going to be the bass player before I even got there . . . because that was my style. I was a rock 'n' roll bass player. That was my roots, rhythm and blues. I wasn't a frustrated guitar player."

For once, Leee and Jerry were in agreement. Jerry wanted Leee to spend a few minutes privately with Billy to make sure he understood what he was getting into. Leee: "I went out and sat with Billy in a parked car and talked. We talked about everything. I was pretty frank about Jerry and Johnny's drug addiction, which he knew about. We didn't talk about music much. We talked about the fact that he'd never be rich, and that he was just doing this because somebody had to keep Johnny performing. And he was real cool with that, so I was cool with him."

Jerry knew Billy was their man. He liked that Billy was a professional bass player and that he was not a personality that he had to compete with. Hell was a "star." Billy was a bass player. That suited Jerry just fine. For all Hell's talents as a wordsmith and stylist, being a solid rock 'n' roll bass player was not one of them. Jerry and Johnny could be the stars.

ONE
TRACK
MIND

12

THE HEARTBREAKERS BEGAN REHEARSALS, NOT ONLY TO BREAK in Billy, but also to replace all of Richard's songs. "Blank Generation," "Hurt Me," "Love Comes in Spurts," "New Pleasure," and "You Gotta Lose" were out, with "Chinese Rocks" the only song remaining that Richard had had a hand in.

New songs were written and quickly learned. By the Heartbreakers' next gig, on July 23, they had eight new songs, six of which were originals, with the Contours' "Do You Love Me" and Bo Diddley's "I Can Tell" being the two covers. Johnny brought four new tunes: "Baby Talk," "I Love You," "It's Not Enough," and "Born to Lose." Walter and Jerry collaborated on two songs: "Take a Chance with Me" and "Get Off the Phone."

While "Baby Talk" was an all but straight-up rip-off of the Yardbirds' "I Ain't Done No Wrong," it contained some of Jerry's strongest drumming yet. His repeated rolls introducing each verse are a direct homage to Gene Krupa's drumming with Benny Goodman on "Sing, Sing, Sing," where his rapid-fire snare rolls bring the song to its magnificent climax.

"Get Off the Phone" exhibits some of the same thinking behind Jerry's drum parts in the original "Love Comes in Spurts" and the Dolls cover of "Somethin' Else," with Jerry throwing in an extra snare hit besides the standard two and four. This time he does it throughout the bulk of the song. It's surf rock, done at such a fast tempo it becomes punk rock.

It was Jerry's idea to partner with Walter on writing, satisfying several of his concerns. Without Hell in the band, Jerry didn't want Johnny to end up in a position as de facto leader and conspire with Leee, whom he did not trust, to call the shots. By co-opting Walter, who was also looking to improve his station in the band, he could keep Johnny's power in check. Walter also had more of an understanding of songwriting than Jerry did, taking his skeletal ideas and turning them into finished songs.

According to Walter, "Jerry had a lot of [songs]. 'Can't Keep My Eyes on You' . . . was Jerry's. He had the rhythm [and he] could play guitar a little bit. . . . He had the first verse and the lyrics. Same thing happened when he had 'Take a Chance with Me' and a few other ones. He wasn't that good with the words, so he would just come up with an idea for a verse or a chorus and then I would fill it out."

As a drummer, Jerry wrote song snippets that had a solid rhythmic structure, giving Walter a strong foundation to work with and making it relatively easy for the band to come up with an arrangement quickly. Walter also preferred writing with Jerry as opposed to Johnny. "John was always a million miles away, thinking about drugs or this, that, and the other thing."

With their new songs, the band could assess Billy's impact immediately, and they liked what they heard. Even the earliest live bootlegs of "I Wanna Be Loved" with Billy, compared to versions with Richard, reveal the Heartbreakers as a pure rock 'n' roll band. Hell's artistic vision, which he hoped to impart to the Heartbreakers, was now gone. The new Heartbreakers embraced a pre-Beatles style of rock 'n' roll that had more in common with Gary U.S. Bonds than with Arthur Rimbaud. Billy was the final piece of the puzzle. Tommy Ramone may have said it best: "The Heartbreakers were different with Richard Hell. It was more bohemian and arty. When Hell left they became more like New York jet-set street kids."

As they rehearsed, the band got to know Billy. Walter: "He was sort of an outsider. He was a speed freak and we were all junkies. Right away, there's a conflict there, because they move at different speeds." His choice of illicit substances notwithstanding, Walter's assessment of Billy turned out to be somewhat of a paradox. "He wasn't really a dimwit, but he was sort of slow."

Despite their different drugs of choice, Billy and Jerry were simpatico musically. Billy particularly loved playing with Jerry. "He was rock solid," said Billy. "I was a stickler for time. I didn't slow down. I didn't speed up. I flowed with Jerry so well. Very little was discussed."

With a new band member, Leee realized they needed new photos that didn't feature Richard. They would not only include Billy but give the band a more coordinated look. The resulting shots had all four band members wielding guitars, in smart, thin-lapelled suits and two-tone shoes, or baggy '50s-style trousers. "That was Jerry's idea, of course," recalled Leee.

130

While some shots show Jerry wearing torn, Ramones-type jeans, the bulk of them give the impression that you're looking at a well-dressed '50s gang, which is just as Jerry wanted. Just like he got Johnny to discard his long hair leftover from the Dolls, Jerry got everyone to be more style-conscious. He held the same role in the Heartbreakers that he'd held in Shaker. Walter: "Jerry was the one who was coming up with the most ideas as far as clothes to wear, and images, and what songs we want to do covers of, and what looked cool and what didn't, [and] how to present ourselves. . . . He was more '50s than, say, the Ramones or the punk rock guys, but it was a natty style that was different that no one had seen, because they had just come out of the glam rock scene and the hippies in the '60s."

But the music was paramount, and that now had more pre-Beatles inclinations. The rest of the band came to love music through exposure to '60s English groups like the Beatles, the Stones, the Who and the Yardbirds. Jerry exposed the band to American '50s artists like Eddie Cochran and Gene Vincent.

Clothing and music weren't the only things associated with the '50s that Jerry was into. He was known to make unflattering remarks about people based on their race or religion. He was already known as Nigs to his friends, the nickname arguably carrying with it racist overtones. "He said terrible things about Jews," recalled Leee. "He said terrible things about gay people and black people. I was trying to think of some extenuating circumstance that would say he was joking in a way. No, he didn't. He did hate Jews and black people and homosexuals. We could always come up with a reason. I mean, homosexual is easy: Jerry was afraid he was homosexual himself. But he couldn't have been afraid he was a black person, or afraid he was a Jew." But what of Jerry's long-standing friendship with Buddy Bowzer, or his time spent with Art Steinman and his family? "That's the old racist thing," added Leee. "A racist can have a personal friend who's black or Jewish, and they somehow don't seem to count in the overall hate of the race."

While it may be true to say that Jerry's racism was just another attempt to blame a set of "others" for the negative state of his life and career, the cognitive dissonance that Leee refers to was found not only in Jerry, but also among some of the New York punk scene at large, and in popular music fans far and wide. Many followers of beloved black artists like Chuck Berry, Diana Ross, Donna Summer, and Bob Marley still held deep-seated or institutionalized racist beliefs. Coming up in the 1950s, those feelings were extremely common among whites, even in highly integrated cities like New York. It was a hangover of American immigration and distrust of anyone different—Irish, Polish, German, Jews. No one was immune.

Writing for the *Village Voice* in 1979, Lester Bangs called out the racism, including his own, so easily found in New York's punk scene, in an article titled "White Noise Supremacists." After hearing racial epithets and insensitivity too often, Bangs stated, "Those words are *lethal*, man, and you shouldn't just go slinging them around for effect."[1] He continued, "If you're black or Jewish or Latin or gay those little vernacular epithets are bullets that riddle your guts and then fester and burn there, like torture-flak hailing on you wherever you go."[2]

Whether Bangs was aware of it or not, other Dolls would have been fitting examples in the piece. Referring to guitarist Barry Jones, Thunders was heard to say, before going onstage with the Idols, "I want to get up and jam, but it's full of niggers." A few years later he'd write and perform "Just Because I'm White," which contained liberal use of the N-word. Arthur's band the Corpse Grinders released a single in 1978 called "Rites, 4 Whites," an undeniably winking, and accepting, reference to racism. For Jerry, it was a vestige of his '50s urban street-gang tough front. But these songs represented a tolerance for racism, not to mention sexism, or homophobia, in the guise of nihilism, artful provocation, or some misguided sense of cool.

These contradictions were indicative of an inherent split in Jerry's personality. Walter: "He wanted to be this type of '50s icon. One of these guys with a girl on his arm, where he was the man, a girl was a girl. It wasn't like the free love of the '60s. He liked this image of himself as being a tough guy, down-to-earth, but then he also had this big, glaring problem that he was a drug addict . . . and couldn't get away from it, so it was like the image of himself had a big crack down the middle. . . . You could just get this sense . . . he was sort of conflicted."

The new Heartbreakers debuted at Max's on July 23, 1976, with Blondie and the Fast opening. Already a big draw on the underground scene, the new lineup fostered lots of curiosity, making this show as packed as any.

It was also curious that Jerry was now singing lead, his vocalizations filled with "whoops" and other exhortations, on "Take a Chance with Me." Not coincidentally, his old pal Peter Criss sang lead on several Kiss songs, at least one on each of their albums. These included "Nothin' to Lose" and "Black Diamond," both of which Kiss performed for national television audiences on ABC's *In Concert* and NBC's *Midnight Special*. Their newest album, *Destroyer*, was certified gold less than two months after its release and contained the song "Beth," on which Peter not only sang lead but also had a cowriting credit. If Jerry was to keep up with

Peter, he needed to be more than just a drummer: He had to write songs and sing lead.

Note was made of Jerry's vocals in a review of the show in the *New York Rocker*, credited to a writer by the single name of Nancy. Her full name was Nancy Spungen. Nancy had access to the Heartbreakers, as not only did she know the names of the unrecorded songs in their set, but she was aware of a song the band was working on but had yet to play live, Thunders's "Dead or Alive."

In 1976, Nancy was an eighteen-year-old groupie, stripper, and prostitute from the Philadelphia area, with a reasonably privileged and educated middle-class background. She scored high on intelligence tests but exhibited behavioral issues at a young age. She was the quintessential "does not play well with others" young lady.

She spent time at a school for girls with "special needs" and by the age of sixteen had attempted suicide at least twice. As a teenager, she got to know rock stars coming through Philadelphia, claiming to have slept with members of Bad Company and Aerosmith. Eileen Polk recalled Nancy as "jaded. She had seen it all. She was just angry and like most kids she hated her parents. She wanted to do what she wanted to do, and she did it and she had no apologies."

"Nancy had one of those passions for rock 'n' roll that very few people have,"[3] said *Punk* magazine cofounder Legs McNeil. "She knew everything about every album."[4]

Nancy came on the New York scene in December of 1975. She quickly met and roomed with Sable Starr, who'd left Los Angeles a few years earlier to be with Johnny Thunders. She spent her nights at Max's and CBGB looking for a rock 'n' roll boyfriend. Nancy particularly loved the Heartbreakers, and her favorite Heartbreaker was Jerry. Eileen saw her at every Heartbreakers gig. "I think her explanation was that they were so cool that she brought drugs for them. She was just interested in having a guy in a band as a boyfriend. And that wasn't happening."

Nancy's strategy to find a boyfriend in a band was to attract him with sex and drugs. She was known to have had relationships with Richard Hell, Iggy Pop, and Dee Dee Ramone, each one an intravenous drug user. She claimed to have had sex with Jerry, which he denied. Leee Childers wasn't so sure, though. "He was a complete junkie, and all the negative aspects of how [being] a junkie can affect you. He would rob you, lie to you, fuck your girlfriend, fuck your boyfriend, just so he could rob their purses."

While Leee possessed a raconteur's penchant for dramatic exaggeration, Michelle had similar suspicions about Jerry when it came to what he would do for drugs. She recalled a neighbor of theirs who was gay. "I know something went down between them. . . . I think he had a crush on Jerry. There was a secret I was not privy to there; I could see it in his eyes. He was holding something. Did Jerry do a sexual favor for him? I do not know, but I would not be surprised. . . ."

But Michelle also had insight as to how Jerry used sex to get what he wanted. "Later, after we had broken up, I saw that aspect of him. The way he had become flirtatious, but it was a manipulative flirtation. And I could see through it, after I had gotten some distance. Because by flirting, he could spend the night with somebody, and that opened the door to other things like drugs, money, [a] place to stay, [or] food." It helped that Jerry was "very good in bed," too.

Leee: "He could pretend love. That was part of the whole way he dressed, the way he combed his hair and everything. When he was in bed with you, according to all accounts I have heard, you thought he was in love with you. Every girl I have talked to about that, and it's a lot of girls, have said that they really thought they were embarking on the love of their life. But then that's all it was, just talk. He was very much a charming lover. That is what got him off."

Nancy was loathed or used by those she most wanted attention from. "She was always reviled," said Leee. "It was like a schoolyard; there were bullies, and there were whores, and there were geeks . . . and so everybody was mean to Nancy. I was mean to Nancy."

Some did see her as a person, and not as a junkie whore waiting to be taken advantage of. One friend of Nancy's who did try and help her was a Max's regular named Phyllis Stein. Phyllis had been brought up by her adoptive parents in the Bronx and, like Nancy, was Jewish and loved rock 'n' roll. Unlike Nancy, she finished high school and went on to graduate from a state university. Also unlike Nancy, she seemed to have a somewhat rational head on her shoulders. But very much like Nancy, she also loved Jerry.

Phyllis met Jerry at Max's one night, becoming friendly with him even while dating Blondie's Jimmy Destri and later Philippe Marcadé from the Senders. When Nancy introduced herself to Phyllis at Max's, Jerry cautioned her that while Nancy may have said she was a dancer, it wasn't the type of dancing ballerinas did.

All this activity interacting with women and drugs reflected how Jerry saw women. On one hand, he had traditional needs for female love and companionship. On the other, he learned to take advantage of a woman's trust to benefit his career and now his growing drug habit. Luckily for Jerry, his good looks and standing within the underground rock world made him desirable. "I don't really remember Jerry pursuing women that much," said Eileen. "I remember him being pursued *by* women."

Jerry possessed a certain magnetism that drew people to him, and Leee was aware of it. "We weren't drawn to him because he was a good drummer. There was something very magnetic and very charming, as Suzi Quatro said, to girls and to boys. He was sexually attractive; his personality was very, very attractive. He wanted to be a ten. The only problem with that relationship was him. He could not give someone love, including even Johnny, who, when it comes down to it, was the only person he was in love with. His version of being in love."

By late 1976, Nancy, Phyllis, and Donna also reflected his failing relationship with Michelle. Since the beginning of the Heartbreakers, Michelle had known the two of them were running on fumes.

They gave up their big apartment on the Upper East Side after the loss of his regular Dolls income. In the mid-'70s, the economy in New York was at its worst since the Great Depression, with the city teetering on the edge of bankruptcy. Michelle lost her job and received unemployment insurance. "We got evicted twice," recalled Michelle. "We moved when the lights were off. It was the lowest of the low."

Part of the reason they couldn't pay their rent was because Jerry was stealing Michelle's unemployment checks, cashing them at the local supermarket, and using the money for dope. "I had never been on unemployment before. I just thought that maybe they didn't send me a check, or the check didn't come. Now I know you don't *not* get a check. I never really thought that he would do that."

* * *

THE HEARTBREAKERS CONTINUED GIGGING AROUND NEW YORK, with the occasional foray to Boston to play the Rat. The band could now come away with as much as $2,000 on a good night, but after expenses were paid and drugs were bought, there was often little left. Leee had other work as a writer and photographer, and would forgo his 20 percent cut for the benefit of the band, who had no other income. "Not that I was a big hero. It actually was easier to give it to them and get out of there."

Still, the band was always desperate for money. Before Leee, Jerry had taught Johnny the art of getting an advance from the club days before a show to buy dope or to get his guitar out of hock. Once Leee started managing the band, that all stopped.

What little money the band had was used to record a new set of demos at Jay Nap Studio in Staten Island. But the six songs didn't capture the band's live firepower. This attempt to show a more refined and mature Heartbreakers seemed to be an all-but-impossible task.

The band still lacked studio discipline. "Born to Lose" and "Take a Chance with Me" both contained glaring mistakes. While there were efforts to make "It's Not Enough" and "I Love You" sound more poppish with the addition of percussion and background vocals, the band still needed a strong producer. The only recorded song that seemed to capture anywhere near the excitement of the live Heartbreakers was their cover of "Do You Love Me." But even that drops to an emotional low with its superfluous bass solo.

The Jay Nap Studio demos were the result of Jerry trying to take control of the band. Since the departure of Richard Hell, Jerry was the driving force for the band image-wise, and he was now trying to do the same musically. Billy sensed it. "He influenced a lot of what went on and what took place." Jerry had been through enough managers, record producers, and lead singers who thought they knew what was best for the band, only for everything to come out sour. Jerry was now going to take charge.

Unfortunately, the demos didn't create any new opportunities for the Heartbreakers.

Patti Smith had signed to Arista, and Television to Elektra. Even the Ramones had a deal with the semi-independent Sire label. While none of those bands had a reputation anywhere as notorious as the Heartbreakers, Leee thought it was hypocritical of labels to pass on the Heartbreakers because of it. "Every single one of [those] bands is chock-full of junkies but not famous for being junkies. Patti Smith fell off the stage more times than she got on it."

There was, however, a sliver of interest from Richard Gottehrer. With partner Marty Thau, he signed both Richard Hell and Blondie to production deals, where they would put up money to record demos. If a reasonable record deal could be found, they would split everything 50/50 with the band. He'd recently done the same deal, without Thau, with ex–Tuff Darts lead singer Robert Gordon and wanted to use the Heartbreakers as Robert's backing band on his demos. Impressed with the group, he offered them the same deal. Recalled Walter, "At the time, no one in New York was really getting signed to any decent deals. The Ramones had some sort of Mickey Mouse deal for their first album. Blondie [had] another 50/50. Hilly Kristal tried to do the same thing, sign us up for 50/50. It was an outrageous deal because these weren't the kind of deals that regular artists got signed for. But nobody was really signing the punk music, so we almost took the Gottehrer offer."

Thinking back, Leee recalled, "Richard Gottehrer and I talked about it. . . . He couldn't drum up any interest, anywhere . . . because of Johnny's reputation." Leee sensed it would be all but impossible for the Heartbreakers to get a deal in the United States. "The Heartbreakers were too uncontrollable. I was certainly not strong enough. I wasn't like Albert Grossman . . . to say 'I can control them,' like he did with Janis Joplin."

Control is what Michelle sought for her own life, as she was losing all patience with Jerry. There were new threats of eviction, and Michelle, who'd just found a new job, was beside herself. "I went and begged the landlord to let me stay because my cats were locked in the apartment. I was giving them all the money I had from week to week. . . . We were starving."

Jerry had introduced his old friend Elvera to his Ocean bandmate Tom Bakas, and they were now married. They remembered how loyal Jerry had been to them, bringing her platform boots back from England and getting them backstage and into after-show parties when the Dolls played the Felt Forum with Mott. They heard how badly Jerry was doing and paid him a surprise visit. Recalled Elvera, "We went to a supermarket in his neighborhood and we bought him two or three bags of food. He couldn't believe it. He had tears in his eyes."

But Jerry still needed cash for drugs. He came to see Michelle at her place of work, asking to borrow money. "Maybe I was always trying to prove how much I really cared and this was my way of proving it. I was like, 'Look, Jerry, this is my last $15. If you don't get me the $15 back in a few days, in a week, don't ever call me again.' He didn't get me the $15 and I was broke till my next paycheck. That was it. I'd had enough with him. It's over."

# 13 LONDON BOYS

LEEE FOUND NO INTEREST IN THE HEARTBREAKERS FROM RECORD companies anywhere. Until a phone call came from Malcolm McLaren in November, no one knew much of anything about an English rock scene that might hold possibilities for them.

Wayne County, while DJ'ing at Max's, played the Damned's British single "New Rose," which was released on October 22, 1976. That fall, Richard Hell visited Plaza Sound Studios, where Blondie were recording their first album. Chris Stein pointed out a photo of a band in a European magazine with "four guys who look exactly like you!"[1] Hell looked closer and saw Malcolm's name in the article. He saw safety pins, torn clothing, and chopped-up hair, and read that one of them was named Johnny Rotten, easily seen as a takeoff on "Johnny Thunders."

It all finally clicked.

Besides County, Walter was sure that "no one in New York had heard of anything about the British. I remembered reading something in the Sunday paper a couple of months earlier and . . . seeing the Sex Pistols and pictures of a couple of the bands, probably the Clash, and they were talking about the scene in England. That was the only time I'd heard [of it] but no one was talking about it in . . . New York. Everybody thought New York was the center of the world."

The Patti Smith Group went to England in May to appear on television and play at the Roundhouse. The Ramones played two triumphant shows in London on July 4 and 5. Each band had its impact on the locals, with impressed TV viewers and concert attendees including members of the Clash, the Slits, the Sex Pistols, and the Damned. The Ramones were startled by the reaction they got in London, but went about their regular business upon returning to New York a few days later.

Malcolm brought his excitement for the New York scene and the Dolls back to Britain with him in the spring of 1975. His shop had their photos as well as those of Television on the wall, and he talked incessantly of New York City to anyone who would listen. Among his audience were Glen Matlock, who worked at the shop, and Steve Jones and Paul Cook, who were less regular shoppers than shoplifters.

As part of Malcolm's greater vision to upset the status quo and sell clothing, he decided to mentor the three to pursue music, using the lessons he'd learned working with the Dolls, giving Jones the white Gibson Les Paul guitar he'd gotten from Sylvain, who he initially thought might be a possible member of the band. Malcolm also considered Richard Hell for the position, but settled on a local named John Lydon, whom he renamed Johnny Rotten. These four became the Sex Pistols.

Bassist Matlock, guitarist Jones, and drummer Cook were no older than twenty in 1975, having grown up as passionate fans of Bowie, Mott the Hoople, and Roxy Music as well as of the more aggressive '60s pop of Small Faces, the Who and the Kinks. All three had seen the Dolls when they played at Wembley Stadium and on *The Old Grey Whistle Test*.

Rotten was chosen less for his musical ability than for his look and attitude. Still, his lyrics, combined with Glen's abilities as a tunesmith, Jones's Thunders-inspired guitar playing, and Cook's Nolan-like simplicity, made for a powerful sound. With Rotten's and McLaren's political and fashion points of view added to the mix, the Pistols shocked people, reaping attention and press. In a certain sense, they were very much an updated, British version of the Dolls. Like the Dolls, they could play their simple rock with an anger and fury that couldn't be ignored.

By late 1976, the Pistols had signed a record deal with EMI. They were slated to release their first single, "Anarchy in the UK," on November 26, and then to embark on a national tour of Britain to promote it.

The Pistols had only played a total of seventy-one gigs since their inception in 1975, and were mostly known in London. To go national, Malcolm felt he needed to make the bill stronger. But they weren't interested in bringing along just any old EMI stable-mate. The Damned were the only other band on the London punk scene with a record out, so perhaps they could join? As they were signed to the independent Stiff label, though, there would be little financial support coming, outside of that of the additional punters they would attract. McLaren needed more.

He hit upon the idea of bringing over the Ramones. While first considering it as a co-headline tour, the Ramones pulled out, as there wasn't enough time to properly promote it. Malcolm then asked Talking

Heads, but since they did not yet have a finalized record deal, it was financially out of the question.

Malcolm wasn't ready to give up on getting a New York band onto the tour. His last-ditch idea was getting the original New York Dolls back, but David and Sylvain had no interest. However, Leee could promise Malcolm the Heartbreakers, giving him the most notorious two-fifths of the Dolls.

The Vibrators, who had recently signed a deal with Rak Records, were also considered, but declined, presumably not wanting to perform in the shadow of the Sex Pistols. Finally, the Clash were added, and the Anarchy tour bill was finalized.

The Heartbreakers were now ready to throw caution to the wind and join three other bands on a nineteen-show tour of England, third on a bill of four. It was a long way from the limos and room-service champagne of a few years before, but they were getting out of New York. There was hope.

The Heartbreakers were still very much in the dark as to what they were getting into. Billy: "All we knew was that the Damned had a record, and we knew that Malcolm was the manager of the Sex Pistols and that there was a whole new look."

Arriving the evening of December 1, the Heartbreakers were met at the airport by a limousine courtesy of EMI, containing Malcolm and his assistants Nils Stevenson and Sophie Richmond. Loading up their guitars and bags, which contained what they hoped was enough heroin to tide them over until they made local connections, they were scheduled to go straight to a rehearsal hall. On the way over, a visibly shaken McLaren told the band of an incident earlier that day.

Sex Pistols labelmates Queen had canceled their appearance on a live afternoon TV show called *Today* featuring host Bill Grundy. The Pistols had filled in for them, flanked by four equally outrageous Pistols fans and habitués of Malcolm's Sex shop. Among these were Siouxsie Sioux and fellow Banshee Steve Severin. They'd enjoyed the free alcohol in the green room, then joined Mr. Grundy, who supposedly had also done so. Treating his guests with smirking condescension, Grundy proceeded to goad them on live TV until they gave him what he wanted: something outrageous. A few *shit*s and *fuck*s later, the phones were alight.

Walter recalled Malcolm's state of distress in the limo. "'Oh my God, the whole place is in an uproar.' This whole thing was all over the radio and TV."

The band went straight to a shared rehearsal space in Harlesden, playing a set before even speaking to the other groups, all of whom contained members eagerly awaiting the arrival of two former New York

Dolls. The Damned quoted the same Shangri-Las' song, "Give Him a Great Big Kiss," in their single "New Rose" that the Dolls did in "Looking for a Kiss." Mick Jones of the Clash was a longtime Dolls fan, during auditions exhorting drummers to "hit the drums like Jerry Nolan!"[2] Brian James of the Damned was up front yelling, "Go, Johnny, go!" while the Heartbreakers played their rehearsal set.

Glen Matlock recalled speaking to Jerry for the first time immediately after the Heartbreakers finished their impressive run-through. Within minutes, he knew exactly what they were all about. "We were pretty knocked out with the Heartbreakers," recalled Glen. After Jerry came and sat down next to him, Glen mentioned how much he liked "Chinese Rocks" but didn't understand what it was about. "He just looked at me like I was an idiot and went, 'Heroin, boy.'"

Heroin was not a drug seen often among young British punks in 1976. Their substances of choice were beer, acid, and speed.

The tour was scheduled to begin on December 3 at Norwich University. On December 2, the full impact of the Grundy incident took hold, becoming headline news in all the newspapers. When Jerry saw the papers, he threw them on the bed and immediately went after Leee. "He hadn't slept all night because he didn't want to come to England. He had a flair for the dramatic, anyway, but he got every tabloid. And every one of them had the Sex Pistols—not on the cover; they *were* the cover . . . with giant headlines! Even then, because we weren't English—and these papers didn't look like newspapers to us either, they looked like things you got in the supermarket . . . we didn't pay that much attention to it. We just went, 'Oh, ha, ha, ha, ha, ha,' . . . still without realizing the power that came with it, that the whole country was talking about nothing else."

Leee realized that fate had dealt the Heartbreakers an ace. They'd come to England barely known outside of a small sect, but now would be touring the country at the center of a media storm. But Jerry was livid that tour dates could be canceled and the Heartbreakers would be lumped in with this new group of social pariahs. Recalled Leee, "He was able to then prove for a very, very short time, 'See, I told you so. You've gotten us into something horrible.' As it turns out, it was something wonderful for everyone. If they'd stayed in New York, they wouldn't have been a band more than another couple of months."

Jerry noticed the tour posters, which said "Johnny Thunders and the Heartbreakers." Jerry was particularly piqued at this, adding to his general feeling of antipathy toward Leee, Malcolm, and playing third on the bill. In his mind, he was as much a bandleader as Johnny and had just as much cachet, as a former Doll. He no longer had to deal with Johansen or Hell, but now he was worried that Johnny's head would grow. It was just another thing to hate. Leee: "He wasn't in control. He had been forced to go to another country. We were . . . third on the bill, with bands that he hated; and, of course, he hated all bands other than himself, including his own band other than himself. So he was furious."

But everyone was in awe of the New Yorkers, not only because of Johnny and Jerry's stint with the Dolls, but owing to Leee's previous work with Bowie, Iggy, and Mott. These were members of royalty within their midst. Still, the Pistols felt they were the local stars, and were fearful of the Heartbreakers, who dressed and acted like New York toughs. The Damned rode in their own vehicle, but the other three shared a bus. Leee: "It was like a school bus. The Heartbreakers went straight to the back. The Sex Pistols sat in the front, and the Clash were in the middle. The bad boys go to the back, the smelly little ass-kissers sit in the front because they're the stars, and the poor little boys who are just glad to be on the bus at all take any seats they can get. It would have been absolutely foregone for Johnny and Jerry to be in the very back of the bus, back of the classroom, back of everything."

According to Walter, the Pistols seemed to be "snotty little scumbags," but he later found out they were really just terrified to meet Johnny and Jerry. In time, everyone got along, except for Thunders and Rotten, who never hit it off.

Due to the Grundy controversy, opening night in Norwich was canceled. The bus headed for King's Hall in Derby. When they arrived, they were told that the Derby leisure committee wouldn't let the Sex Pistols play unless all the bands first auditioned so the committee could assess their acceptability. The Pistols refused and onward they went, except the third show in Newcastle had been canceled for the same reason as the others. It wasn't until the fourth scheduled show on December 6 at Leeds Polytechnic that the bands got to play.

Leee recalled, "The Clash played. They were just beginning. They couldn't really play, so no one paid that much attention to them. The Heartbreakers went on next after the Clash. They were like old blues musicians. [Johnny] certainly knew his business and Jerry certainly knew his business. Everything just changed from that moment they got onstage. The audience was milling about. Everybody was drinking pints. Nobody was paying attention. And that first note, it was perfect. Everyone stopped and looked at the stage."

Johnny started by asking the audience, "Ain't there any junkies in Leeds"? The band opened with "Do You Love Me."† Leee remembered the moment clear as day. "Four seconds into the song, no one was paying attention to anything else. Johnny and Jerry and me have all said that at that moment . . . The Damned said, 'We're leaving this joint.' Johnny and Jerry, they were good at that first dramatic musical moment, because they weren't moving. Nothing moved. It was just . . . those notes of "Do You Love Me." It caught everyone's attention."

The other bands noticed too. "They were scared. When they saw the Heartbreakers, they thought, 'Oh shit, this is real. We are not real.' And they were right in that respect."

It was obvious that the Heartbreakers were in a league all their own compared to the others. Billy: "They really picked up a lot from watching us, and they knew where they had to go, because we could play."

The show was reviewed in the December 11 edition of *Melody Maker*. Writer Caroline Coon described the Clash's audience as "impassive"[3] and wrote that the Sex Pistols left the crowd wondering "what all the fuss is about,"[4] covering Rotten in all matter of foodstuffs. She notes the Damned's high level of energy and cites the lone positive crowd response as being for the Heartbreakers, whom Coon described as "explosively well-received."[5] Leee agreed emphatically: "The Heartbreakers tore the place apart."

* * *

THE HEARTBREAKERS WERE STILL CLEAR-MINDED ENOUGH BEFORE coming to England to rehearse on a regular basis and write new songs. Walter and Jerry continued their partnership, coming up with what would become a Heartbreakers' classic, "All By Myself." Walter recalled it as the first time he and Jerry truly wrote something together. "He just would play the drumbeat and I played along and came up with . . . a progression . . . . Then he started singing, 'All By Myself,' because it fit the progression. I just wrote the rest of the words and we finished it."

Both "Can't Keep My Eyes on You" and "All By Myself" appeared in the set for the second show of the tour on December 9 in Manchester.

---

† This may have been a skewed memory of Leee's, as the band usually played "Do You Love Me" as an encore, and the song was not on the set list at their next gig a few days later in Manchester.

144

Also in the set was another new Lure/Nolan would-be classic called "Get Off the Phone," which was dominated by Jerry's propulsive drumming.

At that point, the Damned left the tour. Some reports were that McLaren threw them off as punishment for consenting to the Derby request for an audition. Others claim they left of their own volition to pursue their own tour that wasn't bogged down by the Pistols' controversy. Regardless, Manchester favorites the Buzzcocks took their place.

The next four shows—in Lancaster, Liverpool, Bristol, and Cardiff— were all canceled, but a replacement venue was found for the last gig at Castle Cinema, in Caerphilly, Wales, on December 14.

It was at this gig that the first protesters appeared. Walter remembered it well: "The local priest or minister or devil worshiper, whatever he was, he got the whole town out into this parking lot across the street. It was almost like it was a rival band playing a show. They said, 'Take your kids out of here! The devils are in this theater over here!' And parents are waving their hands going, 'Yes, yes, God help us, our father.' We're all looking out the windows of the theater in stitches. And then there's the town's kids and they're in the bathroom . . . stickin' these safety pins through their cheeks to try and be cool . . . and they've got these infections coming out from their face and it's just like, 'God, there really is a scene from hell over here.'"

* * *

RETURNING TO LONDON, THE HEARTBREAKERS, NOW BROKE DUE to all the canceled shows, met Andy Czezowski, a partner in a new club called the Roxy. He and his partners Susan Carrington and Barry Jones were interested in putting on punk shows. Andy, who managed the band Chelsea, offered the skint Heartbreakers a meager £30 to play two sets on December 15. Desperate for a paying gig, the band negotiated a £15 advance and the deal was sealed for their London debut.

Barry Jones recalled the first time he saw the Heartbreakers: "It was sound check at the Roxy. They had a huge presence as a group. The Heartbreakers had a great . . . killer rock 'n' roll set. They had a New York attitude. The sound check just blew us away. Later that night at the gig . . . you could see right up front all these faces: the Clash, the Damned, all the people around at that time. We didn't know anybody that didn't like the Heartbreakers. No matter what you were into they were just straight, gutsy rock 'n' roll."

The bands went back on the road to resurrect the tour, and immediately, five more shows were canceled. Luckily, McLaren booked a return engagement at the Electric Circus in Manchester on the nineteenth, which was notable for the number of bottles thrown. This was followed by the canceled Birmingham show, now replaced by Cleethorpes. A successful show was pulled off at Woods Centre in Plymouth on the twenty-first, followed by a second, hastily added show at the same venue, to replace a cancellation in Torquay on the twenty-second. The two remaining shows, at Penelope's Ballroom in Paignton and the Roxy Theatre in London, were both canceled.

Throughout the tour, the Heartbreakers took careful notice of the appearance of the English bands and their associates. Jerry and the rest of the New Yorkers had known for years how to shop inexpensively. While Lydon had also done so, most famously when he was first seen by McLaren wearing a homemade "I HATE PINK FLOYD" T-shirt, McLaren gave the Pistols free clothing from his shop, which fans in turn would buy from him at top dollar. Leee recalled, "They had all these clothes, bondage pants and all that ridiculous stuff. And we all made so much fun of it the minute we saw it, [like] the big angora sweaters." During the first limo ride from the airport, Leee mistook Nils for the "Sophie" he'd been speaking to on the phone due to his pixie haircut and fluffy "jumper" (Brit-speak for "sweater"). The Heartbreakers had their natty suits and motorcycle jackets, but the English had taken things beyond anyone in New York.

"The British kids dressed a lot better than the US kids," recalled Walter. "In New York, it was just leather jackets and ripped-up jeans. We were just a little neater than the other guys were. The British took it another step further."

While Jerry may have been broke, he was considered a star by members of the Clash and the Pistols. He was a veteran of real rock wars, with battle stories aplenty. With all the off days on the tour, there was plenty of time for Jerry to regale the group with tales of the road. "He did love telling stories," Leee recalled, "and that makes for a good raconteur. The stories were so well told and so funny. I would hear some of them over and over. . . . He would keep total strangers enthralled."

Walter had similar recollections. "He still wasn't strung out right then, so he was upbeat a lot more. . . . He'd get along with anyone, so he'd start telling a story and laughing along with it, so you'd just laugh along with him. He'd be making fun of a song by some other group, or he could be talking about something that happened in the Dolls and he'd be fuckin' hilarious. He used to be shaking his head like a little rooster and giggle. . . . It was this infectious way of getting everyone busting their guts just laughing."

Leee: "He had a wonderful stand-up comic type of side to him where he could make people laugh. And he had a good sarcastic sense of humor. He and Johnny both. I used to call them queens because they had that kind of West Village, old-time-homosexual sense of humor. It was hilarious when both of them got going at once."

Another result of the canceled gigs was the extra time spent in hotels, leading to extra time spent in hotel bars drinking, finding out the next show was canceled, then doing it all over again, with the occasional trashed hotel room thrown in for good fun. Sometimes drinking wasn't enough, particularly to those with the proclivities of the Heartbreakers. Jerry claimed that his habit was so bad he couldn't sleep on the Anarchy tour, but Walter, who roomed with him many nights, said that wasn't quite accurate. "He'd fall asleep in the middle of the night. He'd get up and he'd walk around for twenty minutes. That's sort of like a mild withdrawal. It's not the really bad ones, but even John would leave the tour every now and then and run back to London for a night when he knew we were going to have a day off and find someplace to score."

Jerry claimed to have shot up Johnny Rotten for the first time, which Rotten vehemently denied in his 1994 book *Rotten: No Irish, No Blacks, No Dogs*. However, in his 2015 book *Anger Is an Energy: My Life Uncensored*, he completely contradicts himself, confirming that he tried heroin with Jerry out of curiosity, trusting Jerry to guide him through it, as he was Irish like him. Leee had seen Jerry introduce people to heroin before. "He would turn people on to heroin constantly. It was a horrible thing to do."

In total, only seven gigs were played on the tour, several of them added as last-minute replacements. Each Heartbreaker received £20 each per week, equal to about $34, for the whole of the Anarchy tour. It was now Christmas. They were in a foreign country and broke.

14 SO ALONE

AS THE TOUR ENDED, SOME OF THE HEARTBREAKERS LUCKED OUT, staying at the home of designer and Clash roadie Sebastian Conran. Billy drew the short straw, sleeping in a dismal loft at the Sex Pistols' rehearsal space. Regardless, with Christmas upon them, they all missed their homes and families.

There was, however, a Christmas party held at the home of journalist Caroline Coon, to which members of the extended punk rock community were invited. Among those attending were members of the Pistols, the Clash, the Damned, the Slits and the self-invited Heartbreakers. Others included Billy Idol, Siouxsie Sioux, and future Sex Pistol Sid Vicious, who befriended Leee after the two tearfully shared a listen to an old Jim Reeves Christmas album together.

No fond memories of the Heartbreakers are held by Coon: "They wrecked the place, rang up a huge international telephone bill, stole money and property, and gave heroin to young, vulnerable people." Her most scathing vitriol was saved for Johnny: "What a rude, violent, ugly pig he was!"

Leee liked to call the Heartbreakers "misbehavers." "The Sex Pistols misbehaved in a predictable, *acceptable* way. The Heartbreakers misbehaved: They took drugs, and they stole things, and they lied and they cheated. They were real bad boys."

Leee tried to keep everyone's spirits up however he could. "We were so broke, in an effort to keep things from getting too miserable, I told every Heartbreaker they could have one treat a day. Johnny Thunders always got a little tube of Smarties, which is like M&M's, and . . . Jerry Nolan would get a big, green Granny Smith apple . . . marginally more healthy than Johnny's Smarties."

Jerry had started a methadone program before leaving New York, but found it difficult to get on one in England, especially traveling from city to city. With the added difficulty of copping on the road, he was in bad shape by tour's end. He'd also acquired a taste for cocaine in New York, especially mixed with a shot of heroin, the cocktail known as a "speedball."

While Jerry went through withdrawal, Johnny Rotten suggested he try an over-the-counter flu medicine called Night Nurse, which is similar to the American product NyQuil and was used by many to quell drug withdrawal symptoms. Jerry drank two bottles' worth and began experiencing bizarre hallucinations, some sexual. After returning to his room, with the heroin leaving his system, other pleasure centers began to feel sparks again. A massive sexual urge overtook him. Jerry masturbated, letting go a colossal amount of spunk. Afterward, he slept like a baby, and was relieved to wake up to the realization that he had kicked heroin. The last few weeks of the tour were a joy. But once the band were back in London, temptation brought him right back to using heroin again. It was an endless cycle that no amount of Night Nurse or masturbation was ever going to cure.

With the tour over, the band wanted to return to their girlfriends and drug connections in New York, but Leee resisted. With punk rock in the newspapers every day, he knew that London held promise for them. His immediate need was to get enough money for them to eat, but if he could keep them in the public eye, he knew he could get them a record deal.

Their next show was January 3 at Dingwalls, which sold out. Dingwalls had been in existence since 1973. With a capacity of about five hundred, and run by former Deviants and Pink Fairies roadie and road manager Dave "the Boss" Goodman, Dingwalls welcomed punks as well as pub rockers, and all manner of freaks and '60s holdovers. "That was the night I thought we might produce something," recalled Leee. "These were punters, people who might buy a record."

After traveling to the Netherlands to open for the Sex Pistols—where the locals weren't lined up with pitchforks and torches ready to lynch them —they returned to the Roxy on January 11, where the London punk phenomenon had truly exploded. "It was like a whole different world," recalled Walter. It was pure mania. New York didn't have anything like pogo dancing, gobbing, bondage trousers, or people with safety pins in their faces.

Watching at the Roxy was John Perry, lead guitarist for the Only Ones. "You could see Jerry had an R&B background. It was obvious from this one Heartbreakers show that he knew how to pace a set—and remember, please, you're talking about a time and a place where most of the bands didn't know how to place a kit of drums let alone structure a set. Compared to the sort of musicians, especially the drummers, playing down the Roxy, Jerry stood out a mile. . . . [He] was like a Hendrix among a bunch of Saturday morning music store kids."[1]

The band was well dressed for New York, but in London, they exuded a subdued cool compared to the locals. Marco Pirroni, who later joined Adam and the Ants, described their look as "sharp. They always had the best clothes." Even though the Ramones had come to London six months earlier wearing their matching motorcycle jackets, it was the Heartbreakers who helped establish it as the de rigueur accessory of the well-dressed punk. They also had two-tone versions: basic black with white lapels. Classy stuff. Marco: "They came over, and all of a sudden, everything was there."

After seeing them at the Roxy, Marco recalled, "people were kind of blown away by how tight they were, how like a real band they were. They weren't shambolic, or stopping and starting, and they were in time, and they were in tune. And, to us, this was kind of, wow . . . real musicians."

On March 2 and 3, the Heartbreakers played two nights as part of a celebrated week of New York bands headlining the Roxy, with Cherry Vanilla and Wayne County coming over from New York to cash in on the London punk rock craze.

At the March 2 show, the Heartbreakers played the same night as a prerelease party for Marc Bolan and T. Rex's latest album, *Dandy in the Underworld*. Jerry told more than one person that Marc was smitten with him, trying to pick him up several times.

The March 3 show was effusively reviewed in *Sounds* by Giovanni Dadomo, who described the Heartbreakers as "phenomenal, delivering great songs . . . matched only by the style and proficiency of everyone concerned. Right now this just has to be one of the finest young bands in the country—period. I just can't see any way they won't be enormously successful with any audience that likes real rock 'n' roll music, no matter what their previous tastes. See them *now* and be amazed."[2]

Not everyone liked the Heartbreakers, though. The artier bands like Wire thought they were just a junked-up version of Chuck Berry. Others thought their lyrics and attitude were derivative and hedonistic compared with the Pistols and the Clash, who were fueled by anger and had a hard political bent that dealt with real working-class issues. There was a line in the sand, and the Heartbreakers were squarely on the rock 'n' roll side.

Record labels started sniffing around. Arista, Virgin, CBS, and France's Skydog all were showing interest in the Heartbreakers. Even EMI, despite having dropped the Pistols after the Grundy affair, gave them a look. The A&R representative talking up the Heartbreakers at EMI was Mike Thorne, whose production credits include Wire's first three albums, 'Til Tuesday's "Voices Carry," and Soft Cell's giant hit "Tainted Love." With his sights set on Wire, Siouxsie and the Banshees, and the Heartbreakers, he pressured EMI to start a punk imprint. Mike saw the Heartbreakers multiple times. "They were tremendous."

EMI proved gun-shy, leaving the winner of the sweepstakes Track Records, who once upon a time had been within a hair's breadth of signing the Dolls until the death of Billy Murcia scuttled the deal.

Before signing on the dotted line, the Heartbreakers returned to New York to sate the immigration authorities. Without a girlfriend, Jerry looked for a new female sidekick. He approached Phyllis Stein with an offer: quit your job, come to London, and live with me.

Though attracted to Jerry, Phyllis was in a relationship with Philippe from the Senders, and declined. When Jerry returned to London, he continued calling her with the same request. Before even considering, she needed to be convinced he wasn't using heroin, insisting on speaking to Leee for confirmation. Leee, looking to earn a brownie point with Jerry, lied and vouched for him. Phyllis fell for it but wouldn't give up her job or apartment, agreeing only to visit him in London.

Phyllis didn't reveal her plans to Nancy Spungen until the cab was waiting outside to take her to the airport. She knew Nancy was obsessed with Jerry, and volatile. As expected, Nancy went ballistic, telling anyone who would listen that she was going to kill Phyllis, sometimes holding a knife in her hand to emphasize her anger. Nancy was determined to get to England and find Jerry.

By the time Phyllis arrived in London, the band had signed with Track, receiving a £50,000 advance plus temporary housing. In February, Track paid for demos of "Let Go," "Chinese Rocks," "Born to Lose," and "All By Myself," with the first three receiving a final mix. Track then recorded two sets at the Speakeasy on March 15, planned for later release. The live tracks didn't see release until 1982, under the title *D.T.K. Live at the Speakeasy*, with *D.T.K.* being gang-speak for "Down to Kill."

The Speakeasy gig exemplified why the Heartbreakers were viewed as "tremendous." Their fierceness was unstoppable on this night. At the core was Jerry, in command behind a mouthy and overly hyped-up Johnny. Haranguing audience members for their lack of enthusiasm, Thunders repeatedly counted off the songs at breathtaking speeds. Jerry repeatedly ignored him and reset the pace, unmoved by any deviation. Noted John Perry, "The majority of punk bands started songs very fast [and] then as the chaos began, accelerated. Jerry kept time. . . . There you have the difference between Innocence and Experience . . . [and] . . . Amphetamine Sulphate and Heroin."[3]

All recordings were engineered and coproduced by Speedy Keen, a songwriter, and multi-instrumentalist in his own right. Previously Pete Townshend's personal chauffer and flat-mate, he boasted songwriting abilities that led Townshend to record his composition "Armenia City in the Sky" on the Who's *Sell Out* album. Townshend then formed a band around Keen, producing the recordings himself, including the single "Something in the Air," which hit number one. The record has been on constant rotation on radio stations and in film sound tracks since 1969. His CV and nonjudgmental attitude about drugs were enough to sell the Heartbreakers on him. After all, everyone knew he hadn't earned the name Speedy through any prowess in track and field.

Both Leee and his attorney Peter Gerber were aware that label heads Chris Stamp and Kit Lambert were eccentrics. There were also rumblings of legal troubles with the Who, the label's biggest cash cow. Track hadn't released an album since Golden Earring's *Switch* in 1975, surviving mostly on back catalogue and compilations from the Who and Jimi Hendrix. Another odd element of the deal had the band contracting with a holding company called Chris Stamp Band Limited, as opposed to Track itself. As protection, Gerber had the rights to all the band's master tapes revert to the Heartbreakers in case the label went south.

Still, the band felt they were amongst kindred spirits. Boosting their confidence, an article appeared in the April 23, 1977, edition of *Billboard* magazine's International section with the headline "New Directions for Track Label Planned by Hall." It read, "After a long spell of inactivity, Track Records is being revived under the managing directorship of Mafalda Hall, former Arista director of international operations."[4] Industry veteran Danny Secunda would continue to serve as manager of A&R and produce the Heartbreakers' records. With label head Chris Stamp producing their demo, it seemed the band had full support of the top brass at the newly revitalized label.

But they were odd ducks, which suited Leee and the band just fine. "They were a little scary to straight people," said Leee, "which is why we ended up on Track, because they weren't straight people."

It was now full steam ahead.

Before recording began, Peter Criss's wife Lydia appeared on US television to accept Kiss's People's Choice Award for Peter's composition of "Beth." The award was for Favorite New Song of 1976, which they shared with Rick Dees for his "Disco Duck," both beating out Captain and Tennille's "Muskrat Love" for the honor. A recorded performance of

Kiss performing "Beth" was also shown, with Peter singing his composition alone onstage. Fortunately for the sake of Jerry's fragile ego, he was in the UK and missed it.

In Essex Studios the Heartbreakers laid down "All By Myself," "Can't Keep My Eyes on You," "Get Off the Phone," "I Love You," "I Wanna Be Loved," and "Let Go." Next they moved to the Who's larger Ramport Studios and cut "Baby Talk," "Born to Lose," "Chinese Rocks," "Do You Love Me," "Going Steady," "It's Not Enough," "Pirate Love," and "One Track Mind," which contained the music previously used in Richard Hell's "Love Comes in Spurts."

Billy and Walter recall Jerry being very efficient in the studio, needing few takes to get things right. Jerry felt both New York Dolls' albums were filled with bad takes, and wasn't going to let that happen again. He invariably made the final call on all takes, though they came relatively easily. As for his playing, "He had his parts down," said Walter. "He didn't have to do too many retakes or practice things. Sometimes he'd try and get a different snare sound . . . or tom-tom sound." After playing some of these songs for as long as two years, he was as ready as he'd ever be.

Phyllis stayed at the band's flat on Denbigh Street in the Pimlico section of London with Jerry and Billy. Track was paying for the flat as well as for maid service, which, combined with Billy's penchant for cleaning while on speed, meant the apartment remained in relatively good shape. There was, however, the issue of the bathroom. The walls and ceilings were speckled with blood, the invariable by-product of the Heartbreakers needle cleaning process.

Phyllis naively assumed it was from other band members and guests, but soon realized Jerry was joining in. She also found out he was getting only £5 a day from Track to live on. At that point she'd had enough. She waited for Jerry to head to the Track offices to collect his £5, caught a cab to the airport, and flew back to New York.

As the band recorded, their partying continued. Keith Levene, an original member of the Clash and later of Public Image Ltd., recalled, "If anyone came and completely brought a plague to London, those fuckers did."[5] Walter couldn't deny it. "We brought the whole allure. There was plenty of heroin around but it was just the older rockers [who] were doing it like Jimmy Page. . . . The punk scene itself, nobody was doing dope that we knew of." The London kids were using speed and LSD, and smoking pot and hash. "They looked down on heroin."

Jerry knew the Heartbreakers were bringing something eerie yet seductive with them. He reveled in it, seeing it as a badge of honor signifying outlaw bravery. It established him as a "man," while the guys in other bands were just "little boys." Jerry put it this way: "When it came down to the real nitty-gritty shit, throwing works on the table and cooking up some junk, they got scared."[6]

But even the Heartbreakers were scared when Nancy Spungen arrived in London.

She was carrying Jerry's Fender Stratocaster, the one with dice for control knobs, which he'd hocked before leaving for the UK. Once he knew she was coming, he used her to bring the guitar so he could sell it, never telling the rest of the Heartbreakers or Leee.

Just a few hours before she found Jerry in London, she ran into Leee on Carnaby Street. He tried to stop her. "Both of them were inherently evil users of everyone else around them, and just let heroin completely inundate over everything else in their lives. She had no heart and no soul, no love, no capacity for love, only greed. And so, naturally, she wanted Jerry."

Despite Leee's attempt to intervene, Nancy found out where the Heartbreakers were staying and arrived guitar in hand. Jerry took the guitar and kicked her out. But by the evening of March 15, Nancy was at the Denbigh Street flat, annoying Nils, his girlfriend Simone Stenfors, Johnny, and Jerry. Jerry hid from Nancy, in the same bed as Nils and Simone, just to avoid her. Luckily for Jerry, she would meet Sid Vicious, who had just joined the Sex Pistols on bass. She turned him on to heroin, and just as when lightning struck the cold body of Frankenstein, a monster was created. Leee recalled thinking, "This is probably a bad turn of events here."

* * *

AT THAT SAME MARCH 15 GIG, JERRY RAN INTO YVES STEPHENSON. Yves had first met Johnny in 1972 when the Dolls came to England. She kept abreast of what Johnny was up to, seeking out the Heartbreakers when they came to England in December of 1976. "We were all at the Speakeasy Club, and Viv Albertine and Johnny sort of 'got it together.' Jerry was initially a shoulder to cry on but he was so sweet and kind that I soon fell for him. I didn't even smoke cigarettes, let alone take any drugs, but they never flaunted it in front of me. I guess I was pretty naive to it all. I vividly remember them playing the Ramones first album to me—another . . . life changing event."

Jerry gave her a set of little black-and-white boxing gloves that previously hung from his leather jacket. For a short while, Yves and Jerry were an item. "I know I was at one point supposed to be going to New York to meet his mum."

Yves recalled portions of the recording sessions: "Speedy Keen [was] shaking this huge chain over the recording desk and uttering some words like chants." Speedy and Danny Secunda were far from acting like the adults in the room. Walter recalled, "They had a bottle of Rémy. . . . Danny was the one who used to bring most of the coke. Speedy was like Johnny. He was sort of a wild guy. I didn't think he was out of it, although sometimes by the end of the night he'd have a little bit of a loop on."

Once the band signed with Track and they started writing checks, Jerry made sure he got his share. Leee recalled, "Jerry said, 'I need a set of drums.' And of course he named the most expensive possible set of drums . . . handmade in candy pink with chrome everywhere . . . and he needed two of everything. He said, 'If something breaks, sometimes it could take weeks to fix. I need to have two full sets.'" Jerry got his two sets. Incredulously, Leee added, "One full set he sold immediately." As this kit showed up years later, he'd only hocked it. But Leee was right in assuming the worst with Jerry.

Mixing began on March 22, followed by more gigs in London, Liverpool, Winchester, Birmingham, and Cheshire, with the band then returning to London for two more shows. The Heartbreakers were red-hot, with press reports from Tony Parsons of *NME* describing the Hull gig as "the nearest thing I ever saw to Beatlemania."[7] People waited anxiously for a record. To meet that need, there were endless mixing sessions.

A single was released on May 20 of "Chinese Rocks" b/w "Born to Lose." Initial orders reached twenty thousand, but something was suspect. Dee Dee Ramone and Richard Hell had written "Chinese Rocks," but Johnny and Jerry were listed as cowriters. Johnny claimed to have written a line or two, but Jerry's contribution is unknown. Richard put it into perspective: "Well, anybody who takes anything Jerry Nolan or Johnny Thunders says at face value— Ha!"[8]

Additionally, as on the Dolls' two albums, the sound wasn't quite right. The drums, particularly, sounded off, like wet paper bags and cardboard boxes. Jerry was diplomatic but honest in the British music weekly *Sounds*: "I think it's okay but not great and it should be great, I think we performed on it great, played great and the production could have been great, it was just good."[9]

Still, through the murk, you can hear Jerry's exemplary playing and ideas. John Perry: "That one simple idea of playing a rolling passage on the toms through the whole of each chorus is brilliant. Simple but dramatic. Makes the record sound like nothing else. I know Krupa was his hero, but the only other drummers I can think of who might have made a similar move are Moon and Baker."[10]

Throughout the *Sounds* article, Jerry is articulate and self-assured, mentioning how he enjoys working with Speedy Keen but tactlessly adding that he wouldn't want him to produce all the band's records. Even more shocking, he adds: "This band is a band out of business, not out of friendship.[11]

Perhaps it was a slip of the tongue, but this was quite a revealing statement. Roxy partner Barry Jones said, "We didn't know they were fighting like girls."

Leee and Jerry's mutual antipathy was no surprise, but Jerry was also having issues with the band. His allegiance would flip from day to day. Walter: "Jerry was a volatile character. I think if he'd been investigated, they would have found out he had something like bipolar disorder, because some days he's hilarious. He'd have the whole bus fucking laughing, and the next day, he'd be depressed for the next week. He really had different personalities. I guess you'd call it manic-depressive. He'd be mad at me one week or Johnny the next week and then there'd be all sorts of 'who's friends with who' this week."

His relationship with Johnny was complex, to say the least.

Walter: "John always looked up to Jerry as a father figure." Jerry's influence over Johnny loomed large. Johnny learned about Eddie Cochran and Gene Vincent from Jerry, and about the clothing from the same era. But there was more to it than just clothes and music.

Billy Rath: "[Jerry] had a big influence on Johnny. I remember once Johnny . . . bought a pair of cowboy boots. He wore them onstage that night. A picture was taken and Jerry wrote on it some wisecrack. I never saw the boots again."

Jerry lobbied Johnny to have the recordings remixed. Leee: "They did a mix with some inexperienced engineer and the whole thing sounded raw. . . . I thought it sounded wonderful [and] that was what they wanted. But Jerry didn't like it. In those days, what Jerry didn't like, Johnny didn't like and that was the end of it."

Besides the remixes, there were endless, drug-fueled overdub sessions. Walter: "A lot of wasted nights and time and money." Producer Danny Secunda's memories are consistent with Walter's: Secunda recalls Leee giving Johnny a snort of smack as motivation to rerecord guitar parts, leading to more chaos.

Throughout the fall, mixing sessions were held at Ramport, Advision, Olympic, and Trident studios, with the goal of making their record sound as powerful as the band's live sets. While mixing continued, a cover story in *ZigZag* hit the stands featuring a lengthy interview with Johnny and Jerry. Once again, Jerry did most of the talking. Much of the article centered on Jerry's youth as a gang member, and on the origins of the title of their soon-to-be released debut album, *L.A.M.F*, gang-speak for "Like a Motherfucker." This was the image Jerry and the band wanted to portray. They wanted to be seen as authentic tough guys from the streets of New York.

Johnny and Jerry claimed to be finished with drugs—a complete lie—while at the same time promoting a single about heroin and announcing they wanted to change their name to the Junkies, thanks to the success of Tom Petty and the Heartbreakers. It was all an ill-advised attempt to prepare the Heartbreakers for national consumption while trying to stay rebellious in a new, British punk rock world.

* * *

UNTIL LEEE GOT JOHNNY AND JERRY ON A BRITISH METHADONE program, they acquired it illicitly if they couldn't score smack. Leee and Gail Higgins coordinated getting the pair's daily doses.

Gail came over to the UK in the early spring to act as tour manager. She had briefly dated Jerry in the early '70s and was Johnny's old roommate and a cousin of his first Dolls-era girlfriend, Janis Cafasso. A tough New Yorker, Gail was well aware of Johnny and Jerry's sly ways. Her experience gave her the skills she needed to handle this bunch of junkie swindlers.

Gail: "When they were in London they were allowed to be enrolled in the methadone program for registered addicts, but the doctor was located miles out of town. They would not even think of taking the train, so . . . a taxi took them to Harrow to get their methadone."

Leee: "They couldn't just go down to Boots and get their methadone like the English junkies could. We couldn't get on National Health. We had to be enrolled in a clinic, and the clinic was in Harrow. They would go and lie to the doctor, who knew they were lying. They knew he knew that they were lying. Then he would hand Dibbs two quarts of methadone. Quarts!"

Dibbs Preston, a former soul boy turned rockabilly, also surfed the punk scene. He met Leee and Gail on their nightly search for attractive young boys, befriending the Heartbreakers. A Harrow native, Dibbs would sometimes drive Johnny and Jerry to the clinic. Leee: "Dibbs—I'm sure with all manner of cajoling, lies, and fibs—managed to get [the methadone] back to me." Leee was concerned they would either sell it or take too much at once and overdose.

Johnny and Jerry both wanted their doses first thing in the morning to prevent even the slightest withdrawal symptoms but might have different plans once they received it. "I lived in Islington and I would have to get up and go all the way over to Kings Road to give Jerry his, and then to Mayfair to give Johnny his. If I was five minutes late, the phone would be ringing where Gail was. . . . I'd have to take the bus. I couldn't afford a taxi [and] I didn't have a car. And, of course, the whole time then, I would have to watch them take it and they'd have to give the little cup back to me, because Johnny wasn't taking it. He'd drink it, talk to me, sometimes . . . for five or ten minutes. I'd leave. He'd go into the kitchen and spit it out in a glass so he could save it up, so he could OD on it. He'd have to keep it refrigerated, and [drink] the whole glass. Then he went to the hospital, which is like a junkie form of recreation. Jerry would take it right then [and] go out and get heroin anyway."

During the endless recording and mixing process, Jerry stopped seeing Yves, under circumstances no one can recall. He sent out feelers through back channels to Michelle in New York, having a mutual friend call her at work. Michelle: "I knew he was calling per Jerry's request, to feel me out. 'Jerry's doing really good. He's cleaned up his act . . . and he wants to pay your rent.' I was just like, 'No. I don't want anything from him.'"

Near Jerry's birthday in May, Michelle softened and sent him a birthday card, which was Jerry's green light to call her directly. "He said, 'Quit your job and move over here. It's really good.' I said, 'I'll take my vacation and come over and see you.' We had a couple of conversations, and there was this one last conversation, he said, 'You know what to do, Michelle. You'll know what to do if you love me.'"

After Jerry had stolen what little she had, Michelle had turned her life around. She was working in a respectable advertising agency and paying her bills. Her bosses wouldn't let her go and took the opportunity to talk some sense into her. "They knew that the relationship was a bad one for me. My independence felt good. I didn't want to be walking in the snow with no money." She concluded that it was best to stay in New York. She'd heard about Phyllis going to England to be with Jerry and realized that "people were just waiting in the wings for him to leave me. It must be awfully nice to just have a ton of women standing out there waiting for any little thing to go wrong."

Jerry began dating a teenager named Esther Herskovits, who'd previously dated Barry Jones and was the sister of Barry's friend Steve

Dior. Described by Eileen Polk as an "innocent" and a "waif," she came to New York with Jerry when the Heartbreakers' immigration and work permit status necessitated a trip back to the states. While there, the band played five sets at the Village Gate in the West Village from August 18 through the twentieth.

Before the Village Gate shows, Jerry called Michelle, inviting her to come. To her surprise, Esther was there. "She was like sixteen and absolutely gorgeous. My jaw just dropped. She was just like a Playboy bunny . . . the quintessential rockstar girlfriend. Ugh, it was painful."

"Esther was his trophy," remarked Arthur's wife, Barbara Kane.

Jerry stopped by Michelle's apartment unannounced. "He rings the bell" 'Can we leave our stuff here?' I was really pissed." He still had a key to the apartment, so he let himself in later to retrieve the bags. "There was a note when I came home from work, scribbled . . . cryptically saying something about ending it. 'I'm happy now. I hope you'll understand, blah, blah, blah, I'm moving on. Found something better for me.'"

If there was still any doubt in Michelle's mind, she now knew for sure, it was over between her and Jerry.

The Village Gate shows were the band's first in the States since November 1976. "That was the peak of the Heartbreakers," recalled Walter. "It was probably the best shows [we] ever played in New York, only because we were so tight from touring for six months." Old Dolls roadie Desmond Sullivan came to see the band. "It was incredible. It was one of the best shows I ever saw in my life."

Recording of the shows were finally released in 2015. The band were high on speed the first night but seemed to find their regular intoxicants the other nights. It mattered none, as they played with a ferocity previously unseen on US soil. In fact, they blew out the PA system about three-quarters of the way through their first set.

Jerry's drum sound is more like his vision of what drums should sound like than on any of the Dolls or Heartbreakers recordings to date. With his regular kit still in England, he used rented drums. Jerry normally liked lower tunings, hoping for depth of sound. On the "Chinese Rocks" b/w "Born to Lose" single, it just came across as lacking resonance. But on this night, in this club, with the rented kit, and with Brooke Delarco at the sound board, it worked. The snare and kick drum both hit you right in the chest like a blast from a shotgun.

As usual, the band's appearance was just as important as the music. They'd left New York looking better than any other band and returned still looking better than any other band. But the band had absorbed life at the center of the UK punk hurricane and no longer looked like a modernized version of Dion and the Belmonts. They sported leather pants, cropped and spiked hair, and neckties with open collars. Jerry's hair was platinum and he wore a shirt that looked like a print from Malcolm's shop. To all in attendance, they were a new and improved Heartbreakers.

The band did a photo shoot with Roberta Bayley for the cover of their soon-to-be-released album before returning to England. Jerry wore a blue mohair jumper and Johnny a junkies button. The band looked like members of a street gang. Roberta: "I went to their rehearsal space somewhere down on Crosby Street and . . . shot a few rolls, mostly outdoors, with a flash as it was nighttime. I rushed over and got the film developed in two hours. We looked at all the photos that night on a projector and narrowed it down to five images. Then everyone agreed on one and Walter drove to JFK and put that slide on a plane to London. That was the cover."

During the Village Gate run, besides shooting the Heartbreakers' album cover, Bayley came up with the idea of getting all five New York Dolls to reunite for a series of photographs as part of a retrospective in *Punk* magazine. In an inspired twist, the location chosen was Gem Spa on St. Marks Place, the same site depicted on the back cover of their first album.

When it was time for everyone to arrive, Jerry was a no-show, causing Syl to stingingly joke how Jerry, the replacement for original Doll Billy Murcia, was "never really a Doll anyway."

Using all power of persuasion, Roberta convinced everyone to give it another go the next week. While everyone now had shorter hair, except for David, who tucked his into a red cap, they no longer wore platforms, off-the-shoulder tops, gold lamé, or Norma Kamali jumpsuits. All of them looked more "punk," particularly Jerry with his chopped blond hair, skinny tie with open collar, pointed suede boots, and pleated pink pants with studded hem. It would be the last time all five Dolls ever appeared together.

The success of the Village Gate shows did not temper Jerry's displeasure with the album mixes. He returned to the UK before the rest of the band to attempt a remix of the record himself. He was tired of allowing so-called professionals, who knew nothing about his music, to make decisions about his records. He considered himself the real leader of the band, and he was going to get in there and get things right. He'd heard the three Sex Pistols singles, which sounded like an army bursting through your front door. The Damned's "New Rose" and the Clash's "White Riot," as well as their albums, while somewhat shambolic, still were roaring flames of sound. Even the Ramones' two albums, though cheaply done, still sounded fresh and blistering in comparison. In Jerry's mind, only he could salvage the record. He told Leee: "'I'll quit the band!' So, he was brought ahead, secretly, of the other band members." Upon reflection, Leee was still angry: "They should have killed him."

In the end, he couldn't salvage the record. He just created another version of "bad." Yes, the drums were loud. But it was a clattering and discomforting sound. Track insisted on using the mixes they'd chosen and planned to move forward with the Heartbreakers' *L.A.M.F.* on the scheduled October 3 release date so it would be on shelves for the Christmas season. The band agreed to acquiesce to the label's wishes— all but Jerry. True to his word, he quit.

L.A.M.F. is reviewed glowingly in the major British trades. *NME*'s Julie Burchill gave it a thumbs-up, saying, "True Romance rules here with rough brilliance. . . ."[12] *Sounds*'s Jon Savage heaped on his own praise in his four-and-a-half-star review: "This could be the party album of the next few months."[13] Jerry received accolades from Savage, who commending his "battering-ram drumming"[14] on "Baby Talk" and "Pirate Love."

But even these beaming reviews noted the wanting sound. Burchill pointed out the "ham-fisted, Loch Ness–dredging production of Speedy Keen and Daniel Secunda, who deserve at the very least to have their ears cut off."[15] Savage noted what all involved in the process know only too well: "They can't seem to get it quite right."[16]

But why did it sound so bad? Some blamed the mastering process, the last step in preparing a recording for transfer to vinyl. Walter blamed the band. "We used to play flat-out loud." Leee thought it had to do with the endless overdubs, which he felt had left the sound muddy and lifeless. Speedy Keen was blamed because he wasn't professionally trained as an engineer. Drugs were blamed as everyone involved was on something or another throughout the process. Mike Thorne laid the blame on everyone: "It's just incompetence all around. Incompetence and indulgence."

A large portion of the blame must be placed on the shoulders of Speedy and Danny. Neither of them had the track record or experience to produce and engineer a great record. Compared to Sex Pistols producer Chris Thomas, they pale in comparison. Chris coproduced (without credit) and played keyboards on several tracks of the Beatles *White Album*, mixed Pink Floyd's historic *Dark Side of the Moon*, and produced four of the first five Roxy Music albums. Bill Price engineered the Pistols album and produced the first Clash album. He'd previously engineered and mixed Mott's two great post-Bowie records, *Mott* and *The Hoople*, and had worked with Beatle Paul McCartney. As amateurish as the Pistols and the Clash may have been as musicians, they were in experienced and professional hands while recording. The Heartbreakers were not.

But few people blame Jerry and his role in determining the sound of his drums. The one thing recordings of Maximillian, the Dolls, and the Heartbreakers all had in common was Jerry. His lack of success in getting his sound right in the studio hang over all of these recordings. Whatever fire Jerry could light under his bandmates as well as the audience was not enough to fully shine inside the cold walls of a recording studio. Danny Secunda, who had little to offer on the making of *L.A.M.F.*, was pissed that Jerry wanted a different drum sound after the drums had been recorded. As in his relationships with Teddy Vann, Todd Rundgren, and Shadow Morton, Jerry was unable to come to any sort of mutual understanding, or healthy relationship, with his producer, the authority figure in a recording studio. Peter Jordan opined, "[Jerry] wasn't articulate enough or together enough to actually assert himself in the studio to get what he wanted done." Whatever vision Jerry had in his mind of what drums were supposed to sound like, he could not get it across.

As for Leee, his feeling was, "It's the biggest, hugest, fuck-up in the history of rock 'n' roll." *L.A.M.F.* would see a remix in 1984; a reissue in 1994, when alternative mixes were released; and a four-disc retrospective in 2012, when even more mixes were dredged up. Such is the mythology of this record that it seems like trying just one more time and just a little bit harder will allow its greatness to finally shine through.

While *L.A.M.F.* was universally panned for its muddy sound, there were more fans than just Savage and Burchill. As the years rolled on, young Henry Lawrence Garfield of Washington, DC, and the slightly older Paul Harold Westerberg of Minneapolis would find some sort of personal validation in the record's combination of brute force, pop sass, and gritty urban authenticity. Garfield and Westerberg would form two of the pillars of '80s alt rock: Westerberg with the Replacements, and Garfield, working under the name of Henry Rollins, in Black Flag. The Replacements would cover "I Wanna Be Loved," in their lovable drunken style, and write "Johnny's Gonna Die," about Mr. Thunders's seemingly inevitable pursuit. As for Rollins, he would visit *L.A.M.F.* over and over years later on his *Fanatic!* radio show.

The Replacements captured the spirit of the Heartbreakers as well as anyone, with their general who-gives-a-shit attitude standing in direct contrast to the seriousness of alt rock bands like REM, the Cure, or the Smiths, who were then the smart alternative to corporate rock. Additionally, Rollins's Black Flag may have been at the vanguard of the hardcore punk scene, but the sheer brutality of their musical attack, and

Rollins's unrelenting willfulness to go head-to-head with any lunkhead in the audience, made them as much the spawn of the Heartbreakers, as any band of their time.

These were just two of the faithful who would sing the praises of *L.A.M.F.* But the number of fans who bought the record never grew beyond that of a cult, and sales never accumulated significantly. For his part, Jerry took no responsibility for any of the problems with the record. "It was everybody else's fault," said Leee. "Always." After trying for a year and a half to keep Jerry in the drummer's chair, Leee was beside himself. He had put up with endless abuse from Jerry, sacrificed for him and the band by waving his rightful 20 percent fee, and run all over town to get Jerry methadone, and *now* he was quitting. He saw satisfying Jerry as an impossible task. "He hated every gig I booked. He hated every soundman, every van driver. He hated Track Records, it turns out for . . . no reason. It's like saying, 'I hate retarded people.' You don't hate them; you just don't sign contracts with them! He just hated anything that wasn't his idea and completely under his control."

To Jerry, when no one stood by him to hold up release of *L.A.M.F.*, it was an act of disloyalty and yet another abandonment, this time by his whole "family." But the part he could not face was that he was as responsible for it as anyone.

Jerry stayed with Esther and licked his wounds, planning his next move. He'd met Esther's brother Steve and remembered his friend Barry from the Roxy. With his pedigree from the Dolls and the Heartbreakers, and his resourcefulness, he could start anew. Like Richard Hell, he could start his own band.

The Pistols were banned from playing throughout most of England, so the Heartbreakers got Paul Cook to sit in on drums for several gigs through the early part of October. But as good as Paul was, he had his limitations. Swinging songs like Gary U.S. Bonds's "Seven Day Weekend" were beyond him, as were '50s-style drumbeats. The band brought over Spider, who'd played the Dolls Hippodrome gigs when Jerry had hepatitis. "He was not that good, and he just turned out to be a drug buddy for John," recalled Walter. They even tried Rat Scabies from the Damned, but his style was more Keith Moon than Charlie Watts. A deal was struck that would benefit all parties: Jerry would fulfill the tour commitments until the band could find a replacement, but he would be paid as a hired musician. And this was how Jerry would finance his next move.

This was a headline tour, with the Heartbreakers topping the bill over Siouxsie and the Banshees, the Models, the Killjoys, or Slaughter and the

Dogs. With their debut album out, this should have been a joyful time for all, the culmination of more than two years of struggle. Instead, Jerry could barely contain his disdain for the other Heartbreakers. He would not pose for photos with them and stayed to himself.

After an October 14 show in Edinburgh, in an interview with *Record Mirror*'s Barry Cain, Jerry said he left because the record sounded terrible and that the band should have produced it themselves, because, just like the Dolls, outsiders couldn't figure out what to do with them in the studio. He then let loose with a volley at the rest of the band, in terms somewhat cryptic, never naming who he was referring to: "I've discovered he's a coward and I can't work with cowards. He's done things behind my back, he gave in to allow the album to be released, he's only interested in reading about himself in the papers. I can't live with that. He acts more like a middle man in a drug deal rather than concentrating on what he should be doing. The whole thing is a joke and I want out."[17]

But, in a strange turn, Jerry held out hope for his return, saying: "One thing might tempt me back into this band. It's a long shot and I don't know whether it's gonna work. We'll just have to see."[18]

Walter had no idea who or what Jerry was referring to, though probably Johnny, as he got most of the press. The tour ended on October 31, and whatever "thing" Jerry said would tempt him back into the band did not occur. He was out. But he had a plan. . . .

BORN TO LOSE

JERRY WAS DETERMINED TO SHOW HIS FORMER BANDMATES HE could lead a successful band. The Dolls' albums had been reissued as a two-disc deluxe set in the UK, cementing their status as forerunners of punk. Then there was the splash the Heartbreakers had made. Jerry was well aware that he had played on three different albums that were considered ground zero for where rock 'n' roll was now at. Despite being a junkie, he was sure he had the CV and the know-how to get a record deal.

Jerry met guitarists Steve Dior and Barry Jones at the Roxy early on when the Heartbreakers came to the UK, and now that Jerry was dating Steve's sister, Esther, they formed a tight group.

While Barry was away on tour as driver for the British group the Boys, Steve played Jerry some of the songs he and Barry were working on. "Jerry really dug them and wanted to get a band with us," recalled Barry. Steve was taken aback but also knew Jerry was motivated and wanted to show up everyone, particularly Johnny. "It was important to Jerry to show Johnny that he didn't need him; and, if anything, Johnny needed Jerry more. Lovers are like that."

Track paid for demos and offered a record deal. Steve and Barry took the tapes to Virgin, who offered them a songwriting deal. Jerry was only in England on a holiday visa, which didn't allow him to work, though he did anyway. He returned to New York, unable to go back to the UK temporarily due to visa issues, and quickly found an apartment on Eighty-Sixth Street and Broadway. Upon his return, he was welcomed with a photo of Peter Criss on the cover of the April 13 issue of *Circus*. Fortunately, he missed the February 16, 1978, edition which named Peter Best Drummer of the Year for 1977—the second year in a row he won the title.

Jerry held onto a grudge over never hearing from Peter when hospitalized after his stabbing at Max's. This act of disloyalty just made him more envious of Peter's success. Michelle was sure "that was one of the quiet things that was inside his mind that he didn't talk about: some aspects of shame and humiliation." He wanted the success of his new band, the Idols, to rectify the injustice of Kiss's success and his continued failures.

When Steve and Barry called Jerry with news of the offers from Track and Virgin, he answered emphatically, "Don't sign anything! I've got it all here!" Jerry was convinced that the Dolls' old manager Marty Thau was going to handle them. Steve and Barry decided to come to New York. It turned out that Marty had no interest in managing them. In fact, Marty denied ever showing any interest in them. Steve and Barry insisted that he had, but had just become too involved with avant synth duo Suicide. Regardless of the actual truth, the band were now in New York and on their own.

Jerry, Barry, and Steve had decided on the name "the Idols" after toying with "the Nuclear Idols." Steve, whose real last name was Herskovits, and Barry had previously had a short-lived band called the Quickspurts, which contained both Keith Levene and Chrissie Hynde. Jones had also played in various one-offs with Mick Jones of the Clash and Tony James of Generation X. Barry was an art-school dropout who had an eye for graphics, and had created flyers for the Roxy club. They both loved the Heartbreakers, and Jerry loved their style, their songs, and Steve's sister Esther. In rock 'n' roll, that's as good a reason as any to form a band.

The band's first bass player was Simon Cade Williams, aka Simon Vitesse, previously a member of the British punk band Chelsea. Barry and Steve had met Simon at the Speakeasy in London and invited him over to jam. Simon: "It wasn't like just thrashing punk. It was tuneful, like the Dolls." They invited him to come to New York to play in their new band with Jerry.

Simon had never met Jerry, but he had seen the Heartbreakers. Based on Jerry's reputation and the promise of gigs already lined up, Simon jumped at the opportunity to join.

Simon was only seventeen but, like the rest of the Idols, was using what he described as "class-A drugs," mostly heroin. Steve and Barry had shot speed before they met Jerry, but in time, Jerry introduced them to heroin. Simon hadn't yet developed a habit like the others.

Upon arriving in New York, Barry and Steve were met by Jerry, who said to them, while winking, "You left a bag at the airport. We gotta go get it." This was all a ruse to cop some dope without alerting Esther. "We got high that very first night," recalled Barry.

A week later, Simon arrived. During that first month, everyone got the "Jerry Nolan tour of New York." Barry: "This was surreal stuff for an English kid. . . . Everything was an adventure back then . . . me and Steve, a month into Manhattan going like, 'We're in a movie,' because Manhattan was amazing in '78. You had Blondie, Talking Heads, Ramones, Dead Boys. The whole scene was just really exciting. . . ."

Simon saw the band's influences as very New York, as did Steve and Jerry. But Barry was emphatic: "We were doing something that was very English. The punk thing was there, and an influence, but we believed what we did was a direct descendent of the Rolling Stones. It's songs that are repeatable, that are catchy, but are totally guitar based . . . like the Pretenders. We weren't heavy rock, we weren't hard rock, we weren't punk. It wasn't 'I wanna burn down the USA' or 'right to work.' To me, all those were slogans kids knew would . . . get attention. We were . . . writing about rock 'n' roll, which is just sex, drugs, and the music."

Simon saw quickly that musically, "The three of them really knew what they wanted. It was great playing with Jerry behind you. You just thought that this guy was a master at his game." But due to his youth, Simon lacked the confidence and skills to bond with Jerry as a bass player should with a drummer.

The bulk of Simon's conversations with Jerry, outside of music, were about getting enough money together to buy drugs. Then Jerry would go off. The others would give each other a hit but not Jerry. "It was a lot more mundane than people might think." Steve Dior remembered, "The 'great' Jerry Nolan of the New York Dolls at home, just relaxing in his pajamas and socks . . . his glasses on."

As the most experienced member of the group, Jerry handled all their business. He got himself and Steve a gig backing Judy Nylon, half of the duo Snatch, at Max's on May 3, 1978. Judy and her Snatch partner, Patti Palladin, had recruited Jerry to play on their single "All I Want" while in England in 1977. For Judy, looking Jerry up when she relocated to New York made sense.

The Idols' first actual gig was the Blitz Benefit, held at CBGB May 4 through 7, 1978. These shows were held to raise money for recently stabbed and recovering Dead Boys drummer Johnny Blitz. Among those who played were the Ramones, Chris and Debbie from Blondie with Robert Fripp, Sylvain's band the Criminals, Peter Jordan's band Stumblebunny, Suicide, the Dictators, the Contortions, and, with Jerry on drums, the Dead Boys. John Belushi and Divine also made appearances, each with the Dead Boys.

In other efforts to make a living, the Idols backed a character by the name of Dorian Zero. Dorian, whose actual name was Kenneth Passante, was described by Steve as "the biggest fucking loser you've ever met. . . ." He was "overweight" and used "more methadone than [could] kill a fucking horse." Dorian's father owned a restaurant and was supposedly mob connected. Jerry, Dee Dee Ramone, and others latched onto Dorian, as he always had money, acquired in screaming arguments with his parents, and drugs. He was rich and spoiled, and lived in an expensive apartment his parents paid for "just to get him off their backs. He just took an enormous amount of drugs. Just a fucking horrible mess."

Dorian's claim to fame was being the butt of a joke put on by *Punk* magazine founder John Holmstrom and photographer Roberta Bayley, who turned the standard magazine interview on its head by interviewing him because they hated his record. They cared little about him storming off during the interview since they got free steaks and a great story out of the deal.

Recalled Steve, "Jerry used him, and Dorian used Jerry because he was hanging out with a New York Doll." The Idols did a session for Dorian at the Record Plant. "We all got paid, but it was crap. The guy can't sing, for goodness sake."

In the end, Simon left after only a few gigs, realizing he was too young and couldn't cut it. Plus, living with four other people in a little New York apartment proved too stressful for a seventeen-year-old.

After trying out several bass players, including Keith Paul, occasional Dolls and Heartbreakers soundman, they turned to Jerry's old Dolls compatriot Arthur Kane. Arthur had returned from the West Coast to start a band with Rick Rivets called the Corpse Grinders, and, in a turn of good fortune, his ex-girlfriend Connie had moved on to Dee Dee Ramone. Arthur was overjoyed to play with a member of the Dolls again.

It took Esther some time to realize how involved with drugs everyone was. Eileen Polk: "Esther was a sweet, naive, beautiful English girl who was just new to it all. I think that Jerry impressed her, but I don't think she knew what she was getting into." Arthur's wife Babs agreed to a point: "She wanted to be with Jerry, and she wanted to be put up on the pedestal of being a rock 'n' roll girlfriend. She was naive, but not that naive. Her front was her naïveté, but . . . deep inside, [she] knew what was going on, and she knew how to play it."

When they first got to New York, Esther believed that Jerry was only on methadone. But after getting his morning methadone, he'd start looking for heroin. Babs: "He'd get up . . . and his whole demeanor was shaky. He would be pale and not able to really relate to anybody.

He'd . . . get out the door and get his methadone . . . and then . . . go on the hunt for the heroin. The whole day was spent accessing the drugs. Then you'd watch his personality change into a more aggressive person."

Half black, and darker skinned than the rest, Barry was chosen to cop with Jerry most often, easily blending in as Puerto Rican. Sometimes Dee Dee Ramone would join, but the Ramones put a stop to that whenever they could. Barry recalled copping with Jerry: "He was very street-smart. He had the blue overcoat tied around the waist. He wouldn't wear the pink pegged pants; it would be some other nondescript stuff and he would pull a black beret over his bleached-blond hair. He knew how to behave where you didn't set off alarms."

Despite their heroin dependency, the Idols were a functioning band, writing, rehearsing and gigging. Musically, Jerry acted as mentor and teacher, regaling the younger Idols with tales of his idols, using them as aspirational examples. He talked to them about the two Genes: Vincent and Krupa. Barry: "He loved Gene Vincent. He talked a lot about Gene Vincent's style. They had to have style . . . or Jerry wasn't interested." Steve: "He worshipped Gene Krupa. If you watched him play drums, you thought you saw Gene Krupa. That tribal rhythm. A lot of floor tom . . . He had the style, he had the attitude . . . he had showmanship. That's what Jerry really liked: the showmanship."

Jerry trained his younger, less-experienced bandmates as if they were in the military and he was their drill sergeant. Barry: "He taught us the basics. It's like joining the army: this is how you march; this is what you do under combat. . . ." Steve saw him as a mentor, "for good or worse. To me, I was in boot camp. I was a willing soldier. He wasn't like a person who barked orders. It was fun to be in a band with Jerry . . . even though we were struggling."

But it wasn't all fun and games, according to Barry. There was a right way and a wrong way to do things. The right way was Jerry's way. "He had these goddamn rules: Jerry had this thing about loyalty. Loyalty was huge to him. Loyalty to your friends. Loyalty to the band was paramount."

Jerry taught them his rules of stagecraft. Take pride in yourself, and never do what Johnny Thunders did. Steve: "He didn't go onstage, fall over, and nod out. Thunders sometimes was just a clown, a rock 'n' roll clown. But Jerry was never that. He was always of the utmost professional persona and always looked finely dressed. He took pride in his music and the way he looked and his performances."

Jerry's second rule of stagecraft: You always had to look your best. "His clothes were always impeccable," recalled Steve. "He would drum in a three-piece suit . . . Total showman."

Most of all, there was the music. To Jerry, it was about feeling something special. Barry: "When you're onstage . . . part of it's act, part of it's what you rehearsed . . . but if you're lucky, and can hook into 'the zone,' a lot of it just comes and you might not ever repeat what you played. That's what Jerry was about."

Like Johnny Thunders before, Steve and Barry loved watching Jerry play, even if it meant turning their backs to the audience. "He was always such a joy to watch," said Steve. "It was more fun, like being on a train ride with him."

Friday and Saturday Max's gigs had a built-in crowd, helping the band develop a small following. But something happened in September that changed the focus of the band. That something was the New York arrival of Sid and Nancy.

The Sex Pistols had broken up in January of 1978, and Malcolm kept releasing Sex Pistols material with alternating lead singers. Sid sang lead on Eddie Cochran's "Something Else" and "C'mon Everybody" and Paul Anka's "My Way." In the ensuing months, with his equally self-destructive partner Nancy Spungen at his side, Sid became even more of a walking car crash than he'd been on the Pistols' ill-fated US tour, using any number of drugs, but particularly heroin, to numb himself. With Nancy egging him on, they decided that New York would be their new base of operations from which to kick-start his solo career.

Sid already knew all the Idols except Arthur from when the Heartbreakers were in England. He was, according to Leee, a "Heartbreakers groupie."

Nancy was unlike anything Steve or Barry had seen in England. "She was hard-core," recalled Barry. "We thought hard-core was the Roxy club punks. But no, Nancy was much more hard-core than that. Turn a trick in a second just to get a hit."

Nancy showed off her rock star boyfriend to all the people who had maligned her just a few years prior, enjoying her victory lap. But now, saddled with a heroin addiction, it made sense for them to seek out Jerry and the Idols once they got to New York.

Steve recalled, "The first thing we did when Sid come over was put him in a methadone program." Jerry, after taking as much as 80 milligrams a day, had detoxed down to 35. Sid and Nancy were both in such bad shape, they started at the astronomical figure of 110. "Then we talked about playing gigs."

A Sid Vicious gig was booked at Max's for September 7. But, in a move which stung him, Barry was not included. It was originally supposed to be Jerry, Arthur, Steve, and Johnny Thunders, who was in New York, presumably awaiting the October release of his *So Alone* album—his post-Heartbreakers attempt at making it as a solo artist. But if loyalty was of paramount importance to Jerry, why was Barry out? Mostly because they wanted the attraction of a big name like Johnny Thunders, still a draw in New York in 1978. But there was also another reason.

Steve: "It was also the fact that he was black. No one might admit it, but I know that had something to do with it." Arthur's wife Barbara confirmed the reason: "He wasn't white."

Jerry had his concerns about Johnny. Steve recalled Jerry's phone conversation at the rehearsal studio with Johnny: "'Look, Johnny, if you show up looking the least bit stupid I'm walking off.' Meaning, if you show up high I'm walking off the stage."

Johnny never showed up.

Instead of recruiting Barry, they still wanted a ringer . . . who was white.

Steve went over to the Record Plant, where the Clash were mixing *Give 'Em Enough Rope,* and talked to Mick Jones about doing the gig. "He was frightened of the association," presumably meaning frightened to be associated with junkies. In the end, Steve persuaded him to do it to help poor Sid. The irony was not lost on Barry. "Basically, it ended up Steve Dior, who I taught to play guitar; Mick Jones, who I coached his guitar playing; and Jerry and Arthur. My band was getting hijacked."

Roadie Richard Freedman was also at the rehearsals. Although Sid still had a relationship with Pistols manager Malcolm McLaren, Nancy was presenting herself as Sid's manager. In reality, Jerry was in charge, "basically telling Sid what to do because Sid was so out of it. Nancy was keeping him fucked up all the time. In terms of putting on those shows . . . that was all Jerry."

Come the night of the gig, Max's was as packed as it had ever been, with many hoping to see the freak-show circus act that Sid had become on the Pistols short US tour in January. Now Sid was lifeless, occasionally playing the show on the seat of his pants. Peter Crowley recalled, "Poor Sid was in no condition to play. He was sick as a dog." Eileen Polk recalled that he was on "heroin and alcohol, or whatever he could get. He seemed really depressed. People were concerned about him." Ira Robbins, writing for *NME*, noted, "Looking at Sid is no treat—he looks more drugged out these days than before."[1] As for Jerry, Robbins wrote that he was "still a great drummer, [but] also looks like he could do with better health."[2]

The band's set list consisted solely of covers: Iggy, Dolls, Heartbreakers, or other covers those bands or the Pistols already did. In the second set, a shortened version of "My Way" was played, as Sid couldn't remember, or be bothered to learn, all the lyrics beyond the first chorus. Without

Mick Jones, they played three more nights, September 28 through the thirtieth. The Dolls' "Chatterbox" was added for those shows.

Sid was a wreck, acting much like what Jerry feared Johnny Thunders would have been: a stoned mess. Still, Jerry believed that Sid had great charisma and could be a great front man. And, with over $10,000 cash in his pocket after the shows were completed, he cast his concerns aside.

On September 18, a relatively coherent Sid and Nancy, who'd now adopted a British accent, appeared on a local cable TV show with Dead Boy Stiv Bators and his girlfriend, 'B' Girls bass player Cynthia Ross. They announced a Boston show for Sid on September 24 and a planned single, both with the Idols backing him. Neither would materialize.

The Idols kept busy with their own headlining shows through the month of October, including a Halloween bash at the Diplomat Hotel with the Senders and the 'B' Girls. The Sid shows elevated the band's profile. There was also talk of a thirty-city tour with Sid.

On the night of October 11, Barry was headed to a sound check when he received a phone call from Nancy, looking to cop. Barry, a self-described "people pleaser," knew where he could get some Dilaudid, and as the middle man in the deal, he could take a few pills for himself off the top. He arrived at the Chelsea Hotel, where Sid and Nancy were staying, and the exchange was made. Instead of letting him take his money and leave, Nancy insisted he fix her up a hit. Despite Barry's reminder that she was already out of it on downers, Nancy persisted. She claimed to have only taken them to stave off dope sickness, and said she needed the morphine in Dilaudid to finish the job.

Barry: "Well, if you know anything about shooting pills, it's a procedure, not like swallowing a couple with a glass of water. First you got to crush them between two spoons. Scrape the back of the top one so you have all the powder in one spoon, water in, heat under, then filter with your cotton."[3] Barry's good sense prevailed, and he skipped fixing himself. He got to his gig on time. Little did he know it would be the last time he'd ever see Nancy.

On the morning of October 12, 1978, Nancy Spungen was found dead, smeared with blood on the bathroom floor of the room she shared with Sid at the Chelsea. The cause of death was a knife wound to the abdomen. After the police arrived, Sid was handcuffed and brought in for questioning. Sid confessed to killing Nancy, but also made other conflicting statements to the police. Multiple witnesses place others with motive and opportunity at the scene. Sid's prodigious drug intake at the time of death also created doubt as to whether he had the capacity to commit the deadly act. Still, he was charged with murder in the second degree and with depraved indifference to human life.

The next day, Jerry, Esther, and Steve all attended the arraignment, where bail was set at $50,000. Sid was sent to Rikers Island and quickly moved to the medical wing to detox from heroin. There, he received a visit from Jerry and Esther. He spent time at Bellevue Hospital and attempted suicide. Finally bailed out and released, he moved in with Jerry and Esther at Steve's apartment at 47 East Third Street. "I had a two-bedroom flat," Steve recalled. "It was on the Hells Angels block . . . between First and Second Avenue." The Angels owned five buildings on the block, making it safe for all who stayed on their good side.

Sid was provided some privacy in the apartment by a bamboo curtain. "I asked him point-blank, 'Did you kill Nancy?' He told me he didn't. I believe him to this day."

Nancy's death created a media frenzy, with Sid's face on the cover of newspapers and on television. Jerry had already taught him how to lower his profile when copping or going to the methadone clinic, after Sid got ripped off and beaten. That advice went unheeded. Roadies Rick Freedman and Bobby Battery were among the inner circle trying to look out for Sid. Recalled Rick: "I remember very distinctly one night with Jerry, Esther, Bobby, and Sid just walking . . . to one of the little local bodegas on Second Avenue, and just getting mobbed by press. Sid still had bandages on his arms. Jerry and Esther are trying to shield Sid, and Sid just has this completely lost and confused look on his face."

As Sid was still doing dope, someone had to cop for him. Jerry continued to prefer the darker-skinned Barry handle it. "They'd had a raid. . . . The guy at the top of the stairs was screaming, waving a .44 magnum around going, 'I want to see track marks now!'" It was assurance that you were a junkie, not a cop.

Rick noticed Jerry becoming "emotionally attached to Sid" in a fatherly way. He would protect Sid by doling out his heroin to prevent him from overdosing. Recalled Rick, "Jerry had this big bag of dope. I think Jerry was doing three bags and I was doing a bag and Bobby was doing a bag. And then he pulls out, like, fourteen more bags. He said, 'This is for Sid.'"

Despite Jerry, Esther, and Steve's best efforts, Sid continued getting into trouble. There were more suicide attempts, and on December 8, at the Upper West Side club Hurrah, Sid struck Patti Smith's brother Todd in the face with a beer mug and was arrested again. He was not released until February 1, 1979.

Before this latest arrest, Sid had begun spending time at 63 Bank Street with a would-be actress named Michelle Robison, who claimed to have dated Jerry years before. In celebration of Sid's release, his mother, Anne Beverley, who'd been in New York since his arrest, threw him a little party at Michelle's apartment. Per Eileen, in attendance were Sid, his mother, Michelle, Howie Pyro from the Blessed (and later D Generation, among others), Jerry Only from the Misfits, English photographer Peter Kodick, aka Gravelle, his friend Dave, Jerry, and Esther. Peter, however, claims the only other people there were Sid, Michelle, and Sid's mum.

According to Eileen, Jerry and Sid left the apartment after getting $100 from Anne. Everyone assumed it was to buy heroin. Upon their return, they enjoyed dinner. Peter brought more heroin later, which Sid injected. After fifty-five days in jail, Sid had lost his tolerance, causing him to OD. He was revived without calling for medical assistance. Throughout the evening, Sid talked of his plans for a new record and was confident he would be found innocent of killing Nancy.

When everyone left, Sid went off to bed with Michelle and never woke up. He had apparently gotten into the rest of the stash held by his mother during the night and suffered a fatal overdose.

Sid and Nancy were both dead, but the media frenzy continued. If the rise of punk had seemed full of possibilities, to many, it was now over in a blaze of nihilistic, depraved hedonism. In the United States, it was all tabloid-media fodder. Even on the streets of jaded New York, things had changed.

Eileen: "I remember the early part of punk, before people knew it was called punk, as being the most fun, because then if you're dressed like that and you're walking down the street . . . everyone leaves you alone. They just think you're crazy. . . . After Sid Vicious died, everybody would yell out, 'Hey, punk rocker, go back to England.'" Even the levelheaded Peter Crowley acknowledged, "To some extent, we were all buying that 'punk rock' image a little bit, and it was getting into our personalities, but [Nancy] and Sid took it farther than anybody. . . . They took it right into the grave."

Jerry and Esther attended Sid's funeral. Jerry knew he had to get back to his career after losing the possibility of a star-studded, well-paying gig leading Sid's band, but he was stunned by Sid's death. He never felt responsible for Nancy, assuming she got her just deserts based on the life she lived. Sid, however, had assumed Johnny's role in Jerry's life. He felt a fatherly responsibility toward Sid, and had failed him.

The whole Sid-and-Nancy experience of the previous six months was not the only thing shaking up Jerry's world. His old friends and Dolls partners all released solo records and established themselves separately from Jerry.

David Johansen finally got a major label solo deal, releasing his self-titled album in May of 1978. Upon its release, it won the lead review in *Rolling Stone*, where old friend Paul Nelson reviewed it, calling the record "the first genuine masterpiece that the counterculture punk-rock/New Wave movement of the Seventies has produced."[4] With a powerful band, which included Sylvain, who'd cowritten several compositions, on piano and guitar, David's live shows were impressive. They included several Dolls songs and left crowds wanting more. By the fall, he was headlining his own dates and had established himself as a respected artist in his own right.

Syl used the money he made working with David to record demos and start his own band, the Criminals, playing the same clubs as Jerry. They released an indie single by mid-1978 of "The Kids Are Back" b/w "The Cops Are Coming." By early 1979 he'd signed a solo deal with RCA.

Peter Criss's band Kiss had become so ubiquitous that products emblazoned with his face were flying off the shelves worldwide. He'd been on the cover of major magazines, sung on national TV, and, in September of 1978, released his own solo album, which went platinum. He was a millionaire and a star. He had everything that Jerry wanted.

Jerry's old flame Bette Midler was now a regular on talk shows, award shows, magazine covers, and radio. Her television special had won an Emmy award and she was in Hollywood working on her first starring role in the film *The Rose*, for which she was nominated for an Academy Award. She too was a millionaire and a star.

Most upsetting to Jerry, though, was the release of Johnny Thunders's solo album *So Alone* in October 1978. Of its ten songs, three were covers ("Pipeline," "Great Big Kiss," and "Daddy Rollin' Stone"), two of which the Dolls used to perform. Two others were redone Dolls songs ("Subway Train" and "Leave Me Alone," aka "Chatterbox"). It did not sit well that Johnny was so reliant on Dolls-era material. Plus, to Jerry, "Ask Me No Questions" and "You Can't Put Your Arms Around a Memory" weren't rock 'n' roll. But the success of "Memory," probably the most successful of any Dolls-related song ever, must have humiliated Jerry, as he always forbade Johnny from playing any slow or acoustic songs live in the Heartbreakers' set. While Jerry's directives may have been right for a live presentation, they were off the mark on record.

It also galled him that Billy and Walter played on the record and received cowriting credits on "London Boys." Others who appeared on the record were Steve Marriott from Humble Pie and Small Faces, Phil Lynott from Thin Lizzy, Jones and Cook from the Pistols, and members of the Only Ones and Eddie and the Hot Rods. It was a party Jerry hadn't been invited to.

The record was produced by twenty-three-year-old Steve Lillywhite, who'd already coproduced Ultravox's first album and produced Siouxsie and the Banshees' hit single "Hong Kong Garden." Over the span of his career, Lillywhite would go onto win six Grammys and produced major hits by Big Country, Peter Gabriel, the Pogues, and U2. He would also work with the Rolling Stones, the Dave Matthews Band, Talking Heads, XTC, the Killers, Morrissey, Simple Minds, and countless others. Lillywhite helped create the gated-reverb drum sound that defined the '80s. He was a major player, bringing a level of professionalism to Thunders's record that the guitarist sorely needed.

Lillywhite behind the control board gave the record arguably the best sound of any recording done by any member of the Dolls up to that point, if not ever. He took the disorder inherent in any Thunders' project, and created a concise, impactful, and highly listenable record. The single off the record, "You Can't Put Your Arms Around a Memory," became Johnny Thunders's signature tune. It was exactly what Johnny needed, and what Jerry could only wish for.

Steve Dior recalled that after *So Alone* came out, Jerry "wasn't that impressed with it. Actually . . . he was impressed . . . that Johnny actually got the record out." Jerry wasn't as impressed by the drumming, but this may have been a defense mechanism. Steve could tell it hurt him. "It must have been difficult for him to hear Thunders with all these other different drummers."

Jerry slagged off all of Johansen's, Sylvain's, and Thunders's[†] recordings in a July 1978 article in the *New York Rocker* titled "The Jerry Nolan Story!!" He said Sylvain's "The Kids Are Back" 45 "doesn't do nothin' for me."[5] Johnny's single "Dead or Alive" was deemed "not so hot"[6] and Johansen's album was "not so hot at all."[7] He was perplexed by these records:

"I don't understand it. I remember being with these guys and all they talked about was rock 'n' roll. Now they don't even play it! But that's me—if you're not perfect and right-on, I don't even call it rock 'n' roll."[8]

---

† Johnny had only released a single from the *So Alone* sessions by that date: "Dead or Alive" b/w "Downtown."

* * *

JERRY WOULD HAVE HIS CHANCE TO SHOW THE OTHERS WHAT real rock 'n' roll' was after the Idols accepted a singles deal with Terry Ork's new Warner Brothers–backed Ork label. The Ork imprint had released notable underground singles from the nascent punk scene, including Television's "Little Johnny Jewel," in 1975, and Richard Hell's "Blank Generation," in 1976. Now Terry had major distribution, and the Idols were poised to take advantage of it. While it was only a singles deal, it was enough for them to get a foot in the door, as scores of English bands released singles before getting album deals.

Sessions were scheduled to begin in the early part of 1979 at New York's RPM Studios on East Twelfth Street. Before the band could record, though, there were other issues to attend to. Going back to being left out of the Sid Vicious band, Barry had been having problems with Jerry for several months, leading up to Jerry telling him he was out of the group. Steve recalled, "It was a time when Jerry didn't want to play with Barry anymore and that caused tension. There was this period of about two or three months that Jerry and Barry weren't even talking."

Barry Jones: "It was all Jerry. Steve was just following him. He didn't think I was putting in enough effort. . . . We had a meeting. Jerry [was] very high-handed, very rude. We met early morning at this soda fountain, in the East Village. I can remember to this day, him lookin' at me and . . . like Keith Richards, he'd lean his head back and to one side and tell you this is how it is. You did this, you did that. 'And you know what? We have two gigs to play. You're out of the band, but if you're a man, any kind of man, you'll come and you'll play those gigs for us.'"

The two gigs Barry was to play before termination turned into several months of being the band's second-class citizen. Slowly, Barry returned to Jerry's good graces. "I doubled up my input. I made plans, I'd promote. . . . It was never mentioned again until way down the road, when Jerry said, 'I saw the effort you made. I really respect that. You were a man.' He was always about being a man: Face up to shit."

Steve believed Barry's return to status may have been the result of more than Barry just putting in extra effort. A self-confessed people pleaser, Barry came through for Jerry when Jerry was in need, just like he had for Nancy. Steve: "I think Jerry just felt like a schmuck. There were times when . . . Jerry might need 'something.' Barry'd go out of his way to put it together without any strings attached."

Despite once again being in Jerry's good graces, Barry was dealt more indignities. He'd heard comments like "I see you got a nigger in the band" since he first came to the States. Steve tried to broker the race issue between Jerry and Barry. According to Steve, Jerry explained that to him the word *nigger* defined a state of being, not necessarily black people. As far as Jerry was concerned, there were white people that were "niggers" too. "He was always saying, 'I hate fucking niggers.' I was all, like, 'Well, what's he talking about? Is he just talking about black people?' It wasn't all black people. Buddy Bowzer was . . . his friend. It didn't make any sense to me. I've been confused about it all these years as well. Like, exactly how does that work, selective racism?"

Jerry claimed it was the way people acted that made them "niggers." "He used to try and tell me that there were niggers in New York City [that] were different than any other. He said, 'It's just New York.' He says, 'I'll point one out to you.' He's talking about a typical street [person]. A stereotype."

Jerry also had other old habits that wouldn't die. Barry: "He would routinely go to the gig and get an advance and not tell us. We were always pawning our guitars. Then you get an advance from the club. . . . On the day of the gig . . . go get your guitar back. It was all old New York Dolls stuff that he and Johnny used to pull. He taught us all those tricks."

Jerry got the check from the Ork recordings and didn't tell the rest of the band. When they finally confronted him, he patted his breast pocket and said, "Yeah I got the check. I got the check right here. What the fuck"? He was challenging the other band members. "We didn't say anything," lamented Barry. "We pussied out and he'd had the check, all right, and he'd spent the fucking money."

Cracks were starting to appear in Jerry's relationship with Esther as well. Working at Ian's clothing store on the Upper East Side, she'd begun making a life for herself outside of Jerry and the band. "Coke was big," Barry recalled. Esther started using it with the people from Ian's. "She started opening up and going to events at the store."

Jerry, despite his years of philandering, was extremely jealous of Esther's newfound independence. Barry: "He was as jealous and possessive as any man can be of a woman. One, he had this loyalty thing. Two, he had a really, very weird perspective about women. They [were] 'goddesses' or 'ho's.' His mother was in the 'goddess' bit. Esther was in the 'goddess' bit and then she slipped into the 'ho' bit. He slapped her and that was enough for her."

Having an English label with Warner Brothers' backing created the possibility that the band might have some cachet in the UK. They decided it made sense to return there. Steve and Barry went ahead of Jerry to see what they could accomplish ahead of Jerry's arrival. Esther returned to England with them, ostensibly so she and Jerry could have a cooling-off period. But they would never reunite. On the plane ride, she spoke to Barry intimately about her relationship with Jerry, in particular, certain nonspecific sexual hang-ups Jerry had. "That thing about homophobia. I mean, we used to joke, 'Maybe he's gay? Maybe he's just been in denial for years?'"

Jerry was a manipulator of women. Steve: "She was very, very young. She adored him, so he got away with murder. He'd stay out and wouldn't come home. He wasn't womanizing or anything; he was just out doing his Jerry Nolan stuff, probably to do with drugs and God knows what else. She dabbled a little bit, but you're talking about dabbling a little bit. He didn't allow her to really get sucked into the whole shit, which was good."

What was he doing while he was "out"? Stuart Feinholtz, aka Stuboy Wylder, singer with Arthur's Corpse Grinders, had experience with Jerry's secret side.

Stuboy told a story of Jerry bringing a girl by who was visiting from England after receiving a large settlement from an auto accident. Stuboy: "Jerry asked her if she wanted to get high and she said yes. He said, 'Give me all your money.' She gave him like two-fifty, three hundred bucks, and we went and copped a bunch of heroin and came back and gave her like $10 worth and she passed out. When she woke up, Jerry said, 'Well, I gotta go now.' He tried to leave her at my place. I told him, 'No way! Take her with you, because my girlfriend is coming over.' So he took her outside and she could hardly walk, and who comes walking around the corner but Dee Dee Ramone. He lived right next door to me. He sees this cute stoned-out British chick and his eyes like pop out. Jerry introduces her and she's like, 'Oh wow! All these rock stars!' And Dee Dee says, 'I'll take her off your hands.' She is stoned on dope, Jerry took all her money, and now she is with sex deviant Dee Dee. That was pretty much how Jerry treated girls. He had some fabulous, gorgeous, and really loving girlfriends and he always fucked it up terribly and he never cared. He was such a dope fiend. Worse than Thunders. He never stayed with one girl for very long."

PART 4
HURTIN'

On *The Stanley Siegel Show* after the death of Sid Vicious at Max's Kansas City, *left to right*, Gene O'Brian (Max's night manager), Leee Black Childers, Stanley Siegel, Jerry, Esther Herskovits, February 1979. (Photo by Eileen Polk)

The Idols photo session at Max's Kansas City, *left to right*, Arthur Kane, Steve Dior, Jerry (with methadone bottle), Barry Jones, 1979. (Photo by Eileen Polk)

Jerry, 1980. (Photo courtesy of Lesley Vinson)

Passport photo 1982.
(Photo courtesy of
Charlotte Lotten)

At 242 Mott Street,
New York City, 1980.
(Photo courtesy of
Lesley Vinson)

Wedding day,
left to right,
Charlotte Lotten
and Jerry, Chapel
of Gustav Vasa
church Stockholm,
Sweden, June
29, 1982. (Photo
courtesy of
Charlotte Lotten)

Newlyweds, *left to right*, Charlotte
Lotten and Jerry, 1982. (Photo
courtesy of Charlotte Lotten)

Recording Studio, Stockholm, 1982.
(Photo courtesy of Charlotte Lotten)

"Take a Chance with Me" single photo session, 1982. (Photo courtesy of Charlotte Lotten)

Christmas tree in basement of Cat Club, New York, December 1983. (Photo courtesy of Charlotte Lotten)

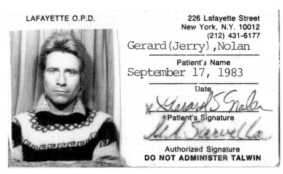

Methadone clinic ID card, New York, September 17, 1983.
(Photo courtesy of Charlotte Lotten)

Passport photos, 1984. (Photo courtesy of Charlotte Lotten)

Finland, spring/summer 1984, *left to right*, Michael Thimren, Rosa Körberg, Billy Rath,
Johnny Thunders, Christopher Giercke, Susanne Blomqvist, Jerry, Charlotte Lotten.
(Photo courtesy of Charlotte Lotten)

New Year's Eve at the Roxy in LA, 1986, *left to right*, Barbara "Babs" Kane, Arthur Kane, unknown, Johnny Thunders, Susanne Blomqvist, Jerry, Charlotte Lotten. (Photo courtesy of Charlotte Lotten)

In Wichita Falls, Texas, 1986, *left to right*, Jerry and Charlotte Lotten. (Photo courtesy of Charlotte Lotten)

On Jerry's Triumph motorbike, Stockholm, *left to right*, Charlotte's father Rolf and Jerry, 1988/89. (Photo courtesy of Charlotte Lotten)

Three Dolls at the Continental Divide in New York, *left to right*, Johnny Thunders, Jerry, and Sylvain Sylvain, 1989. (Photo by Bob Gruen)

From Johnny Thunders Memorial Benefit at the Marquee in New York, June 19, 1991, *left to right*, Sylvain Sylvain, Jerry, David Johansen. (Photo by Bob Gruen)

Spring 1991, for
Village Voice article.
(Photos by Kristine
Larsen)

ASK ME
16 NO QUESTIONS

AFTER ESTHER, STEVE, AND BARRY RETURNED TO ENGLAND, JERRY stayed at the Third Street apartment. To pick up a few dollars, he put aside his grudges and started playing with Johnny, Walter, and Billy again. These were "rent" gigs.

The Heartbreakers used several different drummers during these shows, including Ty Styx, Billy Rogers, and Lee Crystal. A live album was even slated for release from a set of September 1978 shows with Ty on drums. But Walter acknowledged, "Jerry and Johnny always belonged together."[1]

One night, Jerry found himself sitting next to a petite blond from Detroit at the Mudd Club, New York's new hip nightspot, in an industrial-loft section of Soho. Lesley Vinson worked at the *Soho News*, a weekly local newspaper challenging the more established *Village Voice*. Primarily a graphic artist and stylist, Lesley had contacted Jerry the year before, after the death of Nancy Spungen. She recalled, "Somebody said Sid and Jerry were very good friends and I said, 'I'll call him up.' I think he thought we were going to do a story on him. Then I started on what I wanted to know about Sid Vicious and then he just didn't want to talk anymore."

Lesley had recently broken up with her boyfriend when Jerry sat down next to her. "We ended up talking. Of course, I knew who it was." Lesley also played drums and loved the New York Dolls. "I thought, 'Oh my God, Jerry Nolan!' I just liked him so much. But I didn't say that I was that person who called him."

She felt comfortable talking to him. "Something clicked," she recalled, and they went over to his place on Third Street. "It was . . . a hovel. It was one of those typical junkie East Village apartments. There was cat hair and dirt and old food and cat piss and unclean litter boxes."

Lesley was touched by the sad state of Jerry's living condition, as well as his feelings for a cat named Cisco that lived there. "He was a big orange tomcat and I remember thinking, 'Those lives are so sad.' Jerry really loved that cat." Jerry would snuggle with the cat and coo, "My name is Jerry and I have a cat named Cisco." "It was this touching human heart that wasn't rock 'n' roll and drugs. What attracted me to him is that he was . . . a sad guy. Jerry never was the life of the party." A few months later, Jerry met Lesley's mom visiting from Detroit. "She said, 'He seems very nice but very sad.'"

* * *

LESLEY LIVED IN AN UNFINISHED LOFT SPACE ON BLEECKER AND Bowery. When a nicer apartment became available a few blocks away at 242 Mott Street, she jumped at it. It was a one-bedroom, one-bath, third-floor walkup in a building almost exclusively occupied by Italian-Americans. The rent was about $180 a month, cheap even by 1979 standards. Next door was a social club, where low-level wise guys listened to Sinatra and Jerry Vale while drinking espresso or anisette. They had names like Carmine and Nick, and called themselves "restaurantaws," or "entrapinaws."

Despite barely knowing each other a month, Jerry and Lesley moved in together. "Even then I must have been a little bit leery. . . . Nothing was in his name."

Jerry wanted to paint the apartment walls black with flecks of brighter-colored paint. They ended up with fluorescent-blue walls, except for the kitchen. The walls were furry, as they began, but never finished, removing its old wallpaper, leaving its fuzzy backing.

The Mott Street apartment was just a three-block walk from Jerry's methadone clinic at 226 Lafayette Street. Lesley recalled, "Jerry used to get up every morning at like six or seven . . . [as] you had to get your methadone between seven and eight. I'd be sleeping in bed. He was like a shark. He was never tired. So he would pop up, go over to the methadone clinic, get his dose, and would always swing back." He'd stop at Bella's Luncheonette on the corner of Elizabeth and Prince Streets. Bella's looked like Edward Hopper's famous *Nighthawks* painting, but was run by loud Italian-Americans in the heart of Little Italy. Bella's opened early, but at no exact time. "We opin when da cawfee's poikin'." Jerry would get a potato-and-egg sandwich and, with his daily methadone dose, return, sandwich in hand, in an upbeat mood.

But as the day wore on, his mood would spiral downward. "Then he would go out and score, and then he would come back and then he'd go out and score more. . . . He would disappear for hours at a time. I didn't know where he was. He was always on the lookout: how he could make a score . . . and to do that he had to roam."

Meanwhile, the Idols' single of "You" b/w "Girl That I Love" was released in June. It was the best-sounding record of any Jerry had made up to that point. His playing was sympathetic to the song, with nothing taking up as much musical space as his playing on "Baby Talk" or "Stranded in the Jungle." It was straight out of the Ringo/Charlie Watts school of supportive playing, with a beat as fat as a James Brown record.

British DJ John Peel added "You" to his playlist, and Ork felt the band should play gigs in England. "We were literally going to do this tour supporting the Clash," said Steve.

Jerry flew to England with high hopes, but disappointment met him in London when he stopped at the immigration desk. The Heartbreakers had overstayed their holiday visas two years earlier. He was turned right around and sent back to the States. "He shows up at the back door of the *Soho News*, standing with his suitcase. And now he needed twenty bucks before he went home to Mott Street."

"We spent about six months trying to get Jerry over," said Steve. "We didn't have the finances to get a real lawyer or anything. That's what really put an end to the Idols."

Looking back, Barry lamented, "We were going in the right direction musically, but what we couldn't see was that we were just . . . the plague as far as record companies were concerned. We never blew gigs because of drugs, and we never did a bad show, like Johnny. It was just the fact that . . . drugs give you a reputation . . . and we were guilty by association from the get-go."

Now stuck in New York, looking for a gig, Jerry played Heartbreakers rent shows but still had issues with Johnny. Lesley recalled, "He was very proud of himself that he was not a sloppy drug addict. He couldn't stand that about Johnny. 'I could never be like that.' Half of him thought it was an act that Johnny was putting on, how Johnny used to come and stumble onstage and his eyes were like he was always nodding. 'That's just sloppy and it doesn't have to be like that.' That's the only time I ever heard him say anything negative about Johnny. Most people . . . didn't even know that Jerry was a junkie if you hadn't met him."

But Lesley sensed that Jerry was envious of Johnny. "Johnny Thunders without Jerry was still Johnny Thunders. And I think that Jerry without

Johnny, it was harder for him to exist. It was like Johnny was obviously the star. Jerry wasn't a star of that magnitude."

As broke, skeevy, or pathetic as Johnny might be, he was the star, and had a cultlike following. When he was onstage, you couldn't keep your eyes off him. The songs he cowrote with Johansen in the Dolls, like "Personality Crisis" and "Jet Boy," or his songs on *L.A.M.F.*, like "Born to Lose," and his solo work, like "You Can't Put Your Arms Around a Memory," were as good as any from that era. Like Johnny Ramone, he created a simple yet identifiable guitar sound that helped define a genre. His legend grew as he seemingly wasted his talent in a blaze of drug use, making each show, a toes-teetering-on-the-edge-of-a-cliff escapade. Sometimes he would fall over the precipice into the abyss, but if he could balance just right, you would hear rock 'n' roll as exciting as any.

Throughout it, Johnny didn't seem to care what anyone thought, endlessly haranguing the audience and his bandmates from the stage or appearing to nod out during the show. Johnny could have been a contender, but seemed to be trading his chances for a fix. Jerry wanted what Johnny was letting fall by the wayside but, despite his own star quality, simply could not compete. He knew it and it gnawed at him.

* * *

LESLEY AND JERRY BONDED OVER MUSIC. HE LIKED EDDIE AND the Hot Rods' *Teenage Depression*, but his favorite was '50s music. "He talked about 'I Only Have Eyes for You,' by the Flamingos. He'd go through that song like a music analyst. He said, "Listen, you hear where the drums pull out here?' Then he'd go back in and say, 'This is really weird but . . . I really like the way they sing off-key in this.'"

They also discussed how he tuned his drums. "He used to say, 'A lot of people tune the drums too tight. I like to have mine a little bit on the soft side because it gives it this really kind of "boom" at the end. It gives it a deeper sound.' He called it 'jungle drums.' 'That's my sound. It just happens to complement somebody like Johnny Thunders.'"

Lesley felt that Jerry was battling himself—he longed to be with an attractive, educated, intelligent, upwardly mobile, well-connected, and cultured woman, like Lesley. She had a life and prestige he felt he could have had if the Dolls hadn't fallen apart and if he wasn't a heroin addict. "But if you have a girlfriend who's too straight, then you're gonna lose her. The worlds are too different. So it's like this push and pull . . . and so then you've got to somehow introduce her to your world." The world Jerry introduced Lesley to was heroin.

Like many young people, Lesley tried recreational drugs, but never to the point of addiction, and never intravenously. "So Jerry's sitting there. He's got his dope and he says, 'Do you really want to do some of this now?' He's kind of laughing, kind of smiling, and kind of looking out of the corner of his eye. 'Now I don't want you to do this . . . but, if you're gonna do this I've got to be the only person who does this with you.' And I was like, 'Well, I don't know, well . . . yes, yes, yes, I want!' and he said, 'Are you sure? Well, I don't want you to do this, so I'm just going to do this, this one time . . . because I want you to know what this is like and that's all. You have to promise me it's just going to be one time,' at the same time . . . laughing. You could see he was getting a secret kick out of this but at the same time . . . he knew it was really, really, really, really wrong."

Lesley admits she was naive about Jerry's heroin addiction. "Of course, I thought I could be a good influence on him. I remember thinking, 'Wow, this is not just like I've got a cool boyfriend and he's in trouble with the police' or something. He was a person who was really trapped by who he was and the circumstances of how he grew up and his environment. He was very crippled with so many things, and I think that he didn't know how to break out of that."

Jerry rarely let people see his more vulnerable side, but Lesley saw it firsthand. One warm afternoon as she was getting ready for work, something gave her pause. "I asked him if he felt sad or happy about something, and he said, 'I have no real feelings anymore. The drugs take all of that away.' He said, 'I haven't had real feelings for a long time. I don't know what they are anymore. If I want to feel up I shoot some coke. If I want to turn down I do some dope or sometimes . . . a speedball. . . . My emotions are regulated.'"

Lesley was stunned. "And he said that so sadly and it was so poignant. It was so horrible and I didn't even know what to say to him. And that was the thing with Jerry. . . . It would be like you were in a psychiatrist's office. He would say something like that and you'd think, 'Oh my God. How is he so sharp, and so spot-on, and so clear and horrifying in his brilliance?' I thought what he was saying was that he was just lost. He was trapped in some kind of netherworld that he could not get out of. I had this feeling when he talked about it, he could see people and people could see him but he was living in a glass tomb where people couldn't get to him and he couldn't get out. . . .

"I can't remember what I did. You can't say, 'Oh, it will be better.' You can't give them any kind of empathy or sympathy . . . because he's talking about something that is so frightening I can't even imagine thinking about this. But he's describing his life to me. It was one of the few times in my life that I saw a lost soul. He hated himself and so he dulled himself. Poor, poor Jerry. He was so lost."

* * *

ALTHOUGH ONLY THIRTY-THREE, JERRY WAS FEELING OLD AND over the hill. "When we used to talk about things, it would never be about the future. It was always about the past, which he'd talk very deeply about. Jerry used to relive his glory days a lot. He was in his early thirties but he talked like he was seventy."

Jerry took a gig with Joy Ryder and Avis Davis, a Max's band with a single, titled "No More Nukes!!!," that was garnering attention from the anti-nuclear-power movement. Its release coincided with concerts held at Madison Square Garden from September 19 through 23, featuring Bruce Springsteen; Tom Petty and the Heartbreakers; Jackson Browne; Carly Simon; James Taylor; Crosby, Stills and Nash; and the Doobie Brothers. The group performed at an associated rally that was held in Battery Park on September 23, which drew a crowd of over 200,000 people. They performed the song again at a Rock Against Racism event at Kent State University in Ohio, where Jerry joined them on drums.

Joy recalled, "He said he was off the dope and was on methadone and could travel. In the van on the way to Ohio, he downed his entire dosage." When they arrived at the gig, there were no drums there as promised. "Luckily, there was a fan who heard that 'Jerry from the Dolls' was going to be on drums. He was waiting at the sound check, and when he realized there were no drums, he said, 'No problem: I've got a set of pink drums, just like Jerry.'"

Jerry lucked out with equipment, but his addiction was making things difficult. "Now Jerry started getting sick. We get through the show, and some more Jerry fans took him out to cop. Later at the hotel, Jerry has eyes like a reptile. He's high as a kite. We finally all get to sit down and chat. Jerry lights up a cigarette and turns to me and says, 'So, what's a 'mook?' Avis says, "What do you mean"? Jerry says, 'You know, your song, 'No More Mooks.' What's a mook?'"

* * *

LEEE BLACK CHILDERS WAS IN LA MANAGING LEVI AND THE Rockats, a band of mostly British teddy boys he'd met while in England with the Heartbreakers. They were barely twenty years old, with movie-star looks and style aplenty, making up for their lack of musical skills.

Even without a record deal, they'd appeared on *The Merv Griffin Show*, Wolfman Jack's *Midnight Special*, the cover of the *LA Weekly*, and the *Sunday Times* calendar. They were on the brink of success, but their drummer had chosen to move on.

Johnny Thunders had recently relocated to Detroit to start a new band called Gang War with former MC5 guitarist Wayne Kramer. There would be no more rent gigs with the Heartbreakers. The Rockats needed Jerry, and he needed them.

The core of the band was lead singer Levi Dexter, tattooed stand-up-bass player Smutty Smiff, and lead guitarist Dibbs Preston. Jerry knew the boys mostly from hanging around Heartbreakers shows. They'd been exposed to the Heartbreakers' unsavory ways, but Dibbs playing methadone courier was the closest any of them had ever gotten to heroin.

Leee first met them when he and Gail made their nightly rounds in search of cute boys, becoming fascinated by the teddy boy subculture that worshipped '50s rock 'n' roll—they were old enough to recall when the music was new! Teddy boys, or "teds" (the name was short for "Edwardian," which was the style of clothing they wore), worshipped Eddie Cochran, Gene Vincent, Little Richard, Carl Perkins, Jerry Lee Lewis, and pre-army Elvis Presley, and prided themselves on digging up rare B sides and obscure tracks from the likes of Sleepy LaBeef, Billy Lee Riley, Charlie Feathers, or Hank Mizell.

Leee's vision was for the band to be an updated, exaggerated version of rockabilly, with the glamour of the New York Dolls and the raw urgency of punk. Leee knew from watching young bands at CBGB and the Roxy that it didn't matter if they couldn't play. With help from Johnny Thunders, who taught Dibbs a rudimentary Chuck Berry riff, and Billy Rath, who taught Smutty the basic elements of rock 'n' roll bass playing, Levi and the Rockats were born. Jerry ignored the whole process, disdaining anything that Leee held in high regard.

Leee got them into the punk scene, which was quite a feat, as the older teds and the new punks fought each other just like mods and rockers did in the '60s. They played on bills with Siouxsie and the Banshees, and Adam and the Ants, and even did a duet and a short tour with Wayne County.

They decided that greater opportunities could be found in the United States. After helping Leee break into the recently dissolved Track Records' offices to retrieve the Heartbreakers' master tapes, they made their way over, Levi arriving in the spring of '78, and Dibbs and Smutty soon after.

After a U.S. debut at Max's, opening for the Cramps on November 10, 1978, the band settled in LA. Based out of the Tropicana Motel, the first lineup had Americans Dean Thomas on drums and Guy Hemmer on second guitar. They quickly became part of the local punk scene, befriending bands like X, the Blasters, and the Go-Go's; locals like Tom Waits and Rickie Lee Jones; and visitors like Stiv Bators from the Dead Boys. Leee got them on television, in the press, and on the *Louisiana Hayride* in July of 1979, as the first rock 'n' roll band to play on the show since Elvis twenty-five years before.

In the fall, Dean quit and the search for a replacement began. Dibbs, Levi, and Smut all agreed that Jerry was the guy to call. Recalled Dibbs, "He could play swing music, he loved '50s music, and he liked the guys." To the band, it was a marriage made in heaven. To Leee, it was a trip back to hell.

Dibbs had thought Leee would be happy to have a seasoned pro like Jerry help guide them toward competency. But after working with Jerry in the Heartbreakers, Leee was aghast. "I begged them not to take Jerry. He was a horrible junkie, and I had managed to keep the Rockats off of hard drugs. It wasn't enough that Jerry was a junkie, but everyone around him had to be a junkie too. That was just his modus operandi."

Leee's opposition just hardened the band's resolve. Leee swallowed his pride and made the call. Jerry accepted. "He was a good drummer, and we needed one desperately to keep working," said Leee, "so I gave him really strict rules, which I knew he wouldn't follow." Jerry had to stay on methadone, and under no circumstance could he use heroin around the band or involve them in any way with his drug use. "He was on methadone, which means nothing to nearly all junkies. It just means more drugs. It's the biggest scam in the world. I think a junkie thought up methadone." Leee still had to get up early in the morning to get Jerry his dose, "which he would take either before or after he took his heroin."

The band loved him. Smutty Smiff: "He liked rockabilly, and he definitely adopted the look. He was an amazing dresser, and he had amazing style." As for his playing, "Jerry just had a certain feel to the way he played drums. The way he could swing, and the way he'd use the toms . . ." Dibbs agreed. "He made Levi and the Rockats sound fantastic. Having someone like Jerry . . . sitting behind you, it's going to push you. It's going to propel you. We were a better band for it."

Audience members, such as the Dolls' old friend from Florida, Jim Marshall, agreed: "I remember seeing them before Jerry . . . and they were okay, but they were really more like . . . a pretty-boy kind of thing. With Jerry in the band, they were actually a rock 'n' roll band."

ASK ME NO QUESTIONS

Their first gigs in New York with Jerry were in the fall of 1979, including a three-night stand at CBGB October 25 through 27. Recordings from these performances show Jerry very determined and disciplined, holding the band together with the simplicity the songs called for, but adding a bit of Dolls-like fury when it was called for. But his discipline was in regard to music only.

Leee Childers: "We were playing this little place way downtown, and it was already sold out . . . and he announced like twenty minutes before showtime that he had no drums at all." Jerry had sold his drums. "Fortunately, we were in New York. I was calling everybody up to see if we could borrow drums, and I called Jimmy Destri from Blondie. He said, 'My girlfriend's got drums.' So we got in the taxi [and] got her drums. They were Jerry's drums! The candypink drums!"

But the band drew big crowds, with Peter Crowley recalling that their shows at Max's "tore the house down, and sold almost as many tickets as the Heartbreakers." Plus, in comparison to the Heartbreakers, "they had a somewhat more wholesome crowd."

By the time the band got back to Los Angeles, Jerry was causing problems. Per Leee, "It was the usual trouble with Jerry: disrupting, wanting to take over, wanting to run the band. . . . He couldn't be happy ever, musically. There are always arguments with bands, but these were Jerry arguments, based on nothing." Leee felt that if left to his own devices, Jerry would have turned them into "the Jerry Nolan Five." Jerry also endlessly pestered Leee for money. "Those were horrible times."

Leee and Levi were tight. "Leee always took Levi's side, as opposed to [that of] the rest of the band members," said Levi's ex-wife Pleasant Gehman. "That made it difficult for other people." Dibbs and Smutty noticed, but Jerry egged them on.

It finally came to a head at the Whisky a Go Go in November. In a surprise move, Levi announced onstage that this was the last Levi and the Rockats show . . . ever. "We had this huge fight in the dressing room," recalled Smutty. "I threw a whiskey bottle at Leee."

The band thought it was all over. There was no reason to think otherwise. But Jerry had other ideas.

LONELY PLANET BOY

17

THERE WERE GIGS STILL BOOKED FOR LEVI AND THE ROCKATS, which everyone assumed would be canceled. Jerry didn't see it that way. His plan was to show up at the remaining gigs, with Dibbs taking on lead vocals. Smutty: "If the promoter asked, 'Where's Levi?' we'd say, 'Who's Levi?'" Jerry instructed the band to insist it was like Derek and the Dominos, who never had any band member named Derek.

The Levi-less Rockats played the gigs at the Temple Beautiful, an old Jewish synagogue right next door to cult leader Jim Jones's temple, and went over like gangbusters, gaining enough confidence to continue. Now they would just be called the Rockats.

They decided that Dibbs would be the lead vocalist exclusively, and they'd find another guitarist. Jerry recommended a New Yorker via New Jersey named Barry Ryan who played in the Victims, a Max's band who'd opened some of the Sid Vicious shows.

While Jerry was still in LA, the October 15, 1979, edition of *New York* magazine featured Lesley on the cover under the headline "The Last Word on Punk . . . We Hope." Per Lesley, the article inside "compressed time, exaggerated the truth, and made up quite a few things . . . Docu-fiction. Jerry hated that article because it referred to his drug habit. I just thought it was embarrassing." Still, Lesley's status as a cover girl added to her coolness quotient in New York.

The Rockats decided they'd had enough of LA and moved to New York. Smutty, who was now engaged to Gail Higgins, moved in with her in Greenwich Village. Barry returned to his East Village apartment. Jerry moved back in with Lesley, where he promised Dibbs a couch to sleep on. As for Guy, he'd seen enough, and declined. Florida transplant Tim Scott McConnell agreed to take over Guy's spot, and the lineup was set. An early-January two-night stand at CBGB was the debut of the new band.

In the center of the stage was a simple, baby-pink drum kit. With its oversize hanging tom-tom set up for a left-handed drummer, it was unmistakably Jerry Nolan's. His Dolls Ludwig kit was long gone, and one of his Heartbreakers' Premier kits had been sold to Laura Davis of the Student Teachers. This pink Premier kit was the second one purchased when the Heartbreakers got signed to Track.

While waiting for the band to go on, Lesley spoke with a slim brunette who'd been talking to Jerry, discovering that she'd recently published a controversial book titled *Defector's Mistress*.

Judy Taylor Chavez's occupation was one of the oldest: prostitute. She'd written the book about her experiences with a client who became the highest-ranking Soviet official ever to defect to the U.S.—an undersecretary general of the UN, and a key figure in strategic arms limitation treaty negotiations. As he was paid to be a CIA mole, she was, in a very direct sense, being paid by the CIA to service him on a regular basis, with payments totaling over $40,000 in cash, plus designer clothing and expensive jewelry.

Judy also liked drugs, particularly before she "worked," often smoking opium to psych herself up for tricking. Lesley found her intriguing, "the combination of self-assurance and the expensive attitude that she wore."

The equipment got its last check before the band came onstage. Jerry inspected the drum setup himself. There was no curtain in front of CB's stage, so all preparations were done for everyone to see. In his pink two-piece suit with baggy pants, black shirt, thin white knit tie, pinky ring, and perfectly styled blond post-punk pompadour, Jerry looked like a Lower East Side, punk rock version of Elvis. His white pointed shoes may have been scuffed, and the tip of his tie may have been tattered, but his was a dog-eared chic all its own.

Like CBGB, Jerry was struggling to recapture some glimmer of his past glories. He'd first played there almost five years before, and here he was, still paying his dues. So many, in fact, that he'd remark to anyone who would listen, "Sometimes I think I'm not only paying my own dues, but some other motherfucker's." Lesley: "He knew in his heart of hearts that the Dolls were his big shot."

The show opened with a cover of Billy Harlan's 1958 rarity "I Wanna Bop." Only grizzled collectors or British teddy boys would have known it. It began with a simple drumbeat. Head down, body swaying back and forth, Jerry exuded a hipness that the rest of the band aspired to. It was a simple song, but Jerry owned it.

Jerry brought a maturity to the band's playing that they'd never had. With Buddy Bowzer as the occasional guest on sax, the group was improving musically. Everyone could sense they were far more than just a pretty boy band.

At home, Lesley wondered what Jerry was up to when he'd disappear for hours at a time. Sometimes he'd be with a guitarist who lived on West Broadway who called himself Angel Elektra and played with a band called the Nothing. They spent their time taking drugs or figuring out how to acquire them. Other times he'd hang out at Smutty's apartment while Gail was at work and Smutty went off to his job at a rehearsal studio. Per Smutty, if Jerry had been out all night, he'd shower, borrow some clothes, and make his way over to the methadone clinic. "Then . . . he'd come back with Johnny and Walter and they would all hang out . . . while I was at work, shoot up and then leave."

Barry lived with his fiancé, Maryanne, in a loft on Second Avenue, right behind CBGB. Jerry also spent time there. "I'd go into my closet and a shirt would be gone. When I went back to see if that shirt was back, I'd see on the sleeve there was all these little round blood spots from where he'd been shooting up."

* * *

JOHNNY THUNDERS'S PARTNERSHIP WITH WAYNE KRAMER HAD crumbled, Johnny's junkie capers and ego pushing Wayne past his limit. Johnny returned to New York, and Jerry started playing with him whenever possible. Jerry was behind the drums again for another set of Max's Kansas City rent parties with the Heartbreakers.

Barry's brother and Rockat roadie Kevin Ryan also worked for the Heartbreakers, and found there was usually more work to do before the show than during. "You couldn't do anything until they went and copped. So, we would be in a car after the sound check . . . and we'd drive down to Eighth Street and Avenue C. Once they copped, they were fine." Johnny would often get advances from Tommy Dean and neglect to tell anyone, leaving everyone short at the end of the night. But Jerry caught on quickly, sometimes getting an advance before Johnny. He'd always find a way to pay the roadies early in the night, knowing Johnny might spend whatever was left between sets.

Jerry was behind the drums for several Heartbreakers shows at Max's the weekend of his thirty-fourth birthday, May 6. They were joined by Pretenders lead singer Chrissie Hynde, whose first album hit number one in the UK and number nine in the US that same year. After drunkenly reminding the audience that it was Jerry's birthday, she joined Johnny in an impromptu version of "Happy Birthday," adding, "Can we hear it for the best rock 'n' roll drummer in rock 'n' roll today"? A few seconds later, she chided the nonplussed crowd. "You assholes don't even know what a drummer is!"

Lesley and her friend Felice Mayhem[1] waited at 242 Mott Street to give Jerry his birthday present: a bag of thirty brand-new syringes Felice had stolen from her pharmacy job. Lesley and Jerry first met Felice when Dibbs brought her to Mott Street after a Rockats show for a sexual tryst. Lesley surprised the couple and found Dibbs looking "kind of sheepish. I went into the bedroom and there was . . . Felice. Jerry walked in and he looked at her and he just smiled at me." Jerry could tell that she was of mixed race. "He walked into the kitchen and said, 'That girl's a shine.' He would say things like somebody's a 'shine' or a 'heeb' or a 'gook' and I would think, 'My God, this guy belongs in the Ku Klux Klan.' It wasn't like he was deeply prejudiced, but he wasn't saying them ironically. Those were just the words that he used that probably he grew up with. He thought Felice was fine. It was just this weird dichotomy, and I always put it down to the fact that he grew up in a working-class environment."

Jerry's racist and homophobic side also surfaced after Lesley met the Godfather of Soul. "I had just met James Brown for some *Soho News* article and I was telling Jerry how incredibly cool [he] was. If I ever said I found some guy cool or sexy or good looking, Jerry had this immediate knee-jerk response: 'Oh, that guy's a fuckin' fag!'" Jerry's response was predictable. "He told me James Brown was a 'fag.'"

* * *

THE ROCKATS WERE GAINING ATTENTION, BUT THE BETTER MONEY came from the Heartbreakers' rent gigs. Regardless of who Jerry played with, Lesley would see Judy Chavez. "She always happened to be around. She obviously had cash, which was of course a magnet for Jerry." Lesley was puzzled by the whole relationship. "They were definitely up to something I wasn't a part of." What they were up to was taking drugs.

Jerry could manipulate women, and Judy was no different than the others. Angel Elektra recalled that she would "split for two to three weeks at a time, and she would give Jerry the keys to the house [and] to her jewelry box. This was the deal: Take whatever jewelry you want to maintain yourself, and just leave the pawn slip behind."

Judy's literary agent was Lucianne Goldberg, who besides representing authors Kitty Kelley and O. J. Simpson trial detective Mark Fuhrman is probably best known as the person who advised Linda Tripp to record her telephone conversations with White House intern Monica Lewinsky as they discussed the latter's sexual dalliances with then-president Bill Clinton. Goldberg confirmed that Judy engaged in many "adventures," after the book was published, including a stint where "she had rented a nurse's uniform and was pushing the Getty kid's wheelchair. The one whose ear was cut off." There was also "heroin, yes lots. Nearly died. Mossad agent/boyfriend saved her."

Lesley had always known Jerry was a junkie. What she had yet to realize was how desperate he would get, and what that desperation would lead to.

Lesley was very open with Jerry, believing her honesty would be returned. When Jerry needed money, she'd give him money. When he had money after a rent gig, he'd contribute. But when she didn't have cash, she decided to show him how much she trusted him by letting him use her ATM card. "It was like he'd hit a gold mine." She told him to take fifty dollars, and he did, confirming it the next day. But in time, she realized, "thousands of dollars were gone."

Between whatever secrets he withheld about his relationship with Judy Chavez, and now the missing money, she'd had enough. Lesley left work and headed over to Mott Street to confront him. "Jerry came to the door . . . and he smiled. He said, 'Hey, hi,' and I slapped him across the face. I said, 'You know what this is about. I've got to go back to work for a couple of hours and when I come back I want you to be gone.' He looked at me with kind of shock and also almost with hatred. I hadn't seen that look on his face before, and I left. I remember I was shaking. I was like, 'Oh my God, oh my God! Why am I doing this? Why?' And I came back probably three hours later and he was gone. And then of course I cried . . . and I said, 'Why did I do that?' That was the last time I saw him for a few years."

"Jerry always had girls," said Stuboy Wylder. "He really treated them badly. He would just move in with these girls and steal their money. I remember him coming to my house with a lot of money and being afraid to go back because, as he would say, 'I've been a baaad boy. I emptied another pocketbook.'"

Upon reflection, Lesley thought that "Jerry was incapable of love. . . . You cannot love someone if you don't love yourself and Jerry did not love himself. He had lost himself and respect for himself and I think that was why outward appearances and his facade were so important for him. Jerry was disappointed in himself, but he had certain survival mechanisms to cover it up." Leee said that unlike Johnny, Jerry would never admit to a lie. And Lesley knew why: "Because the facade would crumble. It was really hard to get to know Jerry. He never showed anything. And all girls come to a realization that it's not just enough to love someone if you don't get a return on it. But I needed concrete excuses and I had them."

As for the Rockats, Keith Rawls, who'd been booking a new club in New York called Heat, saw them and realized their potential. He'd previously worked for the William Morris Agency, but, fearing he'd never be more than a small cog in a giant wheel, had decided to strike out on his own. He attempted to manage Gang War, but the usual Johnny Thunders issues surfaced. Johnny "was just a complete . . . catastrophe. Jerry was nothing like that."

Keith immediately set to getting the band on the road, and establishing them as a live act. But he faced another hurdle: Jerry had hepatitis and needed someplace to live and recover. Keith contacted Jerry's old girlfriend Michelle Piza with his tale of woe. Still fond of Jerry, she let him stay with her and nursed him back to health, but promptly caught his malady herself. "It was horrible. I didn't care if I ever saw or heard from Jerry again."

Relatively healthy (or just lucky to be alive), Jerry was now ready to go on the road, but the Rockats were a band with no record deal, just starting to make a go of it on the New Wave/punk rock circuit outside of New York. It was going to be a hard slog, and except for the short stint Dibbs and Smutty did in Europe opening for Wayne County in '78, none of the band outside of Jerry had ever done any real touring. Keith bought the band a station wagon with a trailer to carry the equipment. The band was excited to finally go on the road. But Jerry was resentful that Keith hadn't found him a permanent home. Barry remembered, "I said to Jerry, 'Wow, man. Did you see this station wagon?' He goes, 'Oh, yeah, really nice. When I need a place to live, Keith goes out and spends money on a car.'"

The Rockats drew fans across the country. Their underground reputation, a rising interest in rockabilly, and Jerry's résumé had people interested. "Jerry brought new fans to see the band, but his habit was a lot for everyone to deal with on the road," recalled Kevin. As Leee had learned during his time with the Heartbreakers, getting Jerry his regular dose of methadone was a challenge. "But it was the only way he could hit the road," said Keith.

Before going on tour, Kevin had to sit down with Jerry's drug counselor and work out a plan to get him methadone in every city they'd hit. Kevin: "We were calling Detroit, Chicago, Minneapolis, that whole swing that we always did. It put a big strain on the band because we would have to pack up after every show and get to the next town because the methadone clinics are only open early in the morning."

If Jerry thought there was a chance that the band wouldn't get into the next city in time to get his dose, he would panic. Kevin recalled their vehicle breaking down between two cities. "Jerry gets out of the car while we're calling for a tow, and he starts hitchhiking. And he'd have a pink shirt on with these [pleated] pants: the rockabilly stuff. People passing by, blowing the horn . . ."

While Keith asserted that Jerry was always punctual, Smutty's recollections were different. As far as he could see, "Jerry didn't care about anything at all except for getting high. He was always late. He never cared about anyone else's time or anyone."

But Jerry's years of experience and street smarts sometimes paid off, especially in fly-by-night clubs that tried to stiff the band on their fee. Smutty: "Jerry would make sure that we got paid every nickel that the club owed us." If a club owner, or anyone for that matter, started to give Jerry a hard time, he'd come right back at them. "'I play the fucking drums . . . for you and your club, and . . . people pay to get into your club to buy drinks, to see me play drums. Now, get out of my fuckin' face.' He'd say that to anyone that got in his way."

Kevin saw a more relaxed side of Jerry on the road. "He did not complain about riding in that car. It wasn't comfortable. It was hot, stinky, the rides were long. But I don't ever remember him complaining about any of that, so long as he had his methadone or was able to get high. After that, everything else was like nothing to him."

As in his other bands, Jerry imparted styling ideas and offered haircuts to all. Dibbs: "Jerry cut the best quiff. Style-wise, he helped us a lot. No matter where he was going, what he was doing, he always looked good. He'd spend hours getting ready before he left."

Jerry's idiosyncratic ways of speaking would keep the guys in stitches. He described their hairstyles as "dimensionalized." One phrase he liked to use that made them all laugh was "the judge and the jury." Smutty: "If someone was disagreeing . . . like he didn't want to drive him across town to get some coke, he would be like, 'That motherfucker. Who's he to be the judge and the jury? Who's he to know my life and what I need and what I want?' We'd all laugh because it was always the same shit." They all knew it was Jerry's justification for his addiction, but there was some truth to it. No one else knew what he had to endure.

As the Rockats made their way down south, Jerry became more of a concern. The band was getting press everywhere they went. The crowds were getting bigger, and making their own attempts at '50s styling. "We were really killing people, and it was just an unbelievable scene," Barry recalled. "It seemed like people would call friends in the next city where we were going to and tell them, 'You got to check these guys out.' We could feel this thing building."

But Jerry's habit was jeopardizing their chances for success. Jerry would rip people off for drugs, asking the band to keep the motor running so he could jump in and make a getaway. The band was already annoyed with him from having to leave immediately after each show, passing up all the pretty girls and parties that came with being in a rock 'n' roll band. Kevin remembered, "It put a lot of stress on the band. Yeah, it started to wear."

"One time," said Barry, "we were going to play in Minneapolis the next day. But instead of sleeping at the hotel . . . and getting up and traveling the next day, we had to split right from the gig so we could get his methadone at the clinic at six thirty in the morning. When we got there, he wanted to look clean. He changed clothes and one of our roadies . . . picked up his pants . . . and some works fell out of the pocket. That's when we realized that it was not a good thing, him traveling around with a rock 'n' roll band. We had to confront him about it. He was a little pissed off because he thought, 'Well, some people smoke pot.' He tried to compare it to that."

* * *

FINALLY, THE END OF THE TOUR WAS IN SIGHT, WITH THE BAND scheduled to play one last show in Atlanta before returning to New York. But in Atlanta they couldn't find a clinic that could commit to providing Jerry with methadone. The band went there on faith that it would work out. But it didn't. Atlanta had enough of their own junkies to worry about and didn't need any more from out of town. They refused to service him.

The band tried to get him some dope, without success. He asked fans where he could cop. Still nothing. Kevin: "It's getting later in the day; we go down to the club . . . and we set up. Jerry doesn't come to the sound check. He's in bed. His teeth are gnashing and chomping."

Barry went back to the hotel and found Jerry in his bed curled up in a fetal position, shaking and shivering. "I'd never seen that before. I realized, man, he's got it and it's really not going to work. He was really sick. He couldn't play. We had to put him on a plane and send him home. The funny thing was, as soon as Jerry heard that we were sending him home, he started to get better."

The band's roadie, Larry Hopp, played drums for the gig. The band got paid and made their way back to New York. But they knew Jerry's days as a Rockat were over.

As word made its way around New York, Leee wasn't surprised. "He was completely caught in his own lifestyle. He wouldn't have known how to try to get himself out of it."

The band found a new drummer and in less than a month, Chris Blackwell from Island Records signed them to a million-dollar deal.

18 TAKE A CHANCE WITH ME

AFTER ATLANTA, THERE WAS NO HIGH DRAMA WITH JERRY AND the Rockats. It was mutually understood that he was no longer a band member. Jerry manufactured a story to save face with his closest pals, Angel and Buddy. Angel was told that Jerry had left the Rockats voluntarily after they refused to allow Angel to join the band on guitar. This was a complete cock-and-bull story: The Rockats knew nothing of Angel. But to Angel, it was proof of Jerry's loyalty, surely to be rewarded with injectables.

Jerry continued to play with Johnny when the money was good. When it wasn't, Johnny would use other local drummers. As the legend of Johnny and Jerry grew, young musicians everywhere were glad to play with them for little or no money, just to share a stage with them, earning the right to tell their friends about the night they lent Jerry Nolan their drum kit, or Johnny Thunders their amp. Some of them worked out well enough to become semi-regular band members. One was a young guitarist from Brooklyn named Luigi Scorcia.

Luigi first met Jerry at Max's on a dead night in the late '70s. "This fucking guy comes in with a leather fucking motorcycle jacket with white on the collar, and orange fucking pants from the 1940s. Zoot suit stuff. This guy had fucking golden hair. I didn't know what Johnny Rotten looked like. I knew he had blond hair. I thought it was Johnny Rotten. No, it was Jerry Nolan."

Like many local struggling musicians at the time, Luigi looked up to the Dolls, and seeing one of them out on the town was eventful. Luigi had seen the Dolls in their heyday and loved that they wore feminine clothing but were still "talkin' tough." When Luigi started playing with Johnny Thunders, Jerry was on drums. Sometimes Luigi would play guitar, but if there was enough money to bring Walter in, Luigi might move over to bass. His versatility and ability to take care of the equipment, drive, and show up on time, made him an asset to Johnny, who possessed none of those skills.

Young Luigi loved being around Johnny and Jerry. Jerry impressed him with his clothing style. "He taught me how to dress. He said, 'Clothes are very important. It gives you an identity. It separates you from everybody else.'"

He appreciated that Jerry, like Arthur Kane, never stole the spotlight, always staying back as a supportive band member. He enjoyed taking in the relationship between Johnny and Jerry. Luigi could tell that the two had "a great mutual respect for one another [and] both cared about one another." Luigi swore that Jerry knew what Johnny was going to do or say beforehand. "Jerry knew Johnny's idiosyncrasies. I'd never seen anything like it."

Johnny, Jerry, and Luigi were now calling themselves La Cosa Nostra, making the Johnny/Jerry gang affiliation Italian-specific for the former Mr. Genzale. At a July 3, 1981, gig at Harpo's in Newport, Rhode Island, the opening act was a band called the Daughters. They would go on to be Johnny's opening or backing band for much of the next two years in New England. The core of the band was guitarist Joe Mazzari and bass player Simon Ritt.

Simon had grown up in central Florida, starting out as a drummer, gravitating toward flashier players with large kits, like Cream's Ginger Baker, the Who's Keith Moon, and Rush's Neil Peart. He soon learned to appreciate drummers who were thinking more about the good of the song, like Ringo or Charlie Watts. "Jerry Nolan fit right into that pattern: a guy who didn't have a zillion drums, knew exactly what to do, and [was] just a real tasteful drummer."

Moving to the Boston area, Simon met local musicians, among them guitarist Joe Mazzari. Coming from Florida, Simon felt that he "had as much chance of meeting Johnny Thunders as [of] being an astronaut. Getting to open for Johnny Thunders and Jerry Nolan, and getting to know Johnny as well as we did . . . this is exactly what I had hoped would happen. It was like my wildest dream kind of came true."

At the Harpo's show, Simon was "enthralled" that Jerry was using his kit, overlooking the fact that this was a money-saving convenience. Both Simon and Joe described Jerry as "dignified," and "distinguished," the polar opposite of Johnny. As the two of them transitioned from opening act to becoming part of Thunders' band, they saw the contrast between Johnny and Jerry more directly. Simon: "When Johnny was hurting or wanted drugs, he was a little guy who made a big noise. Jerry definitely carried himself with more dignity. He was a little smoother, a little more discreet. You never saw him do the crazy Johnny . . . little baby hissy fits over drugs in towns in the middle of nowhere: screaming, yelling, getting into fights. Jerry was a class act."

Still, when Jerry needed drugs, he felt he owed no one an apology. Daughters manager Jim Nestor fronted Jerry a few dollars to get high before a show. Simon: "I remember him deriding Jerry: 'You're not gonna have any money left.' Jerry just kinda grinned and [said], 'I love the good high, what can I tell you? I love drugs.'"

At gigs, Jerry was often quiet, staying a few feet from the others, collecting himself before a show. But onstage, it was a different story. Joe Mazzari: "He could just play so carefree and so in the pocket and so flawlessly and so effortlessly and yet when he wasn't onstage, he always looked like he was a little uncomfortable in his skin."

The fact that he said so little made the few words Jerry spoke more valuable. Simon likened him to Jimmy Miller, producer of arguably the greatest streak of Rolling Stones albums, from 1968's *Beggars Banquet*, through 1972's *Exile on Main St.* Miller, who worked with Johnny in 1982 and '83, also used heroin and, like Jerry, spoke judiciously. "When they did talk you had an interest in listening because it wasn't like someone that blabbers all the time . . . and especially for a young musician, you want to catch every morsel you can. It was kind of like a collage of learning experiences that went on."

While Simon and Joe did an estimated thirty shows with Johnny, they only did six or seven with both Johnny and Jerry. Those shows stood out, even more so if Walter was part of the band. Joe: "People in the crowd, if they had any understanding of . . . rock music and where it came from, really appreciated those two guys on the stage. It was always better than whoever else played."

After a good show, Jerry was never demonstrative. There were no group high-fives. But he'd have a satisfied glow to him. He knew he could still play rock 'n' roll like few others. It was like his relationship with Johnny. "It wasn't arms around each other, 'buddy-buddy,' [or] a lot of sentimentality," recalled Joe. "It was a friendship that seemed based on a lot of familiarity with the past. You could tell they were close."

* * *

BY 1982, JOHNNY HAD A NEW MANAGER, A FORMER GERMAN film producer named Christopher Giercke. Christopher set up a European tour for Johnny starting in Sweden, with a TV appearance on a weekly music show called *Måndagsbörsen*, the day of his arrival, March 22. By this time, like Billy and Walter before him, Luigi was using heroin. Luigi had taken a sabbatical from playing with Johnny to tour Europe with Bo Diddley. "I started getting hooked on drugs in England. When they confronted me . . . Johnny called me a 'junkie.' . . . I'm like 'So what are you guys?' Jerry goes, 'This is my medication' and Johnny goes, 'This is how I get well.' And they had a straight face! But what I got out of this story was that they cared about me."

The band arrived in Stockholm late. Jerry, who felt ill on the flight, passed up the sound check. It was decided that instead of performing live on air, the band would be taped for playback on the following Monday. The official reason was a lighting problem due to the drummer's absence that could only be fixed in editing, post-show. It was suspected that the show producers wanted the chance to edit the performance, knowing there was a risk in letting Johnny's performance go out live. This turned out to be correct.

The four songs played were "Who Needs Girls," (which Johnny introduced as Booker T. and the MGs' "Green Onions"), "In Cold Blood," "Who Do Voodoo," and "Just Another Girl." The previous performers were the British synth-pop group Depeche Mode, who appeared with three synthesizers and a tape machine playing the synthesized drum parts. Their playing was exact, and reflected what was coming out of England into dance clubs at that time. What Johnny, Jerry, and Luigi were about to do was anything but exact, or what the kids were digging.

Johnny's antics were plentiful during his performance: He stops playing and sits at one of the tables in the crowd, peppers improvised lyrics with snarled F-bombs, harangues the crowd between songs, asks them which side they were on during World War II, endlessly fiddles with his amps, asks for help from the very white audience by saying, "There must be a few niggers around," bums cigarettes, and slides down a stage prop and sings the remainder of the set lying down on his side. In a closing display of Yardbirds-style feedback, he finishes the set on his ass, guitar squealing. It was a catastrophic performance that never hit the airwaves but, as ridiculous as it sounds, wasn't much different from his usual antics of audience-baiting, begging for drugs from the stage, or stumbling on as if nodding out from a fix.

Throughout the short set Jerry performs valiantly, playing syncopated Bo Diddley– and New Orleans–style rhythms. Even with the muffled sound on bootleg versions of the show, the listener can tell he is remarkable in his determination, never veering from his path of controlled swing, while Johnny plays the fool. At times Jerry looks at Johnny and shakes his head, trying to stop him from going any further over the edge. It was futile.

Deflated by Johnny's performance, Luigi paired off with a local who'd wrestled her way backstage, bringing along a friend as backup. This friend was a writer for a fanzine called *Heatwave*. When her scheduled interview with Johnny was canceled, she continued tagging along, hoping for an opportunity to get a few words from him. She was barely twenty years old, and her name was Lotten Nedeby, *Lotten* being the Swedish version of "Charlotte," Jerry's mother's name.

"Jerry took an instant liking to me," recalled Charlotte, who stayed late enough to miss her bus home. Jerry offered her a place to stay until morning but she was wary. "I thought he was too old. He was thirty-six. But I had several hours' walk home, and he convinced me that he wouldn't try anything, so finally I agreed to stay over." True to his word, Jerry was a gentleman. "All I got was a hug."

The next morning, Charlotte realized the person she'd spent the night with was Jerry Nolan of the New York Dolls. "I saw the tag on his suitcase. I was a big Dolls fan, but he looked quite different then." They said their farewells, and off the band went to their next gig in Sundsvall, ironically, an anti-drug rally and fund raiser. As would be expected, Johnny played the role of Mr. Bungle, the living example of what not to do. Before they could even get to the gig, they saw the newspapers. Johnny was on the front page, under headlines that read, "A Drugged Human Wreck."

On the flight back to Stockholm, the trio broke into the aircraft's first-aid kit, believing it contained morphine. Finding none, they stole some Valium. Exiting the plane, they were met by police. Admitted a remorseful Luigi, "We were like juvenile delinquents." More headlines followed.

Back in Stockholm, the band stayed at a hotel owned by New York transplant Neon Leon's girlfriend. Luigi: "Johnny hates Neon Leon so he burnt a hole in the rug." The chaos continued when Johnny OD'd and turned blue. Jerry revived him. Another day on tour.

Before moving onto London, Jerry called Charlotte repeatedly. "I wasn't that interested. I was breaking up with a long-term boyfriend at the time, and also had a new one and everything was very complicated. On top of that they were on the front pages again for robbing the medicine cabinet."

Jerry discovered that Charlotte worked at a local nightclub and paid her an unannounced visit. "Both my boyfriends were there and furious.

One even hit me. Jerry just came in looking for me and I took the chance of getting out of there. I spent the night with him and the next day he just rang my doorbell with his suitcase in his hand and asked, 'Can I stay here?' From then on, we stayed together. Already after a week Jerry said he knew he wanted to marry me."

* * *

THERE HAD BEEN NO GIGS FOR OVER THREE WEEKS, AND THEY were running out of money. The UK tour began on April 20.

"I came to the hotel room, the door's locked, [and] the guitars got confiscated. . . . Jerry sits me down and says, 'Luigi, don't worry about it. There's money right around the corner. Someone always bails us out.' Jerry was so positive, and [he] was strung out like the rest of us." The bailout came from an added gig at the Venue in London on April 22. In seat-of-the pants fashion, Thunders recruited Generation X's Tony James on bass and former Rich Kid and Iggy Pop sideman Steve New on guitar, switching Luigi over to third guitar. Tony James: "He came over to our apartment to ask me if I would play onstage with them that very night. . . . Johnny taught me thirty songs that afternoon, but I knew most of them already. I met Jerry later that evening just before the show—Johnny was carried in unconscious to the dressing room."

The band continued playing in England over the next month, with Johnny and Jerry staying at Tony's place in Pindock Mews. Tony loved Jerry, calling him "the sweetest guy," and describing him as a "brilliant, solid drummer. Even better, I get to relive all the stories of the Dolls I'd only read about in the past. We spend hours talking into the night."[1]

Between the May 1 show at the Rock Garden and the May 13 show at the Zigzag Club, Topper Headon left the Clash, reportedly due to his heroin addiction. The remaining members of the Clash were all impressed with Jerry from his days with the Dolls and the Heartbreakers, but never asked him to audition. They contacted their former drummer, Terry Chimes. They knew enough not to replace one junkie with another.

Charlotte visited Jerry in London, staying at Tony's flat. "People were shooting up vodka and anything they could get their hands on," said Tony. Jerry continued talking about marriage.

Working for the Concord booking agency, Charlotte helped the band get more Swedish gigs, the first scheduled for June 4 at the Facade in Göteborg. Johnny arrived late for the flight out of London and immediately pulled a syringe from his hat after taking his seat. Things spiraled downward once the show started. Recalled Tony, "Johnny's opening line is 'You're all whores and I fucked all your mothers.' At that point he slithered down the mike stand and collapsed into the crowd."[2] After insulting the audience some more, Johnny played a song that no band members recognized, before exiting. Tony and Jerry vamped, assuming he'd return. He never did. The audience and promoters were not pleased.

Everyone decided to end the tour and send Johnny back to England. Thunders balked, calling them all ugly names. They got in their vehicle and left him. He ran behind, panting, guitar and clothes clutched under his arms. "We put him on the boat back to England," recalled Charlotte.

Back in Stockholm, Jerry's methadone was running out. It was difficult for a foreigner to get on a Swedish program, but there was a way to circumvent the problem. "Being married would make that process easier." On June 29, 1982, while her parents were away, they married in a side chapel of Gustaf Vasa Church in Stockholm. Charlotte acknowledged she was probably too young to understand the commitment. "But I soon grew into it. I was in love. . . . Jerry was Catholic and very serious about marriage. It got to be a very important commitment for me too. Jerry was a committed, loyal and great husband . . . but he did introduce me to smack."

IT'S NOT ENOUGH

19

JERRY AND CHARLOTTE PLANNED ON RETURNING TO NEW YORK when possible, with the intention of getting Jerry a Swedish residency visa before returning to Stockholm. He could then come and go as he pleased, and get on the country's methadone program. But they needed cash. Jerry needed a gig.

Charlotte had two former boyfriends in a band called Teneriffa Cowboys that needed a drummer. One ex-boyfriend was bass player Saile Eliasson. Besides Saile, there were two guitarists: Bonne Löfman, and another former boyfriend, Michael Thimren.

Once Jerry joined the group, Charlotte was able to book them several gigs throughout Sweden. The band continued to play their original songs while adding Jerry's "Take a Chance with Me." Jerry gave the band input on their arrangements, helping them with English lyrics. "It was a big lift for the group," recalled Michael. "It gave the act style." Saile recalled. "He hit hard but he was really consistent. We started to jell playing together."

The band got higher fees with Jerry in the band, but had to pay him more than the others, which they begrudgingly accepted. Still, Jerry bonded with the guys, telling them his tales of gangs, original rock 'n' rollers, and of course the New York Dolls and the Heartbreakers. Jerry took the lead as band stylist, cutting hair and educating his new bandmates on clothing detail. But there was no education relating to drugs, except by example. Saile: "He's the real reason why I was never interested in drugs. He said, 'I really regret I got into this.'"

Charlotte knew Sanji Tandan from the local Tandan record label. Tandan had put out the first records by Finnish glam-metal band Hanoi Rocks, who looked and sounded like an '80s version of the Dolls. To have a New York Doll on their label was attractive. With Teneriffa Cowboys as his backing band, Jerry sang lead. Together, they recorded "Take a Chance with Me," a cover of Chuck Berry's "Havana Moon," and two newer songs, "Pretty Baby" and "Countdown Love." But what started as an album deal would initially birth only a single, as Sanji grew wary of Jerry's drug use and wanted no continued business relationship. "Havana Moon" wouldn't see release until 1985's *Sword: The Best in Scandinavian Rock* compilation. "Countdown Love" wouldn't see the light of day until 1997, as part of a Johnny/Jerry split single, with Thunders's band also doing a version of the same song.

On September 6, before the single could be released, Jerry and Charlotte returned to New York to clear up Jerry's Swedish immigration status. They would be interviewed to determine whether the marriage was real or a ruse only for Jerry to gain residency.

Charlotte was learning how much time and effort Jerry put into grooming. "He smelled good: Mennen's [*sic*] face conditioner, Murray's hair pomade, Vidal Sassoon shampoo, and Johnson's baby powder." He had a tattoo on his right shoulder of a skull with a bloody syringe in its teeth. "It was ugly . . . and he was always ashamed of it. [He] got it while messed up on alcohol or drugs, woke up and said, 'Oh God, what did I do?'" These details would be helpful during the "marriage interview."

Jerry got the permit. What the couple didn't mention during the interview was that they were now both shooting heroin. Jerry had been an addict since 1974. Now he had a life partner to share his habit with. Charlotte had been using drugs daily since she was twelve, but had never used heroin or injected drugs before meeting Jerry.

Their sixteen-year age difference was cause for some conflict. "I'm not very subservient," said Charlotte. "He liked that, but I also think it was a bit of a struggle for him. He wanted me to be me . . . but it was not always easy for him to let me be me."

Charlotte liked to go out and see bands, but Jerry preferred to stay in and remake thrift-shop clothes, write songs, or draw. "He liked to stay at home and he liked to have people over. He liked to cook dinner for people that he liked—but there weren't that many people he liked."

During this period, a film by Lech Kowalski called *Gringo: Story of a Junkie* was in production, loosely based around the street life of a Lower East Side junkie named John Spacely.

Spacely wore an eye patch, the result of a late-night run-in with some high-heeled transvestites. He was universally disliked as an annoying hustler and conniving junkie, but Kowalski was fascinated by these types. At one point, Kowalski followed Thunders around, filming his daily activities, shooting some of a Mudd Club gig on September 30. Jerry was the drummer that night, with Luigi on bass and Walter on guitar.

Luigi recalled: "I'm the first one there. The people who worked [there] are like 'Here come the buncha fucking junkies. . . .'"

Charlotte got acquainted with all the high and lowlifes that showed up for Thunders's shows on her first trip to New York. "We went to the Mudd Club and went backstage and there was Spacely shooting up like a madman. Jerry and Johnny hated Spacely's guts. He was . . . a real lowlife slime bag."

Johnny's reputation was at a low point in the States. Failure followed him wherever he went: the Dolls, the Heartbreakers, his solo record never getting a stateside release, and Gang War. Drugs made him a four-time loser. He wasn't bringing in the crowds or money he once had. Some only came to his shows hoping to be there the night he finally died onstage.

During the decidedly non-PC "Just Because I'm White," Spacely jumped onstage to play harmonica, which he claimed had been agreed upon beforehand. When Johnny pushed him out of the way to finish the song, Spacely began haranguing him, saying, "Ever since his girlfriend left him for a college student in Michigan, he's been sucking shit." It was a reference to Johnny's wife, Julie, the mother of his two children, who'd left him, taking the kids with her. Spacely exited with a stiff right forearm to Johnny's head. Johnny took off his Gibson and went after Spacely just as the cartoon character Quick Draw McGraw would when inhabiting the guise of his alter ego, El Kabong, making a wholehearted attempt to smash Spacely square on the head with his blond TV Junior. As they wrestled in front of the audience, Jerry came from behind the drums to pull them apart.

Moving back to Sweden with Charlotte, Jerry now had a single to promote, "Take a Chance with Me" b/w "Pretty Baby," which Charlotte sagely parlayed into an endorsement from Ludwig drums. Next, Jerry got a gig producing a local band named Pilsner, recording two songs for a single: "I Refuse," b/w "Sleep with You." Each song is in the style of the Idols: fast but heavy rock bordering on punk. After an initial pressing of a thousand, the record faded into obscurity.

After playing more Swedish shows with Teneriffa Cowboys, Jerry should have been happy, the elder statesman of the band, with free methadone from the government. But he grew bored with the slower pace of life in Sweden and wanted to return to New York.

In late summer of '83, Jerry and Charlotte sold whatever belongings they could and gave up their apartment on Sankt Eriksplan in Stockholm.

With a few thousand dollars and some clothes and guitars, the couple flew into New York on August 6. Jerry had a Gibson Flying V, and a left-handed 1962 sunburst Fender Stratocaster that Nancy Spungen had brought to England back in 1977. Charlotte also owned a 1956 Les Paul Goldtop. They dropped the guitars off at David Johansen's East Seventeenth Street apartment and looked for a bank at which to deposit their cash. The plan was to stay in a cheap hotel before finding work and an apartment.

Charlotte couldn't open a U.S. bank account until her information could be verified in Sweden. As the hotel had no safety-deposit box, they kept all their cash and belongings with them or in their room. In an almost unbelievable series of bad luck, it was all promptly stolen. Jerry then sold the guitars, only to lose the money to a pickpocket on the New York subway system. They were now broke and penniless.

They asked Jerry's old girlfriend Michelle Piza if they could stay at her place, but she refused. Per Charlotte's diary, on Thursday, September 1, they met Lesley Vinson, who agreed that they could stay at her work space. But Lesley recalled no such agreement, and by midnight that same evening, they were walking the streets. They did this for two nights, until Saturday, September 3, when they stayed at the one-bedroom apartment of fashion photographer François Matthys and his wife, graphic artist Sara-Jo.

Jerry flew to France for two shows with Johnny in Paris on September 18 and 19, leaving Charlotte alone with the Matthyses. Sara-Jo was also away when François tried to persuade Charlotte to have sex with his coke dealer in exchange for free product. This brought the stay to an end.

Charlotte fended for herself until Jerry's return on September 20, when a friend of his who owned a clothing store let the pair sleep on the shop's floor several nights. Fortunately, Tony Machine came through, allowing them to stay at his place.

Seeing Jerry in his studio apartment, Tony sensed his sadness. "Jerry would be there . . . with an artist notebook doing different logos of the New York Dolls. I don't think he ever got over the Dolls breaking up."

* * *

BEFORE LEAVING THE MATTHYSES', SIMON SPOKE TO JERRY ABOUT playing some shows. "We talked him into doing a gig in New York at Great Gildersleeves. We called it the 'Jerry Nolan Group.'"

Gildersleeves was a block north of CBGB. It was without character, and so uncool that the only artists who played there were bands just starting out, who had no other choice, or those, like Public Image Ltd. or Elvis Costello, who used it for surprise shows, knowing no one would be there except their most dedicated fans.

On October 7, 1983, the Jerry Nolan Group debuted at Great Gildersleeves, with Simon Ritt on bass and Joe Mazzari on guitar, and Walter joining for a few numbers. Simon recalled, "We weren't anywhere in Jerry's league but . . . it's something about him that he would play with a couple of unknowns just for laughs and for some chump change."

The band made a few hundred dollars each, but it was probably more a moment to remember for Joe and Simon than for Jerry. Still, Jerry's playing was as forceful as ever. The gig was a bit unrehearsed, but everyone made it through in one piece.

Jerry was on methadone, only using heroin when he could afford it. For safety reasons, he wouldn't allow Charlotte to cop alone on the street. Handling that himself, Jerry got busted on Mercer Street near his methadone clinic, held overnight, and sentenced to time served. Once released, he made no life changes.

Charlotte found a job at the Cat Club on East Thirteenth Street, where manager Don Hill let her and Jerry sleep on the basement floor a few nights. It was there they spent Christmas 1983, with a makeshift tree cobbled together from extra lights strewn around the club. They saved up enough money to get a cheap hotel room and finally their own apartment.

The band that played at Great Gildersleeves repeated the show at Boston's Rathskeller on January 28, 1984, with Walter joining for the whole set. Jerry made an impact both on- and offstage. In attendance at the packed show was Boby Bear, drummer for local band the Atlantics. "I just remember sitting with my back to the bar, facing out toward the front door, and in he comes, with a girl on each side of him, with two or three in tow. I remember thinking to myself, 'This guy's forgotten more about cool than any of us will hope to know.' Nobody, and I mean nobody, could wear a hat like that man."

In the UK, Alan Hauser of Jungle Records met with Leee Childers, trying to work out a deal for Levi Dexter's post-Rockats group, Levi and the Ripchords. Leee mentioned that he was in possession of the Heartbreakers' Track Records master tapes, including *D.T.K.*, and *L.A.M.F.*, with its numerous mixes, looking for someone to reissue them. While working out a deal, Leee told Alan, "I just don't want to have anything to do with Jerry Nolan."

At the time, Alan felt unsure about a deal for the Heartbreakers catalogue. "Johnny hadn't been heard of for years. Punk had gone, and everything was New Romantic." But he struck a deal with Leee in April

1982. "We first reissued a live album because we thought, 'Oh, *L.A.M.F.*, no one's interested in that.' So we edited the live *D.T.K.* tapes, and . . . unknown to us, that coincided with Johnny coming back to Europe."

In May of '83, Jungle released the three early Track Records demos as a 12-inch titled *Vintage '77*. In October of '83, Alan met Johnny and his manager Christopher to discuss other possibilities, reaching agreement for Johnny to remix the *L.A.M.F.* tapes with Tony James in the coming year. By the time 1984 had arrived, and Leee had established ownership of the tapes, Leee reached a settlement where he relinquished ownership of *L.A.M.F.* and all other recordings to the group. An agreement was also reached for a Heartbreakers reunion tour, a video recording, and unspecified interest in an album of new material.

In a letter to Jerry and Charlotte dated February 18, 1984, Christopher noted that Johnny's "health and mental stability have really improved to an extent that we can start with some more serious work." Christopher added that Johnny was down to 35 milligrams of methadone per day "and further decreasing," hoping that, "Jerry makes good progress too." Then he laid out what he'd negotiated with Jungle on the band's behalf:

- Each band member became an equal owner of *L.A.M.F.*, with an immediate payment of $450 for each of them.
- A biannual accounting to each band member on sales of *L.A.M.F.* and *D.T.K.*
- U.S. and Japanese licensing availability on both records.
- Possible video shoot of gigs at the Gibus in Paris on March 19 and 20, with $100 a day plus food and accommodations.
- Fifteen booked gigs, plus more still in the planning, at $150 per band member per show plus 10 percent "when we break the guarantee."
- A live album from the Lyceum gig in London on March 25, with additional payments of $600 each.
- For his "efforts in getting the tapes back and having arranged a settlement," Christopher was "asking each member for 2½ points of their 20."

While a new record was never explicitly referred to, the letter states (emphasis by Christopher), "maybe you too have written some *new songs*. Johnny has some 5 or 6 and I hope Walter has some new stuff too." Johnny released several records through the early 1980s that were a mishmash of live performances, demos, and acoustic songs, the last of which were arguably often the most satisfying. The *L.A.M.F.* Heartbreakers, together again and with a newly remixed version of their record, would have the potential to rectify all that had gone wrong back in 1977.

Once all parties met, it was obvious where the lines were drawn.

Alan was warned by Leee that Jerry was a "real nasty, difficult piece of work. When I first met them, Johnny would be quite quiet and enigmatic but occasionally he'd say a few words. Billy was just sort of a genial guy; Walter was friendly, but Jerry was very standoffish and sort of didn't say anything, and just sort of stared around a lot. So I thought, 'Oh, yeah, better be careful of Jerry.' I think it was to do with him being either on heroin or methadone or whatever he was on at the time, because it doesn't make people the most communicative."

Jerry would not sign the documents until he could get back to New York to review them. Walter: "I guess he figured he could hold out and get more. He figured out that we'd need him. Chris Giercke was giving John all these tons of drugs . . . so maybe Jerry wanted more of that or more money?" In the end, Jerry signed the documents.

Alan's role as record company executive evolved into that of banker, financing Johnny and Jerry when they visited London, and medical coordinator, taking them to doctors for their methadone prescriptions. They were now being seen by a posh Harley Street doctor with a psychiatric background, who, after periodic therapy sessions, prescribed them several months' worth of methadone and gave them a certified letter allowing them to legally carry high quantities of the drug.

The band played several shows before the Lyceum show on March 25, with the intention of regaining top form for their first London shows together since 1977. This show was videotaped instead of the Gibus shows referenced in Christopher's letter.

Christopher claimed, Johnny consumed eight large vodkas before staggering onto the Lyceum stage, whereupon he began verbally abusing the audience. Whether it was jet lag, the years of methadone turning him into a zombie, or disgust with Johnny, Jerry's playing was lifeless. His beat was unsure, changing mid-verse and even completely turning around during "Pipeline." Walter's recollection was that "everybody was pretty much strung out."

Walter, who no longer had a second career as a pharmacist, had followed his father, a banker, into the world of finance. Still the most rational of the four, he returned to his day job on Wall Street. The band continued through the spring, playing as a trio or with either Henri Paul or Sylvain joining on second guitar. It became obvious to Jerry that while the tour was supposed to be a Heartbreakers tour, Christopher acted solely in Johnny's best interests. His suspicions were confirmed after he overheard Christopher telling Johnny that he alone was the star, and Jerry was expendable. Jerry didn't forget this.

The negative publicity Johnny received during the Heartbreakers' first visit to Europe in '82 led to April gigs in Sweden being canceled due to work permit issues.

On June 14 and 15 the band, now consisting of Johnny, Jerry, Syl, and Billy, performed on television in Madrid. Their set included "Pipeline," "Just Another Girl," "Great Big Kiss," "These Boots Are Made for Walking," "Sad Vacation," and "Copycat," with Johnny joining a flamenco guitarist on "You Can't Put Your Arms Around a Memory." The show was uneventful, and the sound universally bad, Syl's guitar being overly percussive and Jerry's drums overly dampened. Still, unlike at the Lyceum gig in March, Jerry, wearing a bolero hat, was more enthusiastic, though unremarkable in his playing.

During a break in the tour, Jerry and Charlotte returned to Sweden but got careless on a domestic flight, assuming they wouldn't be searched. Caught with syringes and a small bag of heroin, Charlotte thought fast on her feet, making up a story about tour managing and holding for the notorious Johnny Thunders. The cops laughed and let her off.

After having personally received a guarantee that Johnny and Jerry no longer used heroin, Syl realized it wasn't so, and left the tour in August. The Heartbreakers continued as a three-piece, with a weeklong residency at the Marquee in London, August 20 through the twenty-fifth. In a stunning reversal, the shows went down a storm. Carol Clerk from *Melody Maker* wrote, "Thunders came back into town to prove that miracles can happen, looking sharp, playing like a devil and making those songs sound like they always should have sounded. He seemed like the most together person in the whole of the Marquee, all five nights. The eyes alert, the posture confident, the authority re-established . . ."[1] Even Jerry's "Countdown Love" came in for a compliment, being referred to as a song that "rocked and rolled with similar conviction."[2]

Jerry took some credit for Johnny's success but apparently felt no appreciation from Christopher or Johnny. A few days later in Manchester, Christopher was beside himself, struggling to stay afloat financially while band members were using drugs. Trying to get record company interest, he needed the band to avoid behavior that would get in the way of rebuilding their deeply damaged reputations.

Jerry laid it out for Christopher: "Just pay my salary and air fares and I'll do my job to the best of my abilities,"[3]. Charlotte recalled that "Christopher was always on a mission to get Johnny clean . . . be normal, [and] straighten up. I think he thought of Jerry as a bad influence. He wanted to have really straight people around Johnny. Of course, [Jerry and Johnny] were a bad influence on each other."

Christopher's attempt at choreographing the reincarnation of Johnny Thunders was taking hold. Johnny told the press that his days as a drug addict were over. An October return to the Lyceum was a sell-out. Johnny's biographer Nina Antonia recalled it this way: "In Paris and in London, in the mid-'80s they were so big on an underground level . . . the crowds would part for them like the Red Sea when they walked down certain streets. For the last multitude of punk, they were the Kings of Soho."

But Jerry and Billy had seen enough, and quit. Billy had a Swedish girlfriend, and decided to stay and produce bands. Jerry had other plans, and they didn't include Johnny Thunders.

PRIVATE
20 WORLD

AS 1985 GOT CLOSER, AIDS HAD BECOME A VERY SERIOUS TOPIC.
For high-risk groups—such as intravenous drug users like Jerry and
Charlotte—it made sense to get tested.

Charlotte was nervous when she called in for the results. "They were
putting me on hold for quite a while. Then they came back . . . and said,
'You are negative, but we can't find your husband's results. You're going
to have to call back.' My perception was that we were married, we had
sex, we shared needles, either we would have it, or we wouldn't. So I
called him and I said, 'Oh great, we didn't have it, we're negative!'"

When she called back later to verify Jerry's results, she received a
sobering response. "They said, 'We are sorry . . . your husband is positive.'
So I had to call back Jerry. I felt absolutely horrible. And he was terrified.
His first question was, 'Am I going to die now?'"

Charlotte requested a counseling session from the clinic, who agreed
to see them right away. Charlotte and Jerry understood they would need
to have protected sex and stop sharing needles from here on out. They
had no idea whether they could share a toothbrush, a razor, or even a
bath. They'd once talked of having children. That was now out of the
question. Johnny's girlfriend Susanne had their daughter, Jamie. "He
couldn't do that for me. Things like that . . . they got to him."

Except for Charlotte and his doctor, no one knew about Jerry's illness.
"He wouldn't even tell the dentist," who already knew he had hepatitis C,
and took precautions. Jerry was afraid of being stigmatized, losing their
apartment, facing ridicule, or never getting another gig. He was also
afraid Charlotte would leave him. She did her best to reassure him, but
he felt alone.

Despite his HIV status, Jerry showed no signs of illness, declining
any experimental treatments, fearing the side effects. Per Charlotte, he

said, "'If I start feeling sick . . . I might come see what medicine they have around then, but until then, I just want to live like it's not there.'"

* * *

CHARLOTTE BEGAN WORKING FOR A COMPANY CALLED Scandicore, one of the world's largest poster companies. They printed posters of anything from pinup girls to rock bands to sunsets in Palm Beach. As the art and licensing director, Charlotte traveled the world, meeting with studio executives, band managers, photographers, and artists to acquire rights for posters.

In early 1985 Jerry got a call from Barry and Steve from the Idols. Their current band, the London Cowboys, had records out and gigged regularly. They wanted Jerry to join them for tours of Europe and Japan.

The Cowboys were more middle-of-the-road than the Idols, with a sound more akin to Billy Idol than to punk. Steve Dior described it as "guitar-based, chorus, verse. Nothing 'out there.' It's pretty much what you'd recognize as a rock 'n' roll song." The band had been around since 1980, and had at various times included the Clash's Terry Chimes, Generation X's Tony James, and the Sex Pistols' Glen Matlock. The band for the two legs of this tour included either Glen or Alan D'Alvarez on bass, Hanoi Rocks' Andy McCoy or Gerry Laffy along with Barry on guitars, Steve on vocals, and Jerry on drums.

Since the demise of the Idols, and though they'd once tossed him out of the band, Jerry had grown closer to Barry. In the early '80s Barry lived in New York, working as Peter Crowley's assistant at Max's. This kept him in Jerry's orbit. "I had my girlfriend who was a dealer so that kind of made us closer. I would look out for [Jerry] and I earned his trust."

Having Jerry in the band was a plus, both for his steady drumming and for selling a few extra tickets, but there was a downside. "We had to sort of babysit him. I had to pay for his flight to come over. I had to look after him, which I did and was plenty happy to do. That was part of the gig of having Jerry in a band."

Getting high was still a top priority for Jerry. Barry recalled "a couple of times where he said, 'I can't play,' and we'd have to find something. He was still getting high like crazy. That was the major problem. It never went away."

Jerry's reputation as a drug addict preceded him. Throughout the '80s, scores of major-label artists were aware of Jerry's skills. Their own bands would break up, or they'd start new bands, or their old bands would reform in different incarnations, with different drummers. These bands and artists included John Lydon and his Public Image Ltd.; Chrissie Hynde's Pretenders; the Clash; Mick Jones's Big Audio Dynamite; Generation X and then Billy Idol; Blondie's Debbie Harry; the Ramones; Mink DeVille; Lords of the New Church, formed by Stiv Bators (Dead Boys) and Brian James (the Damned); Iggy Pop; and David Bowie. None of them called Jerry to audition.

In the latter part of 1985, Charlotte gave Scandicore an ultimatum: With so much of her time spent traveling to the states, she wanted an apartment in New York, as well as a guarantee that she could spend as much as three months there annually. She got her way, acquiring a company-paid apartment at 320 East Forty-Ninth Street, near the UN building.

In 1986, Johnny pissed off his road manager, who left with band funds in the dead of night. His band, who thought Johnny had shorted them on cash, threw his clothes out the window of the Chelsea Hotel. His relationship with Susanne was also on the rocks. Christopher also left, leaving Johnny to work out his own problems, both business and personal. Walter offered a final summation of Johnny's relationship with Christopher: "Like millions who had come before and would come after, they always thought they could change Johnny, and they never did. They ended up blowing their money or blowing their lives to try to fit Johnny into the round hole that the square peg would never fit into."

At times like these, Johnny invariably turned to Jerry. Nina Antonia: "If it was the end of Johnny's world, which it was periodically, it was Jerry he'd go to . . . to pour his heart out. Jerry was sort of stoic. He was strong and silent to Johnny's sort of fieriness."

While mouthing off onstage, Johnny gave more than just hints about how he felt about Jerry. During yet another late-'70s rent gig at Max's, Johnny referred to Jerry as "my compadre in chief." At a gig at Irving Plaza in '86, despite Jerry not being behind the drum kit that night, during an extended version of "Gloria," Johnny laid across his speaker cabinet to tell the audience that Johansen was just a "Maynard G. Krebs," but Jerry was a "real friend."

By 1986, Johnny was back in Stockholm trying to repair his relationship with Susanne, and reconnect with Jerry. As Jerry was less social than Charlotte, Johnny often talked with her, telling her about the screw-ups he regretted and how lost he was without Jerry, even saying that he couldn't figure out what to wear without him. Johnny finally came to Jerry asking him to play with him yet again. Jerry made it clear that he was only interested if it was a 50/50 proposition and Charlotte could road-manage. Johnny accepted.

Jerry joined Johnny in London to work on a record that French label owner Marc Zermati and Japanese journalist Gaku Torii were backing, featuring a Japanese rockabilly singer named Jimmy Kurata. The album, called *Trouble Traveller*, was to have been produced by Johnny, but he only managed to produce one side. For those sessions, the core band was Johnny, Jerry, and Glen Matlock. The other side was staffed by Elvis Costello's long-standing drummer Pete Thomas; Bob Andrews on keyboards and Martin Belmont on guitar, both from Graham Parker and the Rumour; with studio bass player Dave Wintour rounding out the group.

During the sessions, Johnny and Jerry fought each other for control. With some sarcastic flair, Glen Matlock recalled an incident: "They set the drums up and got a bit of a sound going and suddenly Thunders said, 'I don't think your drums are sounding too great Jerry. Don't they need some tuning?' 'Tuning? I tuned them in 1973. Why should I tune them again? It's always something with you, you little shit. I'm not doing it!!!' That was the excuse for not doing anything. But it had nothing to do with that. It had something to do with an argument over some girl in 1979 as far as I knew." In another instance, Jerry supposedly hit Johnny with a wine bottle, leaving him whimpering like a child.

The recordings are fine as far as both bands are concerned, although Jerry does sound a little rushed on the beat compared with the Pete Thomas sides. Still, the record was never released in the States, ending up a minor blip on Johnny and Jerry's career screens.

Soon after the recording sessions, Johnny, Jerry, Glen, and guitarist Matt Kellett played London's Dingwalls on May 13. Throughout the set, Johnny was spooked, suspecting the former band members who threw his clothes out the window in New York would be at the show to exact more revenge. Afterward, Matt made a disparaging remark about Johnny. According to Nina Antonia, "Jerry got so pissed with this guy he broke a plant pot over his head."

Jerry wanted Matt out and knew who he wanted in: Barry Jones. A tour was set for July in Japan, September and into October in Australia, plus seven shows in Spain in November.

Barry knew that Johnny didn't want him in the band. "[Johnny] didn't respect either Steve or me just because we were the competition for Jerry. So Jerry talked to him: 'Barry's the guy you need. He's a kick-ass rhythm player.'" Johnny deferred to Jerry, and Barry was in.

Barry was game. "Got to Sweden and [Johnny] was straight. One of the few times he'd actually cleaned up. He was playing great guitar."

Barry loved playing with Jerry. "We would really connect onstage. When it worked, it worked fantastically. [If] he did a little skip beat or some new thing I'd look around at him . . . catch a smile. He always knew I would hear it. Sometimes we would blend so well. It was like I was the bass player almost, the drums and guitar were so in tune."

They played a few warm-up gigs in Sweden before making the trip to Japan. After a respite and two gigs in Italy, it was off to Australia. Barry Jones: "[Jerry] would chuckle like, 'Ike, ike, ike, ike, ike, ike.' He was very happy about something . . . and he goes, 'You're not going to believe this. I'm so fucking jazzed.' Johnny had come to him and said, 'You were right about Barry.' He was really proud to be vindicated."

The band didn't get high in Japan except to smoke Thai stick. It wasn't until they reached Australia that they indulged in anything stronger. Heroin was readily available, and all, except Glen, partook.

Glen was a drinker, making him the odd man out in a band with three junkies. In retrospect, Barry could see how skewed their thinking was. "Johnny and Jerry would call Glen 'the Waiter' because they could not relate to him as an alcoholic, which is really weird, considering that they played with Arthur, who was also an alcoholic. They're going, 'We gotta get another junkie in the band.' They were serious! 'He's an alcoholic. He don't fit.' God, that was so fucking crazy! I loved Glen. I didn't want it to happen. I thought they were very unfair to Glen, who to me was a great bass player . . . and was a great band member."

Glen described his time in the band as being like "a spare prick at a wedding." Jerry tried to get Glen to join in using smack, exhorting him not to be a "party pooper." "Once or twice I did, but it didn't do much for me . . . and I know my limit. If you get involved with that, you want to do even more. I didn't. And I don't like being told what to do."

Some of their flights were eighteen hours long, with lengthy drives in between. The long amount of time on the road took its toll on the band and the crew. Barry: "Got to Australia and the first gig we had, Peter Noble, this Australian promoter, got drunk. . . . We got up a couple hours later to drive to the airport. The guy was still drunk. He rolled the truck. . . ."

Charlotte was there as tour manager, asleep in Jerry's lap when the truck toppled over, leaving him unconscious. Charlotte, Barry, and Glen were thrown from the vehicle but Jerry remained inside. Concerned that it might catch fire, they broke the window to get him out. Glen helped smash it in, inadvertently kicking Jerry in the head. When it was all over, Jerry had a broken right collarbone and Johnny's girlfriend, Susanne, a concussion.

Being left-handed, Jerry used his right hand to hit the snare drum, repeatedly, with great force. Barry recalled, "They strapped his arm to his chest so that he could just move . . . from his elbow down, for the snare drum snap, and they miked up his snare drum loud." Doctors agreed that Jerry could play if he could handle the pain, and the painkillers. With his years of experience playing under the influence of drugs, Jerry never missed a show on the tour.

After a break in Sweden, it was off to Spain, where Johnny got up to his old tricks. The promoter had "heaps" of cocaine, and Johnny went at it with gusto. Barry: "That was probably my most uncomfortable time with them, because Johnny was out of control."

In Barcelona, Johnny wanted a speedball after the show, so the promoter had to get him some heroin to go along with his coke before he would go onstage. Said Barry, "They were pleading, 'After the gig we'll get you anything you want!' And Johnny's like, 'I ain't goin' on till it's here!'" He knew from experience that it's often more difficult to cop after a show. There was a curfew, putting the gig in jeopardy. "I can remember looking at Jerry and Jerry's giving me the 'I don't know, it ain't me' look." Johnny finally got his dope and put it into his pocket, and the band went onstage.

The band were embarrassed by Johnny's unprofessional behavior, but the wait created pent-up energy. "That was the best gig I ever did with them. Incredible. I think three songs in I went over to Jerry [and said], 'I feel like I'm in the Heartbreakers I saw at the Roxy.'"

To add insult to injury, Glen was told he should accept less money than promised. "I had a big row with Jerry about it." Glen got his money, but his relationship with Jerry and Johnny was over. "It was a shame. We didn't really part on the best of terms."

The band now needed a bass player for the U.S. leg of the tour. A call went out to Arthur Kane. John called him with the offer, saying he was sober. Though Johnny had jumped onstage with the Idols a handful of times back in '79, this was the first time Arthur, Johnny, and Jerry would play full sets and travel together since 1975.

Charlotte set up the tour, getting the band reasonable guarantees (from $1,500 up to $4,000 for a Saturday night) and percentages of door receipts, plus a quality backline of equipment. Arthur's wife Babs recalled picking everyone up at LAX. "They were basically sober, although once they hit town, they wanted their drugs."

Everyone rang in the New Year together at the Roxy, where they would play a few nights later.

While the East Coast had Twisted Sister, who finally saw mainstream success, after more than ten years of struggle, in 1984 with "We're Not Going to Take It," LA was now the center of what people were calling "hair metal," a more pop version of heavy metal, with a look and attitude taken off the cover of the first New York Dolls album. Mötley Crüe, Poison, and Ratt were all classified under this moniker, selling truckloads of records while being played around the clock on MTV. They lived life using the New York Dolls, particularly Johnny Thunders, as role models. Jerry dismissed them as unoriginal, saying a few years later: "Everywhere I look I see Johnny clones."[1]

Until the rise of Nirvana and grunge in 1991, almost every glam or hair metal band of the '80s had a Johnny Thunders–like character amongst them. Their hair, makeup, clothing, and drug use were in the extreme. What they didn't have was the originality of Thunders or his unmistakable cat-tail-on-the-third-rail guitar sound, much less the humor and intelligence of Johansen. They all played too well, and moved too much in choreographed, spandex-clad step with each other to matter to anyone over fifteen years old. But admittedly, so did Kiss, perhaps a better role model career-wise.

More streetwise were Guns N' Roses, whose debut album would reach number one by the end of 1987. In time, it would sell over thirty million copies worldwide. In 1986 the band would open some shows for Johnny, and Guns singer Axl Rose was in attendance at the Roxy show on January 4, 1987.

Everyone seemed sober and focused for this gig. The opening number, "Blame It on Mom," was smoking hot. On this night, they were a powerhouse of a band.

Arthur, still the immobile sphinx, played simply but effectively, adding in ascending runs that were never fancy but subtly did their job. Barry chugged along in a punk-meets-Chuck Berry style, underpinning the song with appropriate muscle. Johnny sang in a rough-hewn but on-key growl, primarily playing solos, often with his back to the audience to bare his soul to Jerry, the consummate drummer and the epitome of cool: head bobbing up and down, playing a simple but slightly swinging beat, raising his left hand in the air for an extra flourish for each accent like Krupa, and even throwing in a surprise jazz-inflected hi-hat fill in the last verse.

Throughout the show, Jerry's playing was inspired. He broke out a Stax/Volt four-on-the-floor beat in "Pills," then switched it up with the snare only on the beat of two for a portion. In "Chinese Rocks," he changed up his signature tom-tom part in the chorus to a rockabilly snare drum figure. On Willie Dixon's "I Ain't Superstitious," done Jeff Beck style, Jerry never missed a cut, following Johnny's cues, playing a style of music that no band on the Anarchy tour would have dreamt of attempting except the Heartbreakers. During Jimmy Reed's "Baby What You Want Me to Do," Jerry switched over to a rockabilly, rim-shot style.

But many of their shows had small audiences, and as good as the band was, no major record companies were interested. Babs claimed to have connections at Geffen Records, but they were concerned about Johnny's drug reputation. Mötley Crüe, Quiet Riot, and Guns N' Roses all had issues with hard drug use, and they were all acolytes of the Dolls, but they were never as blatant about it as Johnny and Jerry were. Geffen passed.

By the end of the tour, Johnny and Jerry had fallen out again. Alan Hauser recalled that Jerry wanted them to record an album of new material, but Johnny ended up working with Patti Palladin on the *Copy Cats* album. Charlotte: "There were always people that would come and whisper in Johnny's ear, '. . . you don't need Jerry, take the money yourself and get your solo contract,' and Johnny would."

Jerry felt hurt, and took it personally. Insiders felt Johnny was never as good without Jerry as he could be with him. The recent tour with Arthur and Barry was possibly the best Johnny had sounded since Jerry left the Heartbreakers, and it hurt him that Johnny either didn't see it or refused to acknowledge it. Charlotte knew that Jerry "was pissed off that he didn't get recognition." For Jerry, it was about loyalty again.

Jerry returned to Stockholm with Charlotte and tried to make himself useful. Outside of his daily constitutional to and from the methadone clinic, he had his projects. He would collect small, decorative wooden boxes and organize them into personalized sewing kits, one for threads, another for buttons, another for zippers and snaps, and another for sewing needles and tools. He'd collect stickers of angels, fairies, hot rods, or cowboys, frame his favorites, and store the others in another box. He would paint and draw, updating the Club Gentlemen logo from his teenage social club days in Brooklyn with Peter Criss, or sketch a drumstick striking a cymbal. He read biographies, including Charles White's *The Life and Times of Little Richard* from 1984, and Nick Tosches's 1982 book *Hellfire: The Jerry Lee Lewis Story*, stories of eccentric individuals who were maximum profilers who somehow survived life's ups and downs, outran their internal demons, and came out heroes.

By end of 1987, Charlotte could tell Jerry was itching to play music. She tried to put a band together for him, in the process meeting vocalist Henrik "Hank" Eriksson. Hank had a vague idea of who Jerry was but little idea of what was expected of him. "I was pretty nervous going there. But to me, it was a great opportunity."

In his early twenties, Hank attended film school, "partying a lot and [having] no real direction." When he arrived at the audition, Charlotte did most of the talking, giving a summary of Jerry's life and explaining the idea for the band as "kind of '50s with a punk touch to it." They played a Muddy Waters cover, which Hank recalled was awful. After another song, which "sounded even worse . . . Jerry shrugged and said 'Don't worry about it. It's rock 'n' roll.'"

Jerry liked Hank and decided to work with him. The band name changed from the Ellery Bops, a New York street gang, to the Café Racers, a type of motorcycle. At times they were called the Naturals. Another band member, bass player Peder Andersson, recalled the name Jerry Nolan and the Living Sin. Rounding out the band were two guitarists: Stefan Brändström and Patrick Johanson.

Jerry gave Hank an education in his own school of rock 'n' roll. "Jerry was mostly into '50s stuff: Jerry Lee Lewis, Buddy Holly, and Little Richard. His all-time favorite seemed to be Arthur Alexander. We tried to play "The Girl Who Radiates That Charm" with limited success because of its piano-based structure."

Jerry told Hank that when he couldn't find any song ideas, he should work on his profile. "Black jeans, T-shirts, and boots: That was about all I ever wore. Jerry introduced me to detail. When he showed me a black shirt, that's all I saw. 'Check out the stitching, the buttons here and the way it's cut in the back,' he would say. He was great with the sewing machine and needlework."

Charlotte and Susanne were friendly, but Jerry wasn't speaking to Johnny. Said Hank, "They had no contact whatsoever. 'He crossed me.' 'A conniving S.O.B.,' was all that Jerry had to say."

Hank recalled the band doing a dozen or so gigs. But for Hank, there was more to it. "It wasn't just the music, it was a whole world that opened up with all the stories and anecdotes, this new friendship and the sudden sense of adventure that came of it."

Hank reminisced about Jerry and the importance he gave to loyalty. "He used to say 'A band should be like a fist.' United we stand, divided we fall. A band becomes kind of a family, and family comes first . . . and it fit right in to Jerry's fascination with street gangs."

Hank needed a place to stay, and Jerry and Charlotte let him move into a spare room. In return, Hank helped Jerry out. One time, Charlotte went out of town, leaving Jerry with a pile of flyers to deliver to all the local households. "He sat in the kitchen, piles of paper ads all over the floor. 'I promised Charlotte I'd deliver these,' he said, looking completely miserable. 'Charlotte's coming back tomorrow. What if somebody saw me?' So we waited until dark, hoods over our heads, and worked through most of the night. Some of the papers ended up in the trash, but we were brothers in arms after that."

Jerry's suspicion of any lack of loyalty toward him bordered on paranoia. Although they spoke English, the band also spoke Swedish on occasion. "Once when I told a joke in Swedish and the other guys were laughing, he thought we were scheming behind his back or making fun of him. I felt a little hurt, like he doubted my loyalty to him and to the band."

* * *

IN 1988, DAVID JOHANSEN CAME TO SWEDEN AS HIS LOUNGE lizard–like, pre–rock 'n' roll alter ego Buster Poindexter, riding high on the success of "Hot Hot Hot." He'd become the "responsible" Doll, scoring a minor hit with an Animals medley in 1982 and now, as Buster Poindexter, appeared regularly on the American network TV show *Saturday Night Live.* He'd even appeared on *The Tonight Show Starring Johnny Carson*, as traditional a showbiz program as there ever was.

Jerry's bruised self-esteem got the better of him when David called to invite them to his show. The band had discussed going to New York, and Charlotte and Hank thought it would make good business sense to reconnect with David. "Jerry looked like he was having a panic attack," recalled Hank. Jerry couldn't bring himself to go, claiming to have a migraine. Hank sensed that Jerry was intimidated by David's success and "was scared he'd look like a failure in comparison. He took a handful of Valiums and drifted into oblivion."

Jerry still played with the London Cowboys, which was how he met brothers Pete and Paul Wassif. Paul played guitar in the Cowboys while Pete switched between guitar and bass. When Pete met Jerry, he was twenty-one and Jerry was forty-two. Paul was only twenty-five.

The UK-born Wassifs were the sons of an accomplished Egyptian-born oncologist. Though cultured, they had little fatherly influence, as their dad was focused on his work. Jerry stepped in to fill that void.

Knowing Jerry's history with Sid Vicious, Paul saw a parallel between that and the way Jerry related to his younger brother, Pete. "Jerry had a real soft spot for my brother. He used to say my brother's eyes [were] a lot like Sid's, which used to worry me a bit." Pete wouldn't disagree. "Jerry was always there to bail me out."

When the brothers OD'd after a London nightclub gig, Jerry made sure everyone was safe and got home. When they played a festival in Geneva,

Jerry led Pete to safety when he got too high. Paul: "He was a very strong man. You got the feeling that . . . if you were in danger, Jerry would be the guy who will be happy to wield the baseball bat on your behalf."

Jerry imparted to the Wassifs the same lessons he'd shared with bandmates since the early '70s. Paul: "You were supposed to look good. It wasn't an accident. When people pay to see you play, you put on a proper [show]. None of this falling over shit. You don't look like them. You look like you are supposed to be on the stage. [He] told me, 'That's your role. Your role is "We are the fucking entertainers.""'"

Underneath it all was Jerry's drumming. Pete: "He was the best drummer I ever played with. Not technically, but as far as heart and soul goes, absolutely. He meant what he played. And his energy: unbelievable. Offstage he was like an old man, but behind the kit he was never-ending. It was just infectious the way he would grab the tune by the balls and run with it. Even if he was pissed off."

Paul loved the power of Jerry's playing and his creativity. "If he did a fill, it would come in that place that you wouldn't quite expect it, so it was always refreshing. He would make you laugh with what he played . . . like when a joke comes your way and you don't expect it. Even if it's just like how you open the hi-hat slightly or the bass drum comes a beat after you'd expect it."

In London, if he wasn't staying with Steve in Maida Vale, Jerry would stay at the Wassif family home. Their father never bonded with any of the Wassif brothers' friends, except for Jerry. Pete: "My dad, he'd be up at the crack of dawn and quite regimented about his schedule. I'd come down at like noon and Jerry and my dad would be there. Jerry would get up with him . . . and they'd sit and have these intense talks all morning while I was asleep. They got on like a house on fire." Paul added: "He was an incredibly charming motherfucker."

Jerry fell in love with a Triumph Bonneville motorbike he spied at the Wassifs', a '68 that Pete had remodeled. Broke and owing money to drug dealers, Pete was a highly motivated seller. Jerry convinced Charlotte to buy it. It was shipped over to Sweden and "it sat inside the apartment," recalled Hank. "We only took it out for a drive a couple of times." Jerry knew nothing about driving it and didn't have a license. Having driven a moped, Hank knew the basics. "It was great fun. We were kind of stoned and just drove around the house. Jerry never did get it. He was driving in the first gear the whole time. But mostly we posed and took a lot of cool-looking pictures of us with the bike." Jerry finally had the bike that he'd wanted since he was a boy in Lawton, Oklahoma.

THE KIDS ARE BACK

21

IN THE EARLY SPRING OF 1989, SYL PHONED JERRY, ASKING IF HE'D be interested in starting a new band with him in New York. Johnny was also up for it. As much as Jerry enjoyed playing with the "kids" in Sweden, he missed New York, and the prestige of playing with other Dolls was tempting. He was also looking for a little space from Charlotte. "We weren't in the best place with each other," she recalled. "I was busy a lot . . . and my addiction progressed, which disturbed Jerry a lot. I was trying to lie about not getting high." With fifteen years of experience shooting dope, Jerry couldn't be fooled. But he was no angel either. "He'd go cop and miss a plane, and expect me to bail him out." Charlotte started refusing. In those moments, one person he'd call was Phyllis Stein.

Phyllis, who'd had her relationship with Jerry in 1976 and '77, had been out of the scene since 1979. She'd begun using hard drugs and realized the only way to stop was to remove herself from that environment. In the succeeding years, she became successful in advertising, got married, had a child, and divorced a few years later.

She reconnected with Jerry in early '87 when he played in New York with Johnny, Arthur, and Barry. But she wasn't only bailing Jerry out for airline tickets. "He went to her for money all the time," said Charlotte.

Jerry had a long history of using women, including Charlotte, to get cash. Paul Wassif recalled that one time, in a London hotel, Charlotte left band funds in a safe. Jerry and the Wassifs took it to buy drugs, with no regard for Charlotte. Women were expendable. "It was the twisted addict thing." Paul couldn't excuse what they did except to say, "We were dope fiends."

* * *

BEFORE THE NEW BAND WITH SYL GOT OFF THE GROUND, THE Ellery Bops decided to come to New York. While Jerry was in Sweden,

Hank came and stayed at the Forty-Ninth Street apartment. Two weeks later Jerry arrived. He immediately scored some dope and cocaine, telling Hank, 'I just need to get it out of my system.'

Next came the two guitarists. All they needed now was a bass player and rehearsal space before playing gigs. "Even before the others showed up I realized how insecure Jerry felt about playing New York again. Instead of having Johnny Thunders, Walter Lure, and Billy Rath to lean on, he had three unknown Swedish rookies who didn't know their way around the city." Though broke, Hank was finding ways to get coke, Jerry doing the same with dope. "When the other guys moved in, he started to hang out at Phyllis's place."

Jerry neglected to look for a rehearsal space or a bass player. He and Hank argued about money and drugs. Said Hank, "By now I think he was looking for an out." The band was finished. Hank and Jerry didn't speak for over a year.

Jerry still had the Forty-Ninth Street apartment, and after deciding to play with Syl in their still unnamed band, he asked Pete and Paul to stay with him. Charlotte would pop in and out and, despite her own drug use, was considered the responsible one. Pete recalled, "She kind of put us back in perspective. . . . Then she'd go and we'd completely fuck up again. The kind of shit Charlotte really got sick of."

While Sylvain was no choirboy, Jerry had to keep his addiction under control if they were to play together. Syl recruited Max's veteran Danny Ray on sax, and bass player Graham May, formerly with the Vipers. Syl and Jerry discussed songs before the first rehearsal, which was where Danny and Graham met Jerry for the first time.

Danny recalled rehearsals being productive, "shooting through the old tunes. Jerry played like an animal." Syl and Jerry both thought this could turn into a Dolls reunion. Johnny showed interest, even showing up to a few rehearsals. In the end, Johnny was too out of it, completely forgetting about his conversations with Syl. "He looked like Ratso Rizzo in *Midnight Cowboy* . . . carrying his clothes in a black plastic trash bag,"[1] said Syl. There were efforts to get David involved, but between his Buster Poindexter act and various film gigs, he was doing fine.

The band needed a lead guitarist and Jerry suggested Paul. After a few rehearsals, the band got a regular Friday-night gig at the Continental Divide. There was no cover charge but it was a way to develop a following. Said Graham, "It was really like a pub, and it kind of turned into a club, little dive that it was. But it was in a good location down there on St. Marks, or right around the corner, anyway." The band began a run of thirty-six consecutive Friday nights at the club.

Danny: "It was great. We packed that place and we just tore it up. People would dance on tables and on the bar. We had lots of people sitting in, and it was just a real scene."

One regular at the Continental was Simon Ritt from the Daughters, who'd moved from Boston to Third Street on the Lower East Side, a short walk from the club. Simon recalled, "I would sit as far away from Jerry Nolan as if I was across from him on the subway. It was like my weekly drum lesson. I'd be glued to his hands and to watching him. He was just so smooth and effortless."

Paul recalled that Jerry wanted to call the band Dead Presidents, but Syl won out with Ugly Americans. After one show with only Syl on guitar, Paul joined as lead guitarist. "That night Johnny played with us. Sylvain was wasted. He'd done a bunch of coke . . . so he was rubbish. And Johnny . . . he was pretty messed up. It was one of those moments where I think we were playing 'Pills' and I appeared to be the only one who knew how it went."

Jerry and Paul got high as well, but Paul noticed something unusual about Jerry. "It was . . . the first time I saw it hit him really hard. I don't think Jerry got out of bed for two days afterward."

Coming out of his own two-day bender, Paul realized he needed to get into treatment. He wanted to go to rehab in LA, where Barry Jones was, and asked Jerry to join him. "He wouldn't have it. By then he knew he was ill." When Paul told Jerry he was leaving without him, he thought Jerry would be disappointed. "He wasn't. He gave me a bunch of methadone to take with me." With resignation, all Jerry could say was, "No, I can't run anymore."

Paul recalled Phyllis asking him to stay in New York to get clean so Jerry might consider it too. But Jerry wouldn't commit. "I got clean not long after that, and kept thinking, 'I must get in touch with Jerry.'" Paul never saw him again.

* * *

BEFORE THE UGLY AMERICANS FOUND ANOTHER LEAD GUITARIST, they found a manager. Kipp Elbaum had been a promoter in Phoenix and LA. "Come the end of 1988, I had moved up to North Jersey . . . doing more boxing promotions. I was still doing music stuff when things felt right." When he saw that Jerry and Syl were in a band in a small club he went to check it out. "Here are literally a couple of my heroes. I just loved it."

Kipp went for three Fridays in a row. On the third Friday, he and Syl sat and chatted. "We became friends very quickly. They were looking for some help, and I was looking for a project." Kipp became their manager.

The band still needed a lead guitarist, so Kipp contacted someone he'd known since the fifth grade, Burny White, spelled B-u-r-n-y because his playing "burned." He came to the Continental to meet the band and broke the ice by asking Jerry what he thought of the *L.A.M.F.* remixes. After Jerry confessed he'd never heard them, Burny invited him over for a listening session.

"He came over to my house, and I took him to an AA meeting. His influence was a little more powerful, and I fell off the wagon after a while."

Burny and Syl began writing new songs and added them to the bunch Syl had recently written. They did some Dolls songs, like "Looking for a Kiss," and a few covers to round out the set. Syl's "14th Street Beat," "Kids Are Back," and "Teenage News" were in, along with Jerry's "Countdown Love." Covers included Clarence Frogman Henry's "I Ain't Got No Home," the Standells' "Dirty Water," and the Dave Clark Five's "Glad All Over."

According to Burny, Jerry and Syl made the call on the band's repertoire. "I would play a song, just me and my guitar. . . . They would either say, 'Yeah, okay, we can work with that,' or, 'No, no, that's too Springsteenish,' or, 'Too pretty.' Then we would arrange it. Jerry was really good at arranging. I think he was better than Syl was."

Burny loved Jerry's playing, comparing it to that of James Brown's drummers, who had to abide by Brown's rhythmic theory of hitting it "hard on the 'one.'" "He hit that 'one' perfect, and he never overplayed . . . but when you needed that extra little flash, it was there. He just could feel a song out after playing it one time. The second time, he knew where to put those accents, but he never overplayed those accents. He doesn't look to anybody for cues. He knows the fucking song."

Kipp recalled his struggles as manager. "The money wasn't great, and at that stage in the music scene, it was like pulling teeth." In New York, they could draw as many as four hundred people on a Friday night. "But getting out of the city, it was a little tough."

Kipp booked gigs in upstate New York and in New England college towns. After one of the upstate shows, Burny recalled sitting down with Kipp, Syl, and Jerry. "[Jerry] was being very demanding. [He] said, 'Look, I'm not a rhythm drummer. I'm a lead drummer. My drums should be out front.'" Recalled Kipp, "Nobody wanted it."

Burny reasoned with Jerry. "I was like, 'Jerry, the thing that's always made the mystique of Jerry Nolan is that you're back there behind those drums. . . . Drummers in rock 'n' roll look at you for their licks." To put him on a "'pedestal in front of the band, that would be too much arrogance.

You wouldn't be as respected as you are.' He saw the point." Still Jerry made demands, wanting more money, wondering aloud why they didn't have limousines, a record deal, or better gigs.

Jerry still had methadone from his doctors in Sweden and London but was struggling to get back on a methadone program in New York. He told Charlotte that he missed her, although the lack of methadone was also making him anxious.

He went back to Sweden, but after he spent a short amount of time there in August of '89, Charlotte told Kipp that Jerry wasn't happy and wanted to come back to New York. Kipp arranged for his ticket, with a stop in London to see his methadone doctors. He had his pills, and his official letters giving him permission to possess them, but knowing he had more than the permitted amount, he tried mailing some back to the States. Jerry took a few Valiums before the flight and was loopy enough to call attention to himself. When security began questioning and searching him, they realized that between what he had on his person and the envelope ready for posting, he possessed more methadone than was legally permitted. He was arrested and thrown into prison.

Jerry was remanded to Her Majesty's Prison Lewes, in Sussex, and assigned prisoner number N60476. He called Charlotte, who in turn called Kipp. "I hopped right on a plane with a New York attorney." Jerry wasn't allowed his methadone, which was what he'd feared most, more than being without heroin. While Kipp was working to get him released, Jerry wrote a note to Charlotte, dated September 2, 1989. He claimed to have been lied to by jail officials, and sounded afraid and vulnerable.

Kipp arrived at the prison and "found him literally covered with sores, in a pile of puke, hadn't been washed or cleaned or anything." Alan Hauser saw him as he appeared in front of a judge. "He was visibly shaking in the court, and the judge . . . had to stop proceedings and let him sit down. . . . I think he was five days in there." Kipp got him released, after threatening lawsuits. Jerry told Alan he was "determined to kick the methadone and not go back on it."

Despite being off methadone for five days, he got himself a dose as soon as possible, with Kipp getting him into a program the next day. Jerry was grateful, and never brought up the placement of his drums onstage again.

Back in New York, Syl lived with Jerry for a short while in the Forty-Ninth Street apartment while Charlotte was away. Syl was a single dad, raising his son by himself. "Jerry was really taken by the fact that I had my son. And I think that kind of embarrassed him, because [his son] was put up for adoption. He wasn't really proud of that."

* * *

CHARLOTTE REALIZED HER OWN HEROIN USE WAS BEYOND HER control and chose to get into rehab to survive. But Jerry wouldn't go with her. He thought she could go into rehab, and he would just keep living his life as it was. Perhaps he felt that it was useless, as he was HIV-positive. Still, afraid that Charlotte would leave him for good, he committed to trying Narcotics Anonymous.

Charlotte went into treatment in Stockholm, giving up the New York apartment. Jerry had his methadone program and counseling but still resisted efforts to go into treatment. Said Charlotte, "I tried to get him to go into rehab with Johnny . . . [who] offered to pay for it, but he wouldn't go. He was on his methadone and getting off on other things when he had money or someone turned him on."

Jerry needed somewhere to live. His counselor found him a place in Staten Island. He would come into Manhattan often, which is where he met Greg Allen, a singer and guitarist with a band called Whores of Venice. Friendly with Simon Ritt, Greg joined him at Ugly Americans shows at the Continental. Greg loved the band and recalled his first meeting with Jerry. "Jerry was wearing a pink suit. I said, 'You've got to come see our band. We'd like to do a show with you guys.' We were playing at a Hells Angels bar down on Third. He came down with Buddy Bowzer and they liked us. Jerry said, 'Man, it's great, but change the name. It's fuckin' awful.'"

Greg moved to a loft space on First Street and First Avenue, where Jerry would hang out. "He was trying to get it together, but he was dealing with a lot of drugs. [Jerry] didn't want to stay on Staten Island. He said, 'I'm going to stay here for a while.'" Just like that, they were roommates.

Greg was a big fan, still possessing a Dolls scrapbook from when he was a teenager. He loved hearing Jerry tell stories about the Dolls, "stories that you just never heard because they were insane stories. But he loved that band. That was his number one accomplishment in life." Jerry talked of large offers coming in for the Dolls to tour again, always nixed by David. But Jerry never bad-mouthed David to Greg, who had the distinct memory that "he had great respect for David. He really liked him."

Jerry struggled to stay off drugs, but it was hard not to revert to his old ways. "One time this girl came from Rhode Island. She had about a thousand bucks on her, so those guys went out and got coke and dope. It could kill an entire army. I remember sitting in my bathroom with Jerry. . . .

He just looked at me and said, 'I don't even know why I do this shit, but it will get me off.' But he was trying his best to get off dope." Jerry's best wasn't good enough.

While onstage, Jerry would eye someone tasked with copping for him. If they signaled "no," his spirit and performance would collapse. If he was walking toward the stage and saw someone who might be holding, he'd make a beeline for them, leaving the band waiting. "I'd seen him more than once at the Continental shows getting high backstage," said Kipp.

During the winter of 1989, Kipp booked another mini-tour of New England and the Northeast. The weather was cold, and they had two vehicles to choose from: a large Cadillac with no heat, or a tiny Toyota with heat. "Jerry just flipped out. He just felt he wasn't being treated properly . . . [and] . . . deserved more." Graham remembered Jerry missing rehearsals and even some gigs. What sealed Jerry's fate as an Ugly American was a show in Port Chester, New York, at a small club called the Beat.

With generous intentions, Kipp offered to buy Jerry a drum kit. Except for a pink kick drum, all of Jerry's drum kits had been sold, hocked, or lost, forcing the band to rent or borrow kits for every gig. Kipp found an older, used kit, thinking that with some elbow grease it would be usable. "Jerry was thrilled to death. And I said, 'Why don't you come see the kit?' And he's like, 'No, I trust you.' I said, 'I don't know that much about drums, Jerry. It's kind of a beat-up kit.' And Jerry said, 'I can fix whatever you buy so don't worry about it."

Kipp got new heads and professional-grade cymbals for the set. He asked Jerry repeatedly to come and look at it, but Jerry kept delaying. Finally, Kipp brought it to the Port Chester gig. "Jerry freaked out when he saw it. 'This is junk! I'm not going to play on this thing!'" His teetering marriage, his unstable living situation, his years of methadone use, and his HIV status all affected his mental state. At this point he was totally unpredictable.

The club was packed, and Kipp and the band were anticipating a great night. But Jerry was already complaining about the money and the hotel arrangements. The drum kit seemed to be the last straw for his fragile psyche.

As the band began their set, Jerry's anger became obvious to the band and the audience. Burny: "He'd start out okay, and then he'd just start slowing back. And the audience is yelling at him: 'Jerry, come on! What's the matter?' He was just in a bad mood." Jerry started kicking at the drums, knocking them out of the way. Kipp: "It started with one of the toms, and then a couple cymbal stands, and then the kick drum, and then, finally, he ended up hardly playing, just fucking pissed off at the world, on the snare and the hihat. 'I don't want that shit; move it out of the way! This is garbage!'"

Burny and the rest of the band tried to soothe him. "We were like, 'Jerry, calm down. It's only the third song. We've got to entertain these people.' There was hardly any drum kit there." Jerry was having a full meltdown. "We were getting booed pretty bad by the crowd," said Kipp. Danny recalled, "Everything just kind of rolled off the stage."

Jerry walked off partway through the set, leaving the band and the tattered remnants of the drum kit behind. Kipp lamented, "He was going through something in his own head . . . Jerry just didn't care anymore. He just gave up."

When they returned to New York, each band member talked about that weekend with Kipp. Everyone knew that Jerry had to go. Kipp recalled telling Jerry the news. Despite how difficult Jerry made his life, Kipp got no pleasure out of firing him. "I'm firing one of my idols. I'm firing the man to this day that I still call maybe the greatest drummer in the history of rock 'n' roll. It was not easy."

Jerry was surprised. "He was in shock. He played it off like, 'I don't give a shit. It's not going to go anywhere,' but I'm sure he was hurt."

Burny remembers it differently, recalling that Syl did the deed. Not knowing the true circumstances of Jerry's exit from Cradle or the Rockats, Syl said to Burny: "'You know, you guys are the only band that's ever fired Jerry Nolan.'"

Jerry had been arrogant with Kipp while a member of the band. "He kept telling me, 'You don't know what you're doing.' 'We should have a recording contract by now.' 'We should be on a real tour as a support act.' It hurt Kipp to tell him the truth: "'Nobody gives a fuck, Jerry. A lot of the kids don't know who you are.' I'd been talking to record labels, and at that stage of the game, nobody [cared]." The response Kipp got from record companies was, "They were old, has-been junkies."

DEAD
OR ALIVE

22

BY EARLY 1991, JERRY HAD MOVED IN WITH PHYLLIS. SHE LOVED and cared for him at a time when he needed it most. He was broke, at one point even collecting food stamps. His marriage to Charlotte was all but over, and he'd been tossed out of yet another band for his drug use and erratic behavior. He was addicted to methadone, still using drugs when he could get them, and hiding his HIV-positive status from everyone. While Jerry acted like the quintessential tough New Yorker, he was fragile and vulnerable.

Charlotte didn't believe Phyllis and Jerry were sexually intimate. This characterization of Jerry's relationship with Phyllis at this point in time was confirmed by Barry Jones, who described it as "platonic." Therefore, Charlotte saw no need to tell Phyllis of Jerry's HIV-positive status. Said Charlotte, "I don't believe they were lovers. He liked her as a friend, but he needed her to take care of him. He had nowhere to go [and] no way to support himself." Added Steve Dior, "Jerry was obviously in a situation financially where he wasn't able to look after himself, so she was a reliable and consistent friend that way."

Charlotte spoke with Jerry regularly, trying to get him to join her in treatment. He promised her that he was regularly attending NA meetings. "That's when I caught him in a lie, because he'd go to a couple of meetings, and then stop." She realized, "He didn't want to quit." Finally, she decided to threaten him with a specific consequence for refusing treatment: divorce. She couldn't stay with someone whose lifestyle would ultimately kill her.

Jerry couldn't see a life without drugs and chose them over Charlotte. "We were formally divorced in May 1990. The fact that I left him had nothing to do with any shortcomings as a husband, or that I didn't love him anymore. I felt that if I didn't get out of there, I would die."

* * *

JERRY WAS HAVING ISSUES PLAYING. WALTER, WHO'D FINALLY gotten clean in 1988, was focusing on his Wall Street commodities job but still played with his band the Waldos. "He would stop by the Continental [and] sit in but he didn't really play drums that much anymore," said Walter. "He'd been on methadone for so long, he really just turned into a zombie. He couldn't play 'Get Off the Phone' anymore."

Jerry set up an ad hoc gig with Buddy Bowzer for Halloween night 1990 at Cave Canem. The flyer had a photo of Jerry and Buddy, Jerry with a cigarette dangling from his lip, and Buddy with his high-piled pompadour. The flyer said "New York Rocks," and scrawled at the bottom, "Welcome All Dollface Heartbreakers Dressed to Kill." The ad for the sparsely attended gig was literal: the band was only Buddy and Jerry, just sax and drums.

More significantly, a Heartbreakers reunion show was booked for November 30 at New York's Marquee. The gig was featured in the November 28, 1990, issue of the *Village Voice* in the calendar section, with a blurb written by music editor Doug Simmons. It read, "Yes, Johnny, Walter and Jerry are back, with all their hits. It may just be a rent party—like their several 'farewell' shows some 10 years back—though that doesn't mean they won't take you someplace. We saw Nolan walking down Broadway a couple weeks ago, and he still looks the star. Thunders might be another story, but here's hoping."[1]

Like Walter, Billy was also on a more straight and narrow path, having given up drugs and become a pastor and drug counselor in New England. Since he wasn't available for the Marquee show, Waldos bass player Tony Coiro filled in. Johnny had recently been released from a Hazelden drug rehab center, after one of several attempts to get clean. He'd broken up with Susanne, lived in several different locations, and lost contact with his children. He was not at his best when rehearsals began. Per Walter, "John's going to the bathroom every ten minutes just like in the old days, and then he'd play two songs." Then he'd run into the bathroom again. "He'd be in there for twenty minutes, shooting up, trying to find a vein." The other three would roll their eyes and say, 'Thank God we're out of all that bullshit now."

Surprising everyone, Johnny pulled it together for the gig, with everyone helping to put on a quality show. "I figured somebody would be unconscious or we'd forget the songs, but it was all right,"[2] said Walter. "Johnny was in fairly good shape. He threw one of his temper tantrums, but it wouldn't be Johnny without that."[3]

Happiest of all was Jerry, who told Nina Antonia: "I played so well. Walter and Tony said: 'Boy, look at Jerry, how happy he is.' It was great and Johnny admitted it too. . . . He told Walter: 'You know I hate to admit it but, fucking Nigs, what a show.'"[4]

Phyllis was helping Jerry live at a slower pace. With Phyllis supporting him, he was barely playing, and basking in his role as a semiretired elder statesman of New York rock 'n' roll.

He took a small dramatic role in an independent film with local filmmakers Rachel Amodeo and Marc Brady. In the early '80s, Brady had cast Jerry as a writer in a film called *You're Welcome*, later renamed *Achtung Berlin: A Letter from New York*. The project was shelved for lack of funding. In 1989 Brady started work on another film, with Amodeo. Called *What About Me*, it revolved around Rachel's character Lisa Napolitano, who becomes homeless, winding up on the New York streets. Besides Johnny Thunders, musicians Dee Dee Ramone, Nick Zedd, and Richard Hell act in the film, as do Richard Edson, poet Gregory Corso, and *Laugh-In* comedienne Judy Carne.

Rachel thought that Jerry would be great in her film as a gangster. On the day of the shoot, he showed up earlier than the 6 a.m. call time, fully made up. Rachel: "He just really looked like a star. . . . He looked like a gangster."

Rachel never gave her nonactors lines. She gave them situations and asked them to react. "If you give nonactors lines . . . they think too much about the lines they've got to remember." Her instructions to Jerry were, "You've only got to die," and, "This is your last confession. Think about the last things you want to say before you die."

After being gunned down in the street by another gangster, Jerry is comforted by Rachel's character, and then speaks his own written lines:

"I've never been much of a Catholic but . . ."
"I've never told Angela I love her."
"My cigarette! I need a cigarette! I had a cigarette."[5]

After getting his cigarette, he coughs up blood, groans, and, in his last dying breath, utters what may be the single funniest line in the film:

"I have to smoke a lighter brand, I . . ."[6]

"He was fantastic," said Rachel.

* * *

IN THE EARLY SPRING OF 1991 JERRY BEGAN A SERIES OF INTERVIEWS with Doug Simmons of the *Village Voice*. After meeting through a mutual acquaintance, they agreed to meet again for coffee. "One thing led to another and I realized that we should just start doing a formal set of interviews and do this guy's life story."

Jerry started coming into Doug's office at 842 Broadway for the interviews. They met once a week for sixty to ninety minutes for several months. "Maybe twelve to fifteen sessions. He was really serious. We both agreed what we were going to do: a straight chronological life story in which we used him as a history of rock and punk rock, a history of New York style and New York street style, even predating the Dolls."

Jerry talked about seeing Elvis in Hawaii, meeting "Otis," his return to Brooklyn, where he and Peter Criss were in gangs and continued drumming. He analyzed Brooklyn style versus the Beatles' style, his love of Gene Krupa, his dislike of hippies, joining the Dolls, Johnny, Heroin, the Heartbreakers, the Anarchy tour, McLaren, Rotten, Sid and Nancy, and more.

It wasn't easy for Doug to get the story ready for print. "He would go off on tangents or . . . lose his train of thought." Once an interview was over, Doug transcribed it, puzzling it together. "He would jump from Hawaii to the Dolls to Sid Vicious to a memory he had when he was a kid."

About halfway through the project, Doug began mildly confronting Jerry about repeating his stories, and his tangential style. "Finally, [I] said, 'Jerry, this is just going to take too long. I am going to stop you if we've covered certain material . . . and just re-ask a question and bring it back,' to try to keep him on point. . . ."

This temporarily strained the relationship. "It wasn't a terrible fight. I just had to tell him that the project was going in circles." Doug was relieved that at least the stories were consistent when retold.

Jerry also exhibited signs of what Doug believed was illiteracy. "I kept showing him the notes, and said, 'Well, how does this look?' and he's just, 'This is just great! This is fantastic!' I realized he never would specifically say anything about them. That became kind of awkward. I never tested it . . . because Jerry was a very confident and swaggering and larger-than-life character. He just had a sense of command and presence."

Jerry was a high school dropout, and his spelling and grammar skills showed it. Still, Michelle, Lesley, and Charlotte all confirmed that while Jerry did not display reading or writing skills at a high level, he did read books and articles, and wrote lyrics and letters. So what was Doug seeing?

It's quite possible that Jerry was beginning to show signs of an AIDS-related illness.

There is considerable medical data and research on HIV-associated neurocognitive disorders (HAND). According to the National Institute of Mental Health, "(HAND) can occur when HIV enters the nervous system and impacts the health of nerve cells."[7] This, in turn, can impair the activity of nerves involved in attention or memory. Other AIDS-related disorders of the nervous system can also cause any number of cognitive issues.

Doug was careful not to bruise Jerry's ego or pride. "If you are going to be friends with a Jerry Nolan, or a Johnny Thunders, you really had to have enormous patience for this vast ego that could turn on a dime into a very needy, almost childlike sensitivity or vulnerability. I realized that it was just a waste of time to show him the transcripts from week to week. So I ended up putting them together myself."

Doug kept working, building the story from his transcripts, while continuing the interviews. Jerry's candor helped make the story a success. In previous articles, like the one in *New York* magazine in 1979, Jerry had hated public references to his drug dependency. But not anymore. It was all fair game. "He was an addict. He wasn't a criminal. He really didn't have anything to hide. He had no qualms, other than questions of pride. He wasn't vain in . . . an empty sense."

Doug was particularly impressed with Jerry's reasoned analysis as to the origins of punk rock being American. "There was a certain real desire by Jerry to set the record straight. He was there. It was a first-person account. He felt like the Sex Pistols and then the English punks were kind of like cute little kids who were hanging around and looking like the Dolls, and then later maybe the Ramones. They realized that when the New York Dolls came in to town, and Johnny and Jerry Nolan walked in, the Pistols were like short-pants-wearing neophytes. They didn't know the first thing about shooting dope, much less playing rock. And then, later on, to see McLaren, and . . . the credit for punk rock to come from England as opposed to New York, that just really pissed him off. He really felt that it was a historical injustice."

While working with Doug, Jerry began speaking with Johnny again. Despite years of Johnny disappointing, betraying, and abandoning him for a few extra dollars or drugs, Jerry always let Johnny back into his life. He was wary, though. Burny White discussed Johnny with Jerry. "He was afraid that if he was with Johnny, [they] would OD together and die."

Doug noticed similarities between the two. "He and Jerry had a really strikingly similar approach to dress and really similar backgrounds: drugs, fashion, and music. They were really, really peas in a pod."

Jerry told Doug his concerns about Johnny's health. Johnny had swollen feet and had to wear therapeutic shoes. "That was one of the signals that Jerry picked up on Johnny. Style was very important to Jerry: the clothing and how it looked, and then how it all came together. It was very important to him in his whole life." Seeing Johnny wear "these booties . . . Jerry was just appalled. Johnny was in a terrible state."

Johnny was scheduled to perform in Japan. Jerry, alarmed by Johnny's ill health, begged him to check into a hospital instead. Jerry had seen black and blue marks on Johnny's body in places where he wouldn't have shot drugs or been injured, and suspected something was terribly wrong. Johnny acknowledged his advice, but was still going. They said their last goodbyes on Fourteenth Street and Third Avenue, the same spot where Jerry had met Johnny to be "Dollified" after joining the Dolls in 1972. Jerry had the unnerving sense that their relationship was being bookended.

* * *

JILL WISOFF PLAYED BASS IN JOHNNY'S BAND THE ODDBALLS BUT wasn't on the Japanese tour. Johnny told her he wanted to try and get clean again, but this time he wanted Jerry to come with him, and afterward, go to New Orleans to start a new band together. Johnny knew he should probably get into a hospital first but was afraid that if he didn't do the Japanese tour, his career would be finished. "He always thought if he messed up in a big way . . . he'd never work again," said Jill. This was a sizable payday for Johnny, which could support the time needed to deal with his health issues and then go to New Orleans. All he had to do was will himself through the tour.

The new band would consist of Johnny, Jerry, Jill, guitarist Stevie Klasson, sax player Jamey Heath, and Detroit native Karen Monster on second guitar. Johnny, Jerry, and Karen met a few times in March 1991 to exchange song ideas, planning to continue once Johnny returned from Japan. But Jill didn't think Johnny would survive the tour. "[I] was hysterical all that night when he left. . . . He looked like he was about eighty-five pounds."

Despite hospital visits and erratic behavior, Johnny made it through. He stopped in Thailand to pick up some suits and a new tattoo, and saw his doctor in London before spending a few days in Berlin to do some acoustic shows. Another stop in Cologne to work on an all-star version of "Born to Lose," and he was off to New Orleans.

He arrived at the registration desk of the St. Peter House in the French Quarter somewhere between nine thirty and ten the evening of April 22, 1991. The next afternoon, a housekeeper found Johnny curled up under the dresser, dead. He was thirty-eight years old.

The official cause of death was drug-related, but the family never felt that a proper investigation was done. He was allegedly seen with some skeevy locals the night before he died. His room was found in disarray, with many of his belongings gone. In a letter from coroner Frank Minyard to Jungle's Alan Hauser, there was a finding of "an advanced spread of malignant lymphoma (a form of leukemia)."[8] His death, like many things in his life, was surrounded by a shroud of myth that may never be lifted. Perhaps Luigi Scorcia nailed the true reason Johnny died: "There was no one to bail him out. Who always bailed out Johnny was Jerry."

An article in the New York Times in February of 1989 had the headline "Virus That May Cause Leukemia Is Spreading Among Drug Addicts."[9] The article said, "The virus, HTLV-II, for human T-cell leukemia virus, type II, has been found in . . . from 4 percent to 10 percent of a group of drug users in New York, and 20 percent of a group of New York drug addicts who were also suffering from AIDS."[10]

In retrospect, as with Keith Moon, Sid Vicious, or Kurt Cobain, Johnny's lifestyle and the events leading up to his death made his ending seem inevitable. People had been coming to see Johnny die onstage since before the "Catch 'Em While They're Still Alive" poster appeared in 1975. Peter Crowley: "I was kind of surprised that Johnny lived as long as he did." Max's owner Tommy Dean looked out for Johnny, sending him to rehab a few times, and for a full medical workup in 1979. Recalled Crowley, "The doctor's report was that John had the internal organs of a seventy-five- or eighty-year-old man."

* * *

THERE WAS A GREAT OUTPOURING OF GRIEF FOR JOHNNY. JERRY was especially overwhelmed by the news of his friend's death. Steve Dior heard the news and received a call from Jerry. He was "just crying and saying, 'What am I gonna do without Johnny?'"

Johnny's wake was held at the Harden Funeral Home on Northern Boulevard in Flushing Meadow, Queens. Among the mourners were Johnny's immediate family; Jerry and Phyllis; David and Syl from the Dolls; Walter from the Heartbreakers; Danny and Burny from the Ugly

STRANDED IN THE JUNGLE

Americans; crew members Max, Peter, and Desmond; Patti Palladin; Johnny's pre-Dolls roommates and girlfriends Gail, Janis, and Abbijane Schifrin; Lyn Todd; Tony Machine; Bob Gruen; Max's sound man Bobby Belfiore; and Leee Black Childers. Jill Wisoff from the Oddballs came with Cheetah Chrome. Alan Hauser flew in from London and Susanne came in from Sweden. Bebe Buell was there, as was the father of her daughter Liv, Steven Tyler from Aerosmith. Glam metal singer Adam Bomb showed up, and along with Max came Evan Dando from the Lemonheads. Mötley Crüc and Aerosmith sent flowers.

There were also numerous fans, drug buddies, hangers-on, and gawkers, turning the event into what Lyn Todd described as "a three-ring circus, with fights breaking out and people who didn't even know him." People threw themselves onto the casket. Walter called it "a mob scene." Danny Ray called it "a fiasco."

Tony Machine saw Jerry in a limousine on his way to the cemetery. "I can picture the look on Jerry's face: Absolute utter sadness, between devastation and shock. It was like a scene from a movie. Dressed in a suit and in a limousine and going to the graveyard. Johnny Thunders's graveyard."

Leee Childers was at the burial. "It was raining, so we were all in mud and wet, and it was a lot of emotion. Johnny was loved in that heavy-duty, Italian, Queensboy way. People were crying. So, it was a very, very over-the-top, emotional thing."

One of the most emotional was Jerry. Leee recalled Jerry falling twice. "He was a heartbreaking sight at Johnny's funeral. We hadn't spoken then in years, and he came over to me in the graveyard. He was crying and on his knees, and begging me to give him forgiveness for what he did to Johnny. Oh, he knew how evil he was to Johnny."

Some tried to use the opportunity to talk sense into Jerry. Assuming Johnny had OD'd, Burny tried to give him perspective. "He started crying. Not sobbing like a bitch, but tears were coming down his face. I said, 'Jerry, you're alive, man. You were always afraid Johnny was going to take you with him, and he didn't. You made it, so don't fuck up. Don't go out there and cop two bags and say, 'These two are for you John!' . . . all that stupid shit. Then you're doing the same thing that just killed your buddy. Why don't you go home with Phyllis and just take a couple of Valiums and watch TV and smoke pot or something?'"

Bob Gruen also talked to Jerry. "I remember telling him that he was a role model and that it was about time he started taking care of himself. There were a lot of kids coming up . . . looking up to him. He sort of acknowledged it, but it was sort of like, 'Well, that's nice,' but he couldn't really do it."

Nina Antonia saw Johnny's death as an opportunity for Jerry to face his own mortality. But he let others know he had no intention of getting clean. "I don't think it was a wakeup call to stop drugs," said Steve Dior. "He liked his lifestyle. He liked doing drugs. He had no desire to really quit. He was quite happy to take his medicine and then get high once in a while. He was quite adamant. 'Ah, I'll never quit.' I remember being quite taken aback."

On June 19, there was a memorial benefit concert for Johnny's family at the Marquee, the site of the last Heartbreakers gig. Performing that night were David and Syl with Tony and Peter from the Dollettes, Cheetah Chrome, Lenny Kaye, the Senders, Luigi, and the Waldos. Jerry played with Stevie Klasson and Patti Palladin and the show closers, the Heartbreakers, consisting of Walter, Tony Coiro, Joey Pinter, and Jamie Heath. No one played more than four songs, except for the Heartbreakers, who played ten.

Rick Johnson, who worked for a chain of record stores in North Carolina, stopped at the Marquee to bring some items the Ramones were donating for auction. He saw Jerry after the sound check, "holding court," wearing a "sharkskin suit," looking "rail-thin," with a belt that was "way too big for him." Jerry's skin also caught his attention, as it looked like "gray Silly Putty."

The house was packed, Rick Rivets noting, "You couldn't move from your spot . . . the whole night." Jimi LaLumia, lead vocalist for his own Max's-era band the Psychotic Frogs, recounted what occurred when David and Syl hit the stage: "A chant went up of 'Buster! Buster!' which morphed into 'Asshole! Asshole!' To add to the drama, Nolan left the building when 'the Dolls' went on and stood on the sidewalk, smoking cigs until they were off."

"I do remember [Jerry] sitting on the outside steps kind of forlornly," recalled Lenny Kaye. Jerry was upset over Johnny's death, but he was also unhappy being left out of the Dolls reunion. He tried not to hold a grudge toward David for how the Dolls ended, or his refusal to consider the large financial offers to reunite. But not being allowed to play with David and Syl at Johnny's memorial was too painful. Jerry couldn't even watch them play.

Jerry jumped at the opportunity to make things right with Leee. Previously they would have ignored each other, or shown hostility. According to Leee, that night, "we were real nice to each other."

Jerry continued working with Doug to finish the *Village Voice* article. But Johnny's death left him "devastated and grieving," recalled Doug. "He was just deeply wounded. Weeping, even a few weeks later."

When it was finished, Jerry believed he would be on the cover of the quarterly music insert. On July 15, he and Phyllis walked to the magazine stand near the *Voice*'s office that always had the first issues the night before it would officially hit newsstands. Most were there to get a jump on the apartment classifieds, but Jerry was there to read his article. When he saw it, he was stunned to see himself on the front cover. Finally, he was getting recognition for his contributions to rock 'n' roll, a validation of his life's work. What had started out as a "fairly routine feature assignment" had become a ten-page article with a front-page photo. Doug Simmons: "He loved it. He was delighted."

Jerry started to come out of his funk. Phyllis got his Triumph motorbike over from Sweden, keeping it at her place in upstate New York. He was seeing a therapist, who was treating him for depression while coordinating with his methadone program to stabilize him. Between his HIV status, losing Charlotte, and Johnny's death, he'd thought his life was over. He now started to think that he might have a future. Maybe he could even play music again.

HUMAN
23 BEING

JERRY AND PHYLLIS VACATIONED IN LONDON AND PARIS IN THE summer of 1991. Jerry loved shopping, and with all the flea markets and clothing stalls, he was in heaven. They stopped in to see Nina Antonia, who interviewed Jerry for an updated edition of her Johnny Thunders biography, *In Cold Blood*, and talked about helping him write his memoirs. There was talk of Warhol protégé Victor Bockris handling the American portion of his story, and Nina handling the European portions. She thought Jerry was in "really good shape. Phyllis really looked after him." Before leaving, Jerry visited his British methadone doctor. He was still uncomfortable without a few extra doses at his disposal.

Back in New York, he agreed to be interviewed for a BBC documentary on punk rock. Upon its release in 1995, it was titled *Punk and the Sex Pistols*. Mary Harron, who was developing a successful career in film and television, and was one of the original contributors to *Punk* magazine, was assigned to interview him.

With her film crew, Mary met Jerry at Phyllis's Seventeenth Street loft. "He took a long time to come up because he was dressing so carefully, and he looked just fantastic. I think he felt the importance of it and he was going to present himself at his very best."

While she could see that Phyllis "was very caring to him," unlike Nina Antonia, Mary did not think Jerry looked well. "I knew people who had hepatitis C and that's a wasting illness. He was very thin and had that fragile look. He looked ethereal."

In a lengthy interview that covered a lot of ground, Jerry spoke about the early days of the Dolls, their look, their musical ideas, and their influence on what was to become punk rock. He recalled when Malcolm McLaren worked with the Dolls and how he used that experience to put together the Sex Pistols. He voiced his opinions on Johnny Rotten and

Sid Vicious, his recollections of the Anarchy tour, and the ridiculous protests that came with it. His quips and stories, in his singular New York patois, were reasoned and insightful. He was an experienced raconteur who made for good TV.

Greg Allen continued his musical pursuits, getting together enough money to record, and needed a drummer. When Jerry overheard him ask a friend to play drums, he confronted Greg. "He said, 'Why didn't you ask me to play?' And I'm like, 'Because I figured you wouldn't be into it.'" Jerry told him, 'Oh, I love this music.' So we started rehearsing with a friend of mine playing bass, from Rhode Island."

Greg's friend was Vinnie Earnshaw, who played bass with blues and rockabilly bands, backing up rockabilly veteran Sonny Burgess for a spell. Greg and Vinnie were close friends, Greg being best man at Vinnie's wedding.

They started recording at Baby Monster studios in Manhattan. "He seemed a little lost without Johnny," said Vinnie. "He was upset about it and he used to reminisce. Trying to put a band together was the only thing he could do, even though he felt like he couldn't go on without Johnny. With me and Greg he was starting to feel happy."

Jerry liked to poke fun at Vinnie, calling him a "hick," but sometimes Vinnie would tag along on walks. Jerry would point out places he'd been, what club used to be there, or an experience he'd had, often bringing the story back to "his friend" Johnny. On one trip, he told Vinnie about a recent encounter with Rolling Stones guitarist Keith Richards. "It was early in the morning, and Jerry was out for his walk. Keith was in a doorway and he called Jerry over to talk to him, telling him that he should . . . hang in there, and try to put another band together."

Jerry hadn't played regularly for a while, but no one in the session could tell. "He just sat down at the set, messed around a little bit, and it sounded great," recalled Vinnie. Jerry had grown fond of electric blues, telling Vinny he wanted to have a big blues band and play Howlin' Wolf's "Do the Do."

A young Brit named Luke Harris was helping to manage the band's affairs. When the others went back to New England, Luke would be with Jerry in New York. "When I came to New York, Johnny was dead and Jerry was so upset by that. He would go into the Trinity Church downtown near the World Trade Center . . . and light a candle."

As he did with Vinnie, Jerry took long walks with Luke, telling him many of the same stories that were in the *Village Voice* article. New York was one of Jerry's favorite subjects. Music, gangs, fashion—if there was a

New York component, he was interested. He read the book *Gangs of New York*, which is where he found the band's name: the Plug Uglies.

These walk-and-talks he had with Luke and Vinnie were not just daily constitutionals. They were about convincing them that not only did New York have a rich history, but he too had a rich history, and they were intertwined. "I can just remember walking around New York a lot just listening to him talk. That *Village Voice* article is really good, but it was just a taste of what he had to say."

Luke opined on Jerry: "The reason why a lot of people get into drugs [is] a lack of self-confidence. There was something very shy and sensitive and vulnerable. Even walking around town, we would just bump into people, but he would run away from them. Famous people . . . like the guys from Suicide and all sort of New York rock guys."

In April, Jerry reconnected with Lydia Criss, Peter's ex-wife. She mentioned that Peter was scheduled to be in town for a Kiss convention, and she thought it would be a great opportunity for all of them to get together for old times' sake. She spoke to each of them separately about showing up at the Limelight club for a Sunday night event in honor of the convention. Each agreed to come. Neither of them showed up.

A television appearance came in October when TVT Records released a compilation called *The Groups of Wrath: Songs of the Naked City*. Made from demos and early singles of bands Marty Thau had worked with, it included recordings of the Ramones, Blondie, Richard Hell, Suicide, and the Dolls.

The deal for the compilation was the brainchild of TVT employee David Scharff, who knew Jerry from the late '70s when his band the Student Teachers played the local scene, including opening slots for the Idols. CBGB opened a combination record store and art gallery next door called CB's Gallery, also known as the CBGB Record Canteen. TVT held a record-release party there, and a camera crew from *MTV News* did a quick interview with Jerry.

Jerry looked fantastic in a two-tone black leather jacket with red shoulders, and perfectly styled blond hair. He spoke enthusiastically about his new group with Greg Allen and, when asked if it sounded anything like the New York Dolls, laid down a line in the sand: "It'll always be in that groove. Ya know, anything I do will always be Heartbreaker-type, New York Dolls–type of music. I'll never change that."[1]

David remarked that having Jimmy Destri from Blondie and Jerry Nolan from the New York Dolls at the party legitimized it. He looked forward to seeing Jerry for the first time in years. "He was definitely skinnier. He was still a well-dressed man, though. He still wore natty clothes. He still looked like a rocker. And he was still a very cool dude. He was the person that everybody wanted to talk to at this party. Jimmy Destri got a little bit of pull, but here was this guy who was a member of the Dolls, and that was just legend. So he got a lot of attention. A lot of people wanting him to sign stuff and hang out and reminisce a little bit, and he was so affable and so pleasant, and so professional. He really was like he had always been."

Recordings with Greg and Vinnie resumed in November, and they both recall Jerry complaining of headaches and joint pain, but dismissed it as just another by-product of methadone. Luke remembered seeing him at Bella's, where he used to get potato-and-egg sandwiches after hitting his methadone clinic. "He goes, 'I've got this really bad headache. I've got to go home.' He went home and the next thing I hear, Phyllis rings me up and says he's in a coma."

The morning after seeing Luke, Jerry became incoherent before collapsing. He was, however, coherent enough to tell Phyllis's friend Jane, who was watching the loft, that he didn't want to go to the hospital. Nevertheless, she called 911, and an ambulance came to take Jerry to St. Vincent's Hospital just a few blocks south. Jane told the ER doctors that Jerry was a methadone patient. Unaware of his condition, she was unable to tell them that he was HIV-positive.

Once notified, Phyllis, who was in Boston at an event for a client, immediately flew back to New York. When she got to St. Vincent's, Jerry was in the ICU. His face was bloated and his head was shaved, a drainage tube inserted into his skull to relieve pressure. He was unrecognizable, breathing through a ventilator, in an induced coma.

He was diagnosed with bacterial meningitis. By 1991, any hospital in a major city, particularly one in the West Village of Manhattan with its large gay population, knew what they were looking at. After the doctors had been told he was on methadone, they had to put two and two together: He was most certainly a heroin addict, and probably used it intravenously. Meningitis patients are almost always immune-deficient. There was now little doubt: Jerry had AIDS.

Jerry received round-the-clock care from Phyllis, Jane, Johnny's sister Mariann, and her husband Rusty. Lyn Todd, Lydia Criss, and Greg Allen were also among the visitors, pitching in however they could.

Phyllis pinned Jerry's *Village Voice* cover up in his room, to remind the doctors and everyone else who visited that Jerry wasn't just some bloated junkie lying in the hospital bed. All efforts should be made to help him.

256

Jerry had told Charlotte that he wasn't sleeping with Phyllis, so Charlotte assumed Phyllis was unaware of his HIV status. For the sake of Jerry's medical care, she knew it was time to tell her, and did.

Charlotte wanted to come to New York right away, but Phyllis told her not to, adding that she had instructed the doctors, nurses, and guards not to let her in, as it could upset him. "'Don't come here and make a scene.' And I didn't go," said Charlotte.

Back in June of 1990, Charlotte had fallen ill from an unknown, acute allergic reaction. She temporarily lost her eyesight, and only recovered after entering a hospital. "I talked to him afterward and he was like, 'Why didn't you call me'? Charlotte reminded him that they weren't married anymore. "He said, 'You are my wife. You will always be my wife. You shouldn't have been alone.'"

These memories made her uneasy about not going to the hospital. "I just had the feeling that he was waiting for me and that's why he was holding on for so long. That's one of the very few things that I regret in my life."

After appearing to rebound, he suffered three strokes. His health continued to fail, and the doctors determined that he didn't have much time. Rachel Amodeo recalled, "His body just deteriorated really quickly and he didn't even look like himself."

Lyn Todd spent time there, and quickly realized she was on a death watch. "I remember thinking that he would die right there if he knew everybody saw him looking so bad."

Walter came to see him with Tony Coiro. Walter: "His eyes were closed and he was just lying in bed like a corpse. The eyes would blink a little bit. But you had no idea of whether he understood anything or whether he was conscious."

Phyllis maintained that Jerry could respond to her, while the doctors claimed otherwise. Lyn: "We all were convinced he had looked at us, or given a sign he was coming out of it." David Johansen's former girlfriend Cyrinda Foxe visited and insisted that Jerry mouthed to her, "I remember." "I know he said that and no one can tell me he didn't."[2] But what did he remember? "I just thought he meant he remembered his time, the Dolls and everything."[3]

"Everything" could have meant any number of things: his was a life filled with adventures and lived at a pace that few others could claim.

Michelle came to see him after finding out from Corinne Healy that he was ill. Like Cyrinda, she was certain that Jerry responded to her. "I saw him on the respirator. Phyllis said to him, 'Jerry, Jerry,' because he was out of it. I didn't even think he was conscious. And she said, 'Jerry, you have a visitor. Michelle is here to see you.' And right away, his eyes started moving. . . . I saw them trying to roll. And he found me, found my eyes. A lot of expression through the eyes was made between the two of us. He was just basically saying he was sorry." Jerry wasn't one for mea culpas. It was the closest thing to an apology she could ever expect to get from him.

Luigi came to visit, and was overcome. "I couldn't handle it. I wanted to say goodbye . . . but what I remember [was] he was so fucked." Rockat Dibbs Preston visited Jerry and sang him a few bars of the song they'd written together, "Start Over Again." Jerry's mother Charlotte came and stayed with Phyllis for several weeks but returned to Oklahoma, the strain being too much for her.

Phyllis and those closest to Jerry were reeling from the weeks of waiting, as he deteriorated before their eyes. Rachel couldn't stop crying. "There was so much sadness in his eyes. He looked up at me, he couldn't talk and he couldn't move. He was paralyzed at the end from his neck down, and he was almost like a newborn baby, who can see but who can't move. We tried to talk to him, but I just kept crying. I [didn't] want him to see me cry, but I just couldn't help but cry."

Although she wouldn't allow her to visit, Phyllis asked Charlotte to send things of importance to Jerry, as they might reignite some part of his subconscious, setting him on a path to recovery. Charlotte sent Jerry's childhood marksmanship medals and jewelry, including a ring they'd bought together in Thailand. She sent a two-tone leather jacket, adorned with stars and white fringe. It had special meaning to them, purchased in London when they were flush and having a wonderful time together. "Wherever we went, we bought patches from different parts of the world. . . . We kept sewing [them] on the jacket, and it was like a world tour jacket. We both loved that jacket, [and] we took turns wearing it." She never got any of these items back.

Jerry spent eight weeks in the ICU before being moved to a hospice unit. After three and a half weeks, Phyllis got a phone call. Rachel: "Phyllis told me that the day he died, a nurse called her on the phone and said, 'Hello, is this Phyllis Stein? Jerry Nolan has expired,' and she was like, 'He's not a fucking library card!' and hung up. She was really furious about how she was dealt with."

* * *

PHYLLIS FELT THAT JERRY HAD BEEN MISTREATED BY THE DOCTORS, claiming they never gave him the methadone he needed, administering phenobarbital instead. She never forgave them.

Phyllis insisted that Jerry told her if anything ever happened to him, he wanted to be buried near Johnny. But because of his HIV status, Jerry and Charlotte had discussed his death years before. His wishes were very clear, and were confirmed by his mother: He wanted to be buried near her in a simple plot she'd purchased in Brooklyn.

Phyllis and Mariann made the funeral arrangements. Jerry's mother did not attend. Charlotte attended the funeral, even though she hadn't been allowed to visit him in the hospital, and believed that Jerry's final wishes weren't followed.

The funeral was held at the Harden Funeral Home, same as Johnny's. Unlike Johnny's funeral, Jerry's was dignified, with no drama or fights. "Jerry didn't invite emotion like that into his life, which Johnny did," said Leee.

Before the wake, Phyllis and Mariann went in to see the body, to decide whether the casket should be open or not. Charlotte wasn't permitted to join. The casket was left open. Rick Rivets: "I almost thought I was in the wrong room. He just didn't look like Jerry, whereas Johnny looked like Johnny. His hair was gray and . . . they didn't really fix him up like they did Johnny. I was kind of surprised, a little taken back."

Michelle Piza looked at him lying in the coffin. "I felt like all the negativity had washed out of him. It was the little boy . . . the sweet face that I remember seeing before all of whatever that affected him in his life took over. It's almost like his soul was just cleansed."

Also in attendance were Patti Palladin, Luke Harris, Lyn Todd, Danny Ray, and David Johansen. His older friends Tom and Elvera Bakas came with Gregor Laraque. Greg, Vinnie, and Buddy were among the pallbearers. Marc Brady came at the insistence of Dee Dee, who was too overcome with grief to attend. Burny White was there too. "I cried like a baby. . . . I cried like a baby."

Because of his strained relationship with Jerry, Kipp Elbaum decided not to go. Neither did Jerry's brother Billy, who deeply regretted it, saying, "It even hurts to think about it."

Leee came with photographer Patti Giordano. "We went to Jerry's funeral out of respect for Jerry . . . and also for a lot of us it was partly closure too, with Johnny." Lyn Todd: "It was the final straw and absolutely the end of an era."

After the service, the casket was taken to Mount Saint Mary Cemetery in Flushing, where Johnny Thunders is also laid to rest. Everyone shivered in the cold, but no one threw themselves onto the coffin like at Johnny's funeral. The service just went on solemnly, as planned.

After the funeral, Luke shared a ride with a few others. "We got in the car and switched the radio on. Completely by chance, the DJ played a song for Jerry. He played 'Salt of the Earth' by the Stones and everybody burst into tears."

When the headstone Phyllis purchased was finally unveiled, it revealed a large engraving of Christ, surrounded by roses. At the bottom was an inscription, FOREVER IN OUR HEARTS. In the center were two hearts, touching side by side. One said JERRY NOLAN. Below it was Jerry's date of birth, and the day he died. The other heart was empty, presumably for Phyllis.

No one besides Jerry or Phyllis knew for sure whether they were lovers in those last years together. It was clear Phyllis loved and cared deeply for Jerry. But Jerry had decades of experience telling women whatever he had to in order to get what he needed. No one knows for sure how honest he'd been with Phyllis or Charlotte.

Charlotte remembers her conversations with Jerry after she left him, denying any sexual relationship with Phyllis. She recalled a conversation with Phyllis's friend Jane at Jerry's funeral. "She was telling me . . . they weren't having sex. She did ask me, 'Did you and Jerry have sex all the time?' Charlotte responded that they'd last had sex about a year before his death. "I could see [by] the look on her face that she was very surprised."

Despite her regrets, the contradictions, and Jerry's lies, Charlotte believed that Jerry had a positive impact on her life. "I grew up in an environment where I didn't learn a lot of stuff I should have learned. Jerry told me I had a lot of good. Jerry was messed up in some ways, all the junkie shit, but he also had some very good things about him. He had a lot of integrity and a lot of loyalty. He taught me about loyalty, love, trust. . . ."

Charlotte added: "People that have self-esteem [issues] . . . can't be loyal or trustworthy or trust people. . . . I think he carried a lot of pain around. I also think he had a number of disappointments in life. I'm a heroin addict, I work with addicts. People don't just randomly become heroin addicts because they have nothing better to do. Pain: yes. Abandonment: yes. Disappointments in life: yes. Self-confidence issues: at times, yes. Self-esteem; not sure about that one."

According to his old friend Elvera Bakas, Jerry was too ashamed of what he'd become to visit her at the lingerie shop where she worked on Eighth Street. "He came in the store one day. He was all dressed up, he looked really, really good. I said, 'Jerry, I tried calling and getting in touch with you. I can't get in touch with you. What is going on?" He said, 'You know what's going on.' And he says, 'I'm so sorry. I've passed here every day for the past year and I didn't have enough nerve to come in because I don't want you to hate me.' And I said, 'Jerry, I would never hate you. I love you like a brother.' And he knew, because he used to preach to me about drugs. And it hurt him so bad because he couldn't even come in to see me. And then when he did, he felt much better. This is not too long before he passed away. He must have known he was sick. He must have known."

Leee Childers spent the '80s avoiding Jerry and had little good to say about him, if he even spoke about him, until a few years before his own death, in 2014. "It's hard to say good things about Jerry. I want to think only wonderfully about Jerry, but . . . honestly the only really comfortable time, where I felt it was real friendship, was that little last year before he died. It was during that year we discovered that we had always really loved each other. He was jealous of all the attention that Johnny showed me. I was jealous of the affection and servitude that Johnny showed him. We just were in a constant competition."

David Johansen had his own memories of Jerry. "I loved the way he talked, and his phrases like 'L.A.M.F.', about everything. He brought a new vitality to the band when we were in a dark period. He had a way of describing his youth in the most colorful 'Coney Island of the Mind' kind of way. As the main lyricist, it was my duty to represent the group-speak to the best of my ability and Jerry provided a lot of inspiration. The song 'Babylon' comes to mind, with phrases like 'clock my wares,' which is pure Nolan. He was a great drummer in the Krupa Metropole-period style, only better."

From Nina Antonia: "When he told me his story it always sounded like a Nelson Algren story. It always seemed mythical."

It is impossible to think of Jerry without thinking of Johnny Thunders. "When Johnny died, I knew Jerry was next," opined Luigi. "They were inseparables."

"Johnny and Jerry were one of the great unrequited love affairs," said Leee. "They fought like lovers, broke up like lovers, reunited like lovers. Jerry would manipulate Johnny, making him crazy, then Johnny would break down in tears and Jerry would storm off, and Johnny would lay in my lap crying: 'Where's Jerry? I can't live without him, I can't work without him, I can't be without him.' That sounds like lovers to me."[4]

"These two were like a couple of gang members together," said Barry Jones. "They were just into the same thing: getting high and playing badass music. To this day, it's sad. I miss both of those guys. Sometimes I just play old songs and I'll be like, 'Goddamn. They should have both been able to retire with money that wasn't all spent on drugs. They should have had some of the better life.'"

Nina Antonia felt that Johnny and Jerry both knew that they lived a rarefied existence that should be chronicled. "I think there was a sense with Johnny and Jerry, something that they recognized, was that they . . . did want to be . . . made into myths, because they lived their lives like myths."

"He was a great drummer," said Glen Matlock of the Sex Pistols. "There was some kind of way his being encompassed the whole lot of American rock history. He was the embodiment of that. It was more than just playing four to the bar in some song for three minutes. When you saw him play, there was a whole wealth of an American music industry . . . which you don't get with a lot of drummers."

To Tony James, playing with Johnny and Jerry "was a magical time for me. A great experience; getting to play with my generation's Rolling Stones!" To Joe Mazzari, Jerry was "the consummate drummer. For a guitar player to play with Jerry Nolan behind you doing that backbeat . . . that's just as good as it gets."

Paul Wassif: "When you've got a drummer like that behind you . . . they lift you up. They've done over half the job for you. It's got fuck-all to do with what you are doing. You keep sprinkling a bit of fairy dust over the top, and they rock you along. So when someone goes, 'What a fucking great show. They really rock!' Actually, what they are saying is, 'That was a fucking great drummer.' And that's my point: Jerry was one of them. . . . It's like having a steamroller behind you. He was a fucking great drummer."

Clem Burke of Blondie also saw something in Jerry that few other drummers had. "I think Jerry [and] Keith Moon were probably two of the more interesting drummers to come along in rock, as far as somebody you wanted to look at and who had a style, that . . . just really grabbed you. In the context of rock 'n' roll . . . probably he's as good as anybody. They were role models for me."

"He was the best drummer in New York," recalled Rick Rivets. "He just made any band that he played with sound better."

"I have worked with most of the great drummers in rock 'n' roll at one time or another . . . ," said Leee, " . . . and he will always remain the most reliably perfect drummer I have ever worked with. I have worked with Ringo, I have worked with Aynsley Dunbar, I have worked with Ginger Baker. . . . I had to depend on them getting onstage and playing their drums right. And Jerry, as crazy and as heroin-addicted and nutty and mean as he could be, when he got onstage, I knew where I was at with

Jerry Nolan. He was always, always the greatest drummer I have ever worked with. Drumming is not exactly being Mother Teresa, but in the world of drumming, he was Mother Teresa."

Buddy Bowzer and Lyn Todd ran into each other at a bar after Buddy visited Jerry's grave. He showed her pictures he'd taken of the gravesite. "He said, 'I gotta show this to you because if I just tell you, you're gonna think I'm crazy.' He pulled out this stack of photos and on every one of them there was a spiral of smoke coming out of the grave! Buddy said, 'Jerry's still rockin'! His spirit's so strong they can't keep him down.'"

Richard Lloyd had his own view of Jerry's spirit. "You have to recognize at a certain point, there are breaks in the clouds, and you can utilize them to get out, but the suffering that it takes to get out is equal to all the suffering you've avoided through all the years. People can't take that kind of suffering: the man with the golden arm chained to the radiator. You've no clue as to how hard it is to get released when you're having sex with an eight-hundred pound gorilla. It ain't over until the gorilla says it's over. And if you get a break in the clouds, you've got to jump on it. You've got to take it. And you have to have hit some sort of bottom that's lower than physical death. And Jerry didn't. It's called a conversion experience. It just didn't happen to him or Johnny or any of the others. And so they got sucked down. They weren't tied to the mast like Ulysses. Some of us are tied to a mast. Others of us get dashed on the rocks. What can I say? Jerry got dashed."

AFTERWORD

GROWING UP IN THE QUEENS, NEW YORK, SUBURB OF BELLE Harbor (part of Rock, Rock, Rockaway Beach), I was an avid reader of *Circus* magazine. This was where I discovered the New York Dolls. While *Circus* had plenty of articles and photos of drab, sexless bands like Eagles and Bachman-Turner Overdrive, *Circus* also thrived on colorful, sex-oozing artists like Kiss, Bowie, and the Dolls. Honestly, at first blush, the Dolls seemed a little too raw, too street, and too effeminate for this Jewish suburban mama's boy. Besides, as a thirteen-year-old in the summer of 1973, I would have been risking my very existence had I shown an interest in a band of men who wore makeup and women's clothing. Black Sabbath and Emerson, Lake & Palmer were safer choices.

It wasn't until the Dolls appeared on the American television program *Don Kirshner's Rock Concert* in November of 1974 that I first heard their music and saw their drummer, Jerry Nolan, in action. In his spot behind David Johansen, Jerry found himself in almost as many camera shots as their lead singer, giving this viewer ample opportunity to assess his skills and ogle his pink drum kit. I'd been playing the drums since I was five, and so had a different point of view than most. What I saw was a stylish, animated drummer, playing seemingly simple parts. I was curious, but still not sold.

My deeper connection to Jerry Nolan began a few years later, when I was twenty. I was crazy about Jerry's sometime girlfriend Lesley Vinson, who I met at a Devo show at New York's Bottom Line in October 1978. I had a complete crush on her—I'd find excuses to go places she might be, or call her at home. Sometimes a grumbly guy would answer, curtly saying something like "She's at work now." This turned out to be Jerry. When Lesley and I did speak, she told me about "the best drummer in New York," who played on an album called *L.A.M.F.* Still, it didn't quite connect with me.

When she suggested we go to CBGB one evening to see Jerry play with his band the Rockats, I gladly tagged along. Though I'd seen him on TV in '74, at one of the sold-out Sid Vicious shows in the fall of '78, and at an Idols show a few weeks afterward, this would be the first time I'd see him up close.

Before the band came on, while we were standing in the audience, Jerry came over and spoke to Lesley. Though he was right next to me, Jerry and I did not speak. In retrospect, he could probably tell I was a "civilian," with little money and none of the drugs he was looking for. But I could see that his hair and clothes were perfect. His bleached-blond locks were coiffed into a post-punk pompadour that was so much hipper then my mess of a mop. He also wore a pink suit, a black shirt, and a white tie, which put my black jeans and thrown-together togs to shame. I quickly understood why any woman would want to be with him instead of me.

I never actually met Jerry until a spring afternoon in 1980. In the kitchen of Lesley's Mott Street apartment, which less than a year later would be mine, Lesley and I were yammering on when Jerry came through the door. What he was wearing did not register. I was so consumed with finding that sweet spot between fawning and cool aloofness that all I could muster was the feeling of awkwardness. By now I had seen the Rockats multiple times and immersed myself in both Dolls albums, the Heartbreakers' *L.A.M.F.*, and the Idols 45. I was now going to meet the man himself.

Lesley introduced us, and we shook hands before she asked him how Rockats rehearsals were going. He responded by saying he thought they were working on something "the kids" would really like. He then looked down at his shoes forlornly and added, "As if I would know . . ." Before I knew it, he'd launched into an attack on her about how messy the apartment was; then the two of them began to bicker. Sensing I was the third wheel on their bicycle, I beat a hasty retreat, offering to bring them both some coffee from the neighborhood bodega. When I returned a short while later, he was gone.

The very next day, I visited the Mott Street apartment again, only to find Jerry staring blankly at a television set. But what was odd was he wasn't staring at the screen. He was staring at the side of the set, motionless, as if he were frozen in some zombielike state. Through facial gestures and hand signals, I asked Lesley why Jerry was acting so oddly. All she could do was shrug her shoulders and offer a resigned "Ahh, you know."

Jerry left the Rockats that August. They went with an animated but less able drummer before I could even get a shot at the seat. I had work to do.

The event that sealed the deal for me was when Club 57 on St. Marks Place held an Elvis Presley look-alike contest as part of an irreverent celebration on the third anniversary of Elvis's death. Our friend Felice had long, thick, dark hair, making her a perfect Priscilla. All she needed was an Elvis. I was drafted. The ladies pomaded my hair, dressed me up in some of Rockat singer Dibbs Preston's gear and a pair of Jerry's shoes left behind after Lesley kicked him out for stealing her money. They were like Beatle boots, but shorter, and they were terribly beat up and scuffed beyond the point where any reasonable person would even consider wearing them. Still, we shined them up, the girls squealing with delight as I crammed my feet into Jerry's tiny shoes.

We won the contest, with burlesque artist John Sex placing second, despite whipping out little John. Afterwards, several of us celebrated by club-hopping.

With the help of Felice and Lesley, I continued working hard at developing my own "profile," which paid off when Jerry's replacement in the Rockats didn't work out, and I received a phone call from bass player Smutty Smiff. Two days later, after two rehearsals and having inherited 242 Mott Street, I was a Rockat. Through hard work and guile, tongue-tied Claudius was now assuming Caligula's throne.

Traveling with the Rockats, I heard the stories of Jerry's shenanigans, scams, hilarious and ridiculous raps, and prodigious drug intake. I was threatened in New Orleans because of a drug rip-off Jerry had pulled on a previous visit. I heard tales from girls he'd seduced and then abandoned. I also sensed the disappointment fans felt when they realized Jerry wouldn't be playing that night. It was obvious: Jerry had left a mark wherever he went. He was living a mythical, adventurous, and fabled existence. Just walking in his footsteps was an escapade.

Outside of his solo single in 1982, I saw neither hide nor hair of him throughout the '80s. But in July 1991, out of nowhere, he appeared on the cover of the *Village Voice*, with a ten-page feature on his life inside. It was a complete shock. Twenty-five years later people still talk about that article. It validated so much that I felt was important: the Dolls, the Heartbreakers, punk rock, and Jerry's role in all of it. I read that article over and over.

Years before, Lesley had shown me several of the photos in the article, and I'd also heard some of the stories. But what also struck me was that there was so much more that I knew that wasn't in the article: the stories of the Idols and the Rockats for instance. But it was great to see him get his due.

Perhaps it was a sign of providence that I should have acted upon, but the day before leaving New York to move to Seattle, I found myself in Union Square, and there on a crowded street, walking into a pharmacy, was Jerry. I thought about waiting outside for him and politely approaching him. I've gone over this a hundred times in my mind: I'd say, "Excuse me, I doubt you remember me, but . . ." I'd then quickly fill him in on the connections we shared, how I wanted to write a book and talk to him. We'd then have coffee, he'd start telling me story after story, and we'd bond. The talks would turn into interviews, and we'd collaborate on his autobiography. It would turn into a biopic on the scale of *Amadeus*, and a deep friendship—and new successful career—would begin.

The reality was not so lofty. I decided to just leave him be and go on my way.

After moving to Seattle, I was in a record shop called Bop Street in Ballard, one of Seattle's older, Norwegian neighborhoods. The fellow who ran the place had been friendly, lending me books from his private collection as well as letting me into his store room to poke through rare Dylan bootlegs. We started talking and I mentioned I used to play with the Rockats and that Jerry Nolan of the New York Dolls had been the drummer before me. One day I came in and he mentioned that he'd heard that Jerry had died. I figured he meant Johnny Thunders—who had passed just a few months prior—as this was before the internet, and information didn't move as fast then as it does now. Plus, in 1992, no one seemed to care about those guys outside of New York. I figured he'd just mixed the two of them up. Later, of course, it made sense, their deaths being so near each other. They were too close for one to live much longer than the other. The drug use and a broken heart took their toll.

* * *

A FEW MONTHS AFTER JERRY'S DEATH, HIS BIOLOGICAL SON JOHN O'Hanlon, then twenty-five years old, received a letter in the mail. "It was photocopies of the obituaries," he told me. "This was a good eight months after Jerry was already in the grave, and the letter was kind of cryptic. It said, 'Somebody very close to you has died. Maybe you want to know who that person was,' and, 'If you want to know more, contact me here.' So, of course, I did."

John had always known he was adopted, his parents couching it in positive terms: "You weren't given up, you were chosen." He had no great urge to find his birth parents and so was resigned to waiting to search for them until after his parents had passed on, not wanting to upset them. But his parents never dissuaded him from doing so. "So, when this information was dangling in front of me, I sort of felt like I should really know, especially when I saw the pictures. I was like, 'Wow that looks terribly like me in the future.' Without my glasses, I look exactly like him, like we could have been twins."

The letter came from Jerry's mother, Charlotte, who had moved back to Oklahoma after divorcing her third husband. "First I got the letter and I sat on it. I didn't tell my parents that very day. I might have waited a day or two, because I wasn't really sure how to bring it up."

Unknown to John, Charlotte had spent years trying to get to him, even paying private investigators to tail him. "I distinctly remember these instances where people would be coming up to [me] and start to ask questions. I had no idea who these people were or . . . how they found me or anything like that. I know that Charlotte spent a lot of time and a lot of money . . . to have the adoption files opened. She was so obsessed with Jerry and finding Jerry's son that she kind of didn't really regard anybody else's position."

When John finally told his mother about the letter, she revealed that she had been receiving letters from Charlotte for years. "Some of the letters were actually quite threatening, saying things like, 'If you don't let me get to see my grandson I'll find a way with or without you.' They were worried every time I left the house." Cars would pull up to the house with Oklahoma license plates. Strangers would lurk. The O'Hanlons lived with a fear that they'd protected young John from until that day.

He then told his dad, a blue-collar employee of the Long Island Lighting Company since the age of nineteen. "My father was typical: tough guy, Bronx, Irish . . . not able to talk about feelings. He was like, 'Wow, after all these years, she still won't leave us alone.' My father was not afraid of anything, but he just could not understand why this person was causing them so much grief. Tough guy that he was, he actually sat and cried."

John eventually met Jerry's mom, Charlotte. It did not go smoothly. "She arranged a trip to New York. I had no idea she was coming. She thought that I was going to be at the airport . . . with my arms outstretched and saying, 'Grandma!' but she was a complete stranger to me."

Johnny did meet and develop relationships with others who knew Jerry, including his birth mother, Corinne. He drove out to meet her in Queens and spent twelve hours talking to her. John was relieved to find out one thing in particular from Corinne: "I was not born out of some one-night stand with some groupie but somebody that he actually had a very long-term relationship with." John and Corinne continued their relationship.

John also became friendly with Peter Criss's ex-wife, Lydia. "She actually held me the day I was born, and I've seen her a handful of times and she is lovely. I love her."

John also met Phyllis Stein. "When I met her, she had this really great apartment. I went up there and in her bedroom was a complete shrine to Jerry. It was actually quite haunting. She has actually gone to psychic mediums and things like that to try to communicate with Jerry. I've always loved her. She has always been really, really great to me."

Like Corinne, John is unwavering in his belief that Jerry and Corinne made the right choice in giving him up for adoption. He loved his adoptive parents, and voices no second thoughts about what took place. He has no doubts as to Jerry's desire or ability to be a father to a child. "Frankly I don't think he had any intention of being anybody's father. It would have brought out the worst in him."

John does wonder what would have been if he and Jerry had met. "We'd probably be freaking out a little bit, because I think the angle of the story is the nature-versus-nurture theory that it doesn't matter who raises you or where you are or where you grow up, you still wind up having very strong traits of your blood. Don't get me wrong. A lot of me is the creation of my parents: my way of thinking, the way I go through life, my morals, my beliefs. But the aesthetics of who I am and what I am interested in and what I am passionate about have to have stemmed from him somewhere." Before even knowing of his ties to Jerry, John became a DJ, focusing on the sounds and styles of pre-Beatles rock 'n' roll and swing music. "While all my other friends were keeping current— punk rock was going on, and New Wave was going on—I was busy getting into Elvis and girl groups and surf music and Motown and all that stuff. I don't know why or how I ever became drawn to this music. . . . I'm much more interested in that than I was in anything that was going on in my lifetime. I still don't know what to say about it."

* * *

IN THE YEARS FOLLOWING JERRY'S DEATH, MULTIPLE DOLLS collections, both legitimate releases and bootlegs, were issued. Television programs (HBO's *Vinyl*) and films (Todd Haynes's *Velvet Goldmine*) featured their songs. Other artists continued to cover Dolls songs, notably megastars Guns N' Roses, who covered "Human Being" on their 1993 release *The Spaghetti Incident*. Marty Thau claimed receipts from the recording totaled over $300,000. Despite asserting that almost $150,000 was never recouped from their Dolls investments, Thau and Leber-Krebs chose to give all the income from the record to Arthur, Syl, David, Johnny's children, and Jerry's mother, Charlotte.

More than forty years after the band's formation, critics still love the New York Dolls. In 2003 *Rolling Stone* created a list of the 500 Greatest Albums of All Time. The New York Dolls came in at number 213. In 2013 Britain's *NME* created a similar list, putting the same album at number 355. In 2010, *Rolling Stone* also created a list of the 500 Greatest Songs of All Time, listing "Personality Crisis" at number 271.

As for the surviving Dolls, David and Syl kept making records but Arthur struggled, never quite finding his footing. After an alcohol-fueled episode where he either fell, or jumped, out of a window, he joined the Church of Jesus Christ of Latter-Day Saints and soon gave up drinking. Proposals continued coming in for the Dolls to reform, tour, and record, with offered fees rumored to surpass a million dollars. David was always the no vote. It wasn't until dedicated Dolls fan Morrissey curated the 2004 Meltdown Festival in England that David finally accepted. Among those in attendance were Bob Geldof, Chrissie Hynde, and Clem Burke. The demand for tickets was so huge that additional shows were added. The Dolls were a giant success and decided to continue playing and recording, touring the world and adding three new records to their canon through 2011.

Sadly, Arthur was never able to tour or record with the band again, as less than a month after the first two reunion shows, he died suddenly of leukemia. A documentary of Arthur's life was released in 2005 called *N.Y. Doll*; the film was nominated for the grand prize at the Sundance Film Festival. He was also immortalized in song by Robyn Hitchcock in the haunting "N.Y. Doll." Arthur's memoirs, *I, Doll: Life and Death with the New York Dolls*, were released posthumously, in 2009. Johnny Thunders was also profiled in documentaries. While Lech Kowalski's 1999 *Born to Lose: The Last Rock and Roll Movie* never received widespread release, Danny Garcia's 2014 *Looking for Johnny: The Legend of Johnny Thunders* was readily available for viewing in multiple formats. Johnny and the New York Dolls were also briefly portrayed in the semifictional 2016 HBO TV series *Vinyl*. Executive producers included Martin Scorsese and Mick Jagger.

Bootlegged for decades, Bob Gruen's original videos of the Dolls finally saw official release in 2005, under the title *New York Dolls: All Dolled Up*. Covering the years 1973 through the Red Patent Leather shows in 1975, they are as complete a video chronicle of the original New York Dolls as any presently known.

In 1995, Time-Life's ten part *The History of Rock 'n' Roll* paid the Dolls ample respect through on-screen commentary from Malcolm McLaren, Richard Hell, and Joe Strummer. The Heartbreakers, while never mentioned, appeared on screen playing Hell's "Blank Generation." Don Letts's 2005 film *Punk Attitude* paid the Dolls even more homage, with Chrissie Hynde, Mick Jones, and Roberta Bayley all singing their praises. New interviews with David, Syl, and Arthur sit alongside Bob Gruen's live footage as well as clips from *Musikladen* and *The Old Grey Whistle Test*, giving the Dolls their rightful, historic due.

Jerry features prominently in *Please Kill Me: The Uncensored Oral History of Punk*, the 1996 book written by Gillian McCain and Legs McNeil. It is purported to be the best-selling book on punk to date. With Richard Hell, Johnny Thunders, and Walter Lure, he is pictured on the cover in Roberta Bayley's "Catch 'em while they're still alive" photo.

In John Leland's 2004 book *Hip: The History,* in the chapter titled "Behind the Music," Jerry appears on a list of nineteen "tragic drunks and drug addicts,"[1] coming in at number sixteen, between Johnny Thunders and Kurt Cobain.

Besides Arthur, several of Jerry's contemporaries, bandmates, and family members have passed on since his death: the four original Ramones (Joey, Dee Dee, Johnny, and Tommy); Jerry's sister, Rose; his mother, Charlotte; Willy DeVille; Lyn Todd; Marty Thau; Max Blatt; Billy Rath; and Leee Black Childers.

As of 2017, it could be argued that at least ten inductees into the Rock & Roll Hall of Fame owed some sort of debt to the Dolls and the Heartbreakers. In alphabetical order, they are Aerosmith, Blondie, David Bowie, the Clash, Guns N' Roses, Kiss, the Pretenders, Ramones, Sex Pistols, and Talking Heads. Neither the Dolls nor the Heartbreakers have been inducted. However, roadie Max Blatt, who visited the Rock & Roll Hall of Fame with his family, saw the following: "Right when you go through the turnstile, there's a small exhibit. Artifacts from different bands. When I walked through and I went [in], right through the door, bing! There was the bass drum head from Jerry's drums! 'New York Dolls,' with the chick bending over. The thing I handled for all those fucking years!"

It's the perfect introduction to rock 'n' roll.

SELECTED DISCOGRAPHY

This list contains official releases only.

THE PEEPL
Singles

"Freedom" b/w "Please Take My Life," Roaring Records (801), 1967

MAXIMILLIAN
LPs

Maximillian, ABC Records (ABCS-696), 1969

NEW YORK DOLLS
LPs

Private World: The Complete Early Studio Demos 1972–73 (tracks 14 and onward), Castle (CMDDD1405), 1972–73 (released 2006)[1]

New York Dolls, Mercury (SRM-1-675), 1973

Too Much Too Soon, Mercury (SRM-1-1001), 1974

Red Patent Leather, Fan Club (007), 1975 (released 1984)

Night of the Living Dolls (compilation, includes "Give Her a Great Big Kiss"), Mercury (826 094-1 M-1), 1974 (released 1985)

Rock and Roll (compilation, includes "Courageous Cat Theme," "Lone Star Queen," and "Don't Mess with Cupid"), Mercury (314 522 129-2), 1973–74 (released 1994)

From Here to Eternity: Live Bootleg Box Set, Castle (B0007W0KJW), 1973–75/84 (released 2006)

HEARTBREAKERS
Singles

"Chinese Rocks" b/w "Born to Lose," Track (2094 135), 1977

"One Track Mind" b/w "Can't Keep My Eyes on You," "Do You Love Me" (live B side), Track (2094 137), 1977

"It's Not Enough" b/w "Let Go," Track (2094 142), 1977 (released 1978)

LPs

What Goes Around, Bomp (BCD 4039), 1975 (released 1991)

Richard Hell, *Time* (tracks 1–4 only, "SBS Studio Demos"), Matador (OLE 530-2), 1976 (released 2002)

Live at Mothers, Fan Club (FC 95), 1976 (released 1991)

Down to Kill (includes selected SBS and Nap Studio Demos and *Live at the Speakeasy*), Jungle (FREUDCD094), 1975/76/77 (released 2005)

D.T.K. Live at the Speakeasy, Jungle (FREUD 1), 1977 (released 1982)

L.A.M.F. Live at the Village Gate 1977, Cleopatra (2265), 1977 (released 2015)

L.A.M.F., Track (2409 218), 1977

L.A.M.F. The Lost '77 Mixes, Jungle (FREUD 044), 1977 (released 1994)

L.A.M.F. Demos, Outtakes and Alternative Mixes, Vinyl Lovers (901035), 1977 (released 2010)

L.A.M.F. Definitive Edition (includes selected SBS and Nap Studio demos, lost '77 mixes, and other alternative mixes), Jungle (FREUDCD104) 1976–77 (released 2012)

Live at Max's Kansas City Volumes 1 & 2, Jungle (FREUD117), 1979 (released 2015)[2]

Live at the Lyceum Ballroom, London, 1984, ABC (ABC LP2), 1984

EPS

Vintage 77, Jungle (JUNG 5) 1977 (Released 1983)

THE IDOLS

Single

"Girl That I Love" b/w "You," Ork (NYC 2), 1979

JERRY NOLAN

Singles

"Take a Chance with Me" b/w "Pretty Baby," Tanden (Tan Sin 006), 1982

"Countdown Love" (B side only of split single with Johnny Thunders), Sucksex (SEX13 FRA-97), 1982 (released 1997)

LPs

Sword: The Best in Scandinavian Rock (Compilation includes "Havana Moon"), Sword (SWOLP 5) 1982 (released 1985)

JERRY NOLAN BAND
LPs

At Great Gildersleeves, Retro (RET 18), 1983 (released 2014)

JERRY NOLAN & THE PROFILERS
EPs

The Final Recordings, Straight to the Top, 1991 (released 2014)

JOHNNY THUNDERS
LPs

The New Too Much Junkie Business (tracks 1–3 only), ROIR (A118), 1982 (released 1983)

Stations of the Cross, ROIR (A-146), 1982 (released 1987)

Copy Cats (track 6, "Crawfish," only), Jungle (FREUD 20), 1984 (released 1988)

Que Sera Sera (track 7, "Tie Me Up," only), Jungle (FREUD 9), 1985

SNATCH
Singles

"All I Want" b/w "When I'm Bored" (a side only), Lightning Records (LIG 505), 1977 (released 1978)

SID VICIOUS
LPs

Sid Sings, Virgin (V 2144), 1978 (released 1979)[3]

LYN TODD
LPs

Lyn Todd, Vanguard (79436), 1980 (selected cuts)

JIMMY KURATA
LPs

Trouble Traveller, Meldac (MEL-8), 1986 (selected cuts)

LONDON COWBOYS

LPs

On Stage, Underdog (UND2), 1986

Relapse, (compilation, includes Idols 45, and Track Records demos of "Too Right Wing" and "Bigger Splash") Jungle Records (FREUD094), 1978 (released 2008)

ACKNOWLEDGMENTS

This book is dedicated to the primal yet thoughtful art of drumming and drummers everywhere. It is also dedicated to W. C. Fields, Ringo Starr, Bob Dylan, and to my dear mother, Elissa Weiss, who I'm sure is reading this on her Kindle while having a little nosh in Jewish heaven.

The process of writing this book began in 2006 and was accomplished with the help and cooperation of many people. I would like to take this opportunity to thank them.

Special thanks go to Carla DeSantis Black, who suggested I write a book back when we were still children. Her help in transcribing interviews and in reading and editing early versions with a trained and critical eye, and her positive encouragement throughout have been invaluable.

Likewise, special thanks go to Audrey Zekonis, who also read, edited, and critiqued several chapters, coached me on my agent's pitch, and convinced me to attend the Willamette Writers Conference, where eleven agents wanted proposals. I am eternally grateful for all of her tea (code for "vodka") and sympathy. I look forward to returning the favor when her overdue first book is published.

Thanks also go to John Rudolph at Dystel, Goderich & Bourret who believed in me and my maybe not-so-wacky idea for this book. You always "gave it to me straight." A trusted man is he. Mike Edison is thanked for his assiduous editing skills. His humor, encouragement, and passion strengthened me and the book. A mighty sailor on the rocket train is he. Thanks also go to my copy editor, Polly Watson, who masterfully modified my danglers here, there, and everywhere. Smarter than me is she. John Cerullo, Bernadette Malavarca, and Steve Thompson at Backbeat Books: your persistence, attention to detail, and hard work helped make this book possible. A diligent team are ye.

The following people were gracious and generous enough with their time to offer me their personal remembrances of Jerry. Some granted me interviews, either through e-mail, social media messaging, telephone, or in person. Others I might have run into at a gig or, sadly, a memorial. Some only answered a single e-mail, and others spoke with me multiple times for hours on end. Thanks and deep gratitude go to each of them for racking their brains, shedding some tears, sharing a laugh, or venting their spleens: Greg Allen, Rachel Amodeo, Pooky Amsterdam, Peder Andersson, Roni Ann, Nina Antonia, Elvera Bakas, Tom Bakas, Ivan Baker, Charlotte Ballas-Nolan, Roberta Bayley, Boby Bear, Bobby Belfiore, Iris Berry, Peter Blast, Max Blatt, Susanne Blomqvist, Buddy Bowzer, Danny Bracken, Mark Brady, Ernie Brooks, Clem Burke, Simon

Cade-Williams, Nancy Cataldi, Keith Chagnon, Leee Black Childers, Robert Christgau, Cheetah Chrome, Sesu Coleman, Jayne (Wayne) County, Peter Crowley, Alan D'Alvarez, Joseph DeJesus, Maria Del Greco, Brooke Delarco, Vinny DeNunzio, Donna Destri, Levi Dexter, George Diaz, Steve Dior, Dennis Drake, Rob DuPrey, Vinnie Earnshaw, Kipp Elbaum, Angel Electra, Elias Eliasson, Henrik Eriksson, S. Debra Evans, Deer France, Rick Freedman, Donna Gaines, Pleasant Gehman, Lucianne Goldberg, Robert Gordon, Richard Gottehrer, Bob Gruen, Randy Gunn, Dave Halbert, Eva Harris, Luke Harris, Mary Harron, Deborah Harry, Alan Hauser, Corinne Healy, Richard Hell, Esther Herskovitz, Gail Higgins, John Holmstrom, Pat Ivers, Tony James, David Johansen, Rick Johnson, Barry Jones, Mick Jones, Peter Jordan, Barbara "Babs" Kane, Lenny Kaye, Stevie Klasson, Peter Kodick Gravelle, Michele Korolow, Lech Kowalski, Ivan Kral, Gary Lachman Valentine, Jimi LaLumia, Gregor Laraque, Richard Lloyd, Bonne Löfman, Walter Lure, Tony Machine, Mariann Marlowe, James Marshall, Sarah Jo Mathys, Glen Matlock, Graham May, Joe Mazzari, Moby Medina, Kathy Miller, Karen Monster, Elliott Murphy, Chris Musto, Kris Needs, Jim Nestor, Sturgis Nikides, Billy Nolan, John O'Hanlon, Debora Olin, Bobby Paine, Jonathan Paley, Patti Palladin, Alan Parker, John Perry, Mark Pines, Michelle Piza, Alan Platt, Amos Poe, Eileen Polk, Dale Powers, Dibbs Preston, Howie Pyro, Nancy Quatro Glass, Suzi Quatro, Tommy Ramone, Jeff Raphael, Billy Rath, Keith Rawls, Danny Ray, Simon Ritt, Rick Rivets, Cynthia Ross, Ron Ross, Barry Ryan, Kevin Ryan, Joy Ryder, Jon Savage, David Scharff, Andy Schwartz, Bud Scoppa, Luigi Scorcia, Tim Scott McConnell, Daniel Sicardi, Doug Simmons, Stephen Smith (aka Smutty Smiff), Billy Squier, Chris Stein, Art Steinman, Simone Stenfors, Yves Stephenson, Ray Stevenson, Desmond Sullivan, Charlotte Lotten Sunna, Sylvain Sylvain, Marty Thau, Michael Thimren, Billy Thompson, Mike Thorne, Lyn Todd Rude, Sirius Trixon, Dixon Van Winkle, Ned Van Zandt, Jette Vandenburg, Cyndy Villano, Sonny Vincent, Lesley Vinson, Paul Wassif, Peter Wassif, Tina Weymouth, Burny White, Gass Wild, Jill Wissoff, Stuboy Wylder, James Wynbrandt, Tom Wynbrandt, Tony Zanetta, Marc Zermati, and Paul Zone.

Quite a few people and organizations assisted me in a multitude of ways, allowing me permission to quote their work or use their photos, giving me insider tips, painstakingly transcribing interviews, offering words of encouragement, providing needed phone numbers or e-mail addresses, "liking" my work on social media, or supplying some other sort of moral (or immoral) support. I am indebted to all of them. Thank you: Michael Ackerman, Viv Albertine, Steve Almaas, Emily Armstrong, Wren Arthur, Kevin Avery, Michael Azerrad, Laraby Bishop-Sharp, Pete Blecha, Sabrina Booth, Tom Brogan, Cindy Brown, Alice Burke, Robert Burke Warren, Michael Butler, Colleen Casey, Kerry Colburn at the Business of Books, Thea Constantine, Josie Cotton, Charles Cross, Bill Day, Antone DeSantis, Dale Drazan, Michele Earl-Hubbard at Allied Law Group, Megan Erb, Louis Erlanger, Fales Library & Special Collections, Linda Falzarano, Rebecca Federman at the New York Public Library, Robert Barry Francos, Chris Frantz, Angela Frucci, Holly George-Warren, Peter Gerstenzang, Alison Gordy, Nancy Guppy, Christine Hemp, Beth Hester, Darren Hill, Barney Hoskins and everyone at Rocksbackpages.com, Linda Jacobson, Regina Joskow, Kevin Kalicki, Mara Karpel, Steph Kese, Kitty Kowalski, Lynette Kral, Jade Lee, Jan Long Collins, Rupert Macnee, Anuja Maheshka at Viacom, Elise Maiberger, Johnny Marr, Hope Marston, Mike Matheson, Gillian McCain, Legs McNeil, Owen Miller at Viacom, Mike Mindless, Lorne Mitchell, Vicky Mitchell at BBC Vision, Sheila Mullen, Paul Myers, Frank Nolan, Holly Olchek, Amanda Pecsenye at the Rock and Roll Hall of Fame, Spike Priggen, Mark Prindle, Mark Pyskoty, Roddy "Radiation" Byers, Reference Librarian 2 at the Library of Congress, Robin Reul, Ira Robbins, Chris Robison, Emily Rowes, Steven Sachse, Shari Saffioti, Chris Salewicz, Ernie Sapiro, Samantha Schmidt, Nina Shapiro, Mat Snow, Tom Speer, Rew Starr, Jim Sullivan, Jeanne Talbot, Dean Thomas, Roy Trakin, Paul Trynka, Paul Tschinkel, Katherine Turman, George Usher, Amy Watkins at Lawton Public Schools, Dig Wayne, Cynthia Whitcomb, Jon Wiederhorn, Jennifer Worick at the Business of Books, and Peter Zaremba.

A number of people spoke off the record, anonymously, or "on background." Their contributions have been vital, and I offer my sincere thanks.

Special thanks go out to Nina Antonia for the liberal use of quotes from her 1997 interview with Malcolm McLaren.

Extra special thanks are in order for my Uncle Michael, who gave me my first Bob Dylan, Lovin' Spoonful, and Ray Charles records. When I was ten he called one of my favorite books on the 1969 New York Mets a "non-book." I am proud to have now written one. His generous and unending love of life, art, and most of all music, have not gone unnoticed. I love him dearly.

Thanks and love also go out to my dear sister Alicia. She always sang along to the groups on *Ed Sullivan* while I listened with rapt attention. Jeez, that drove me crazy . . . especially since she always got the words wrong. Your awful voice is always welcome noise to my ears.

While I was completing this book, several contributors joined Johnny and Jerry in their eternal rest. They include Charlotte Ballas-Nolan, Max Blatt, Nancy Cataldi, Leee Black Childers, Angel Elektra (Dave Hames), Kathy Miller, Tommy Ramone (Thomas Erdelyi), Billy Rath, Joy Ryder, Lyn Todd, Marty Thau, and Stuboy Wylder (Stuart Feinholtz). Rest in peace.

The most special of thanks go to my wife, Karen, and daughter, Emma. Your love, smiles, support, understanding, and patience make everything better.

NOTES

CHAPTER I

1. Paul Kendall, "50 Years of West Side Story: The Real Gangs of New York," *Telegraph*, July 20, 2008, http://www.telegraph.co.uk/culture/donotmigrate/3556888/50-years-of-West-Side-Story-the-real-Gangs-of-New-York.html.
2. Ibid.
3. Nina Antonia, "Sticks and Style: The Art of Jerry Nolan," *Spiral Scratch*, August 1991, n.p.
4. Ibid.
5. Ibid.

CHAPTER 2

1. Peter Criss with Larry Sloman, *Makeup to Breakup: My Life In and Out of Kiss* (New York: Scribner, 2013), Kindle edition.
2. Ibid.
3. Ibid.
4. Jerry Nolan with Doug Simmons, "My Life as a Doll," *The Village Voice*, July 19, 1991, 18
5. Criss and Sloman, *Makeup to Breakup*.
6. Kris Needs and Dick Porter, *Trash! The Complete New York Dolls* (Medford, NJ: Plexus Publishing, 2005), 69.
7. Kris Needs and Dick Porter, *Trash! The Complete New York Dolls* (Medford, NJ: Plexus Publishing, 2005), 69.
8. Ibid.
9. Ibid.
10. Robin Flans, "CRISS ALIVE!," *Modern Drummer*, February 1999, 62.

CHAPTER 3

1. Pete Makowski, "Johnny Thunders & the Heartbreakers: D*T*K*L*A*M*F," *Sounds*, June 4, 1977.
2. Needs and Porter, *Trash!*, 70.
3. Ibid.

CHAPTER 4

1. Arthur Kane, *I, Doll* (Chicago: Chicago Review Press, 2009), 3.
2. Art Steinman, "The Story of Art Steinman," FromTheArchives.org, accessed January 2016, http://www.fromthearchives.org/nyd/The%20story%20of%20Art%20Steinman.pdf.
3. "From Riches to Rags," *New York Post*, August 4, 1973, 48.
4. "Historic Hotel New Home for Theatre Dream," *Sunday Record* (Bergen County, NJ), March 12, 1972, B-17.

CHAPTER 5

1. Marty Thau, "Legend of the Lipstick Killers," *Popmatters*, June 25, 2002, http://www.popmatters.com/feature/020625-nydolls.
2. Ibid.
3. Ibid.
4. Roy Hollingsworth, "You Wanna Play House With the Dolls?," *Melody Maker*, July 22, 1972, 17.
5. Kevin Avery, *Everything Is an Afterthought: The Life and Writings of Paul Nelson* (Seattle: Fantagraphics Books, 2011), 45.
6. *Once Upon a Time in New York: The Birth of Hip-Hop, Disco, and Punk*, directed by Benjamin Whalley, aired March 5, 2007 (London: BBC, 2007), https://www.youtube.com/watch?v=9UwXKuHrIxE.
7. Ibid.
8. Richard Nusser, "Once More, Death in Threes," *Village Voice*, November 16, 1972, 52.
9. Jerry Nolan with Doug Simmons, "My Life as a Doll," *Village Voice*, July 19, 1991, 19.

CHAPTER 6

1. Binky Philips, "December 19th, 1972: Me, Opening for The New York Dolls 40 (!) Years Ago," *Huffington Post*, December 21, 2012, http://www.huffingtonpost.com/binky-philips/new-york-dolls_b_2347929.html.
2. Ibid.
3. Ronnie Wood, *Ronnie: The Autobiography* (New York:, St. Martin's Press, 2007), 127.
4. *Once Upon a Time in New York*.
5. Barry Miles, "They Simper at Times: New York Dolls, Wayne County: The Mercer Arts Center, New York City," *NME*, 1972.
6. Mat Snow, "Hairspray and Hard Drugs: The New York Dolls," *Q*, January 1995, tk.
7. Paul Myers, *A Wizard, A True Star: Todd Rundgren in the Studio* (London: Jawbone Press, 2010), 64.
8. Snow, "Hairspray and Hard Drugs."
9. Ibid.
10. Ibid.
11. Ibid.
12. Ibid.
13. Ibid.
14. Myers, *A Wizard, A True Star*, 87.
15. Ibid.
16. Snow, "Hairspray and Hard Drugs."

CHAPTER 7

1. Lester Bangs, "Mott the Hoople/The New York Dolls/Dr. Hook & the Medicine Show: Live in Massillon, Ohio," *Phonograph Record*, November 1973.
2. Ibid.
3. Ibid.
4. Ibid.
5. Ibid.
6. Ibid.
7. Nina Antonia, *The New York Dolls: Too Much Too Soon* (New York: Omnibus Press, 1998), 94.
8. Peter Goddard, "Dull, Decadent Dolls Put on Tacky Rock Show," *Toronto Star*, October 29, 1973, D*3.
9. Ibid.
10. Ibid.
11. Nina Antonia, "The First Punk: Johnny Thunders," in "Punk," special issue, *Mojo*, March 2005.
12. Nick Kent, "The New York Dolls: The New York Dolls (Mercury Import)," *NME*, August 25, 1973.
13. Ibid.
14. Ibid.
15. Morrissey, *Autobiography* (New York: Penguin, 2013), Kindle edition.
16. Ibid.
17. Ibid.
18. Ibid.
19. Needs and Porter, *Trash!*, 103.
20. Ibid.
21. Nolan with Simmons, "My Life as A Doll," 22.
22. Antonia, *The New York Dolls: Too Much Too Soon*, 109.

CHAPTER 8

1. Richard Arfin, "The 'Shadow' Reappears," *Goldmine*, July 12, 1991.
2. Snow, "Hairspray to Hard Drugs."

CHAPTER 9

1. Ray Cecys, "Kiss/New York Dolls Allen Theatre June 14," *Scene*, June 20–26, 1974. Available online at http://www.fromthearchives.com/nyd/NYD14_Jun_74.jpg.
2. Ibid.
3. Ibid.
4. Ibid.
5. O. B. Lewis and the Circus staff, "The New York Dolls – 'Too Much Too Soon' or Too Little Too Late?," *Circus*, August 1974, 9.

6. Ibid., 9.

7. Ibid., 9.

8. Ibid., 10.

9. Ibid., 10.

10. *Once Upon a Time in New York.*

11. Janis Schacht, "The New York Dolls-In Too Much Too Soon," *Circus*, August 1974, 20.

12. Ibid., 20.

13. Antonia, *The New York Dolls: Too Much Too Soon*, 149.

14. Ibid., 148.

15. *Once Upon a Time in New York.*

16. Ibid.

CHAPTER 10

1. Snow, "Hairspray and Hard Drugs."

2. Ibid.

3. Ibid.

4. Nolan with Simmons, "My Life as a Doll," 21.

5. Antonia, *The New York Dolls: Too Much Too Soon*, 179.

6. Paul Nelson, "Valley of the New York Dolls," *Village Voice*, May 26, 1975, 131.

7. Ibid.

8. Ibid.

9. Ibid.

CHAPTER 11

1. Jenny Valentish, "CBGB: The Venue from Hell," *Inpress*, January 2006.

2. Richard Hell, *I Dreamed I Was a Very Clean Tramp* (New York: Ecco, 2013), Kindle edition.

3. Ibid.

4. Ibid.

5. David Laing, "It's Been Real: The Real Kids," *Ugly Things*, 1999.

6. Ibid.

7. Ibid.

8. Charles Shaar Murray, "New York: The Sound of '75, *NME*, November 8, 1975.

9. Andy Schwartz, "The Jerry Nolan Story!!," *New York Rocker*, July 1978, 55.

10. Generelli, Carlo. "Johnny Ramone RAW—Last Interview." Filmed March 2003. You-Tube video, 15:16. Posted by "billschannel," Dec. 8, 2010, https://www.youtube.com/watch?v=18i08hEO_xw.

11. Legs McNeil and Gillian McCain, *Please Kill Me: The Uncensored Oral History of Punk* (New York: Grove Press, 1996), 337.

12. Ibid.

13. Nick Kent, "New York: Plug In to the Nerve-Ends of the Naked City," *NME*, March 27, 1976.
14. Barney Hoskins, "The Backpages Interview: Richard Hell—King Punk Remembers the [ ] Generation," *Rock's Backpages*, March 2002.
15. Nolan with Simmons, "My Life as a Doll," 21.

CHAPTER 12

1. Lester Bangs, "The White Noise Supremacists," *Village Voice*, April 30, 1979, 4. Available online at http://www.mariabuszek.com/mariabuszek/kcai/ PoMoSeminar/Readings/BangsWhite.pdf.
2. Ibid.
3. Karen Schoemer, "The Day Punk Died," *New York*, October 19, 2008. Available online at http://nymag.com/arts/popmusic/features/51394/.
4. Ibid.

CHAPTER 13

1. Hell, *I Dreamed I Was a Very Clean Tramp*.
2. Pat Gilbert, *Passion Is a Fashion: The Real Story of the Clash* (Boston: Da Capo Press, 2005), 63.
3. Caroline Coon, "Sex Pistols, Damned, Clash, Johnny Thunders & the Heartbreakers: Leeds Polytechnic," *Melody Maker*, December 11, 1976.
4. Ibid.
5. Ibid.

CHAPTER 14

1. By kind permission of, and copyright, John Perry, in e-mail to author, July 11, 2006.
2. Giovanni Dadomo, "Iggy Pop: Friar's, Aylesbury; Cherry Vanilla, Johnny Thunders & the Heartbreakers, Wayne County, Siousxsie & the Banshees: The Roxy, London," *Sounds*, March 12, 1977.
3. Perry, e-mail to author.
4. "New Directions for Track Label Planned by Hall," *Billboard*, April 23, 1977.
5. Keith Levene interviewed by Jason Gross, *Perfect Sound Forever*, February 2001, http://www.furious.com/perfect/keithlevene.html.
6. Nolan with Simmons, "My Life as a Doll," 22.
7. Tony Parsons, "Get Your Chinese Rocks Off . . . and End Up like Johnny Thunders," *NME*, May 28, 1977.
8. Richard Hell, "Richard Hell—2005," interview by Mark Prindle, *Mark's Record Reviews*, accessed November 17, 2009, http://www.markprindle.com/hell-i.htm.
9. Pete Makowski, "Johnny Thunders & The Heartbreakers: D*T*K*L*A*M*F," *Sounds*, June 4, 1977.
10. Perry, e-mail to author.

11. Makowski, "Johnny Thunders & The Heartbreakers."

12. Julie Burchill, "The Heartbreakers L.A.M.F.," *NME*, October 8, 1977. Available online at http://www.punk77.co.uk/graphics/heartbreakers/8.10.77burchillnmelamfrevie.jpg.

13. Jon Savage, "The Heartbreakers 'L.A.M.F.'," *Sounds*, October 1, 1977.

14. Ibid.

15. Burchill, "The Heartbreakers L.A.M.F."

16. Savage, "The Heartbreakers 'L.A.M.F.'"

17. Barry Cain, "Thunders and Lightning," *Record Mirror*, October 25, 1977.

18. Ibid.

CHAPTER 15

1. Ira Robbins, "Sid Vicious: Max's Kansas City, NYC," *NME*, October 14, 1978.

2. Ibid.

3. Barry Jones, "Had a Gig the Night She Died."

4. Paul Nelson, "David Johansen Goes It Alone," *Rolling Stone*, May 18, 1978. Reprinted in Avery, *Everything Is an Afterthought*, 256.

5. Schwartz, "The Jerry Nolan Story!!," 55.

6. Ibid.

7. Ibid.

8. Ibid.

CHAPTER 16

1. Nina Antonia, liner notes, *Heartbreakers Live at Max's Kansas City Volumes 1 & 2* (London: Jungle Records, 2015), n.p.

CHAPTER 18

1. Tony James, "My Johnny Thunders Story (Part 2)," *Carbon Silicon*, December 31, 2010, http://www.carbonsilicon.com/articles/my-johnny-thunders-story-part-2/.

2. Ibid.

CHAPTER 19

1. Carol Clerk, "Johnny Thunders: The Marquee, London," *Melody Maker*, September 1, 1984.

2. Ibid.

3. Nina Antonia, *Johnny Thunders: In Cold Blood* (London: Cherry Red Books, 2000), 167.

CHAPTER 20

1. Nolan with Simmons, "My Life as a Doll," 24.

CHAPTER 21

1. Antonia, *The New York Dolls: Too Much Too Soon*, 190.

CHAPTER 22

1. Doug Simmons, Calendar, *Village Voice*, November 28, 1990.
2. Jim Sullivan, "Spend Mothers Day with Johnny Thunders: Boston Area Debut for Doc on the Late Punk-Rocker, at the Regent May 11," JimSullivanInk.com, May 9, 2014, http://jimsullivanink.com/?p=2840.
3. Ibid.
4. Antonia, *Johnny Thunders: In Cold Blood*, 222.
5. *What About Me?*, written and directed by Rachel Amodeo (Oaks, PA: Eclectic DVD Dist., 1993), DVD.
6. Ibid.
7. "HIV Associated Neurocognitive Disorders," National Institute of Mental Health, accessed August 2016, http://www.nimh.nih.gov/health/topics/hiv-aids/hiv-associated-neurocognitive-disorders.shtml.
8. Antonia, *Johnny Thunders: In Cold Blood*, 231.
9. Gina Kolata, "Virus That May Cause Leukemia Is Spreading Among Drug Addicts," *New York Times*, February 16, 1989, http://www.nytimes.com/1989/02/16/us/virus-that-may-cause-leukemia-is-spreading-among-drug-addicts.html.
10. Ibid.

CHAPTER 23

1. MTV's "MTV News," originally broadcast October 1991. Used with permission by MTV. ©2016 Viacom Media Networks, all rights reserved. MTV, all related titles, characters and logos are trademarks owned by Viacom Media Networks, a division of Viacom International Inc.
2. McNeil and McCain, *Please Kill Me*, 406.
3. Ibid., 406.
4. Ian Fortnam, "So Alone: The Johnny Thunders Story," Teamrock.com, July 15, 2016, http://teamrock.com/feature/2016-07-15/so-alone-the-johnny-thunders-story.

SELECTED DISCOGRAPHY

1. Combines the previously released demo collections *Seven-Day Weekend*, *Endless Party*, and *Hard Night's Day*.
2. Jerry appears on Volume 2 only.
3. All tracks except "My Way."

BIBLIOGRAPHY

This bibliography lists all previously created, published, or copyrighted works used for researching this book. When quoted directly, citations have been made.

BOOKS

Antonia, Nina. *Johnny Thunders: In Cold Blood*. London: Cherry Red, 2000.

Antonia, Nina. *The New York Dolls: Too Much Too Soon*. London: Omnibus Press, 1998.

Avery, Kevin. *Everything Is an Afterthought: The Life and Writings of Paul Nelson*. Seattle: Fantagraphics, 2011.

Bayley, Roberta. *Blondie: Unseen 1976–1980*, Medford, NJ: Plexus Publishing, 2007.

Bromberg, Craig. *The Wicked Ways of Malcolm McLaren*. New York: Harper & Row, 1989.

Cain, Barry. *'77 Sulphate Strip: An Eyewitness Account of the Year That Changed Everything*. Cambridgeshire, UK: Ovolo Books, 2007.

Chavez, Judy, and Jack Vitek. *Defector's Mistress*. New York: Dell, 1979.

Chrome, Cheetah. *Cheetah Chrome: A Dead Boy's Tale: From the Front Lines of Punk Rock*. Minneapolis: Voyageur Press, 2010.

Criss, Lydia. *Sealed with a Kiss*. New York: Lydia Criss Publishing, 2006.

Criss, Peter, with Larry Sloman. *Makeup to Breakup: My Life In and Out of Kiss*. New York: Scribner, 2013.

Gilbert, Pat. *Passion Is a Fashion: The Real Story of the Clash*. Cambridge, MA: Da Capo Press, 2005.

Gruen, Bob, and Legs McNeil. *New York Dolls: Photographs*. New York: Abrams Image, 2008.

Hell, Richard. *I Dreamed I Was a Very Clean Tramp*. New York: Ecco, 2013.

Heylin, Clinton. *From the Velvets to the Voidoids*. New York: Penguin Books, 1993.

Kane, Arthur "Killer." *I, Doll: Life and Death with The New York Dolls*. Chicago: Chicago Review Press, 2009.

Leland, John. *Hip: The History*. New York: Harper Perennial, 2005.

Lydon, John, Keith Zimmerman, and Kent Zimmerman. *Rotten: No Irish, No Blacks, No Dogs*. New York: St. Martin's Press, 1994.

Lydon, John. *Anger Is an Energy: My Life Uncensored*. New York: Simon & Schuster, 2015.

Marko, Paul. *The Roxy London WC2: A Punk History*. England: Punk77 Books, 2007.

Maté, Gabor. *In the Realm of Hungry Ghosts: Close Encounters with Addiction.* Berkeley, CA: North Atlantic Books, 2008.

Matlock, Glen, with Pete Silverton. *I Was a Teenage Sex Pistol.* London: Faber & Faber, 1991.

McNeil, Legs, and Gillian McCain. *Please Kill Me: The Uncensored Oral History of Punk.* New York: Grove Press, 1996.

Miles, Barry. *In the Seventies: Adventures in the Counterculture.* London: Serpent's Tail, 2012.

Morrissey. *Autobiography.* New York: G. P. Putnam's Sons, 2013.

Myers, Paul. *A Wizard, A True Star: Todd Rundgren in the Studio.* London: Jawbone Press, 2010.

Needs, Kris, and Dick Porter. *Trash! The Complete New York Dolls.* Medford, NJ: Plexus Publishing, 2005.

O'Shea, Mick. *The Anarchy Tour.* London: Omnibus Press, 2012.

Parker, Alan. *Sid Vicious: No One Is Innocent.* London: Orion, 2008.

Savage, Jon. *England's Dreaming: The "Sex Pistols" and Punk Rock.* London: Faber & Faber, 1992.

Savage, Jon. *The England's Dreaming Tapes.* London: Faber & Faber, 2009.

Schneider, Eric C. *Vampires, Dragons, and Egyptian Kings: Youth Gangs in Postwar New York.* Princeton, NJ: Princeton University Press, 1999.

Stanton, Scott. *The Tombstone Tourist: Musicians.* New York: Pocket Books, 2003.

Valentine, Gary. *New York Rocker: My Life in the Blank Generation.* London: Sidgwick & Jackson, 2002.

Vermorel, Fred, and Judy Vermorel. *Sex Pistols: The Inside Story.* London: Omnibus Press, 2011.

Walsh, Jim. *The Replacements: All Over but the Shouting: An Oral History.* St. Paul, MN: Voyager Press, 2007.

Wood, Ronnie. *Ronnie: The Autobiography.* New York: St. Martin's Press, 2007.

ARTICLES

A Dedicated Nolan Fan. Letter to the editor. *Rock Scene*, October 1974.

Aidsinfonet.org. "Cryptococcal Meningitis Fact Sheet 503." Last reviewed May 19, 2014, http://www.aidsinfonet.org/fact_sheets/view/503.

Antonia, Nina. "Sticks and Style: The Art of Jerry Nolan." *Spiral Scratch*, August 1991.

Antonia, Nina. "The First Punk: Johnny Thunders." In "Punk. Special issue, *Mojo*, March 2005.

Arfin, Richard. "The 'Shadow' Reappears." *Goldmine*, July 12, 1991.

Bangs, Lester. "Mott the Hoople/The New York Dolls/Dr. Hook & the Medicine Show: Live in Masillon, Ohio." *Phonograph Record*, November 1973.

Bangs, Lester. "The White Noise Supremacists." *Village Voice*, April 30, 1979.

Billboard. "New Directions for Track Label Planned by Hall." April 23, 1977.

Brown, Pamela. "Heartbreakers." *Punk*, March 1976.

Burchill, Julie. "The Heartbreakers L.A.M.F." *NME*, October 8, 1977.

Cain, Barry. "Thunders and Lightning." *Record Mirror*, October 25, 1977.

Cecys, Ray. "Kiss/New York Dolls Allen Theatre June 14." *Scene*, June 20–26, 1974.

Clerk, Carol. "Johnny Thunders: The Marquee, London." *Melody Maker*, September 1, 1984.

Coon, Caroline. "Sex Pistols, Damned, Clash, Johnny Thunders & the Heartbreakers: Leeds Polytechnic." *Melody Maker*, December 11, 1976.

Dadomo, Giovanni. "Iggy Pop: Friar's, Aylesbury; Cherry Vanilla, Johnny Thunders & the Heartbreakers, Wayne Country, Siousxsie & the Banshees: The Roxy, London." *Sounds*, March 12, 1977.

Dadomo, Giovanni. "Italians Define Rock 'n' Roll." *Sounds*, March 5, 1977.

Dadomo, Giovanni. "Why I Quit the Heartbreakers by Jerry Nolan." *Sounds*, October 15, 1977.

Flans, Robin. "Criss Alive!" *Modern Drummer*, February 1999.

Fortnam, Ian. "So Alone: The Johnny Thunders Story." Teamrock.com, July 15, 2016, http://teamrock.com/feature/2016-07-15/so-alone-the-johnny-thunders-story.

FromtheArchives.org. "New York Dolls—Chronology (New York City early 1971–2012)," http://www.fromthearchives.com/nyd/chronology.html.

Goddard, Peter. "Dull, Decadent Dolls Put On Tacky Rock Show." *Toronto Star*, October 29, 1973.

Heimel, Cynthia. "No Such Thing as Punk." *New York*, October 15, 1979.

Hell, Richard. "Interview: Richard Hell—King Punk Remembers the [ ] Generation." By Barney Hoskins. *Rock's Backpages*, March 2002.

Hell, Richard. "Richard Hell – 2005." Interview by Mark Prindle. *Mark's Record Reviews*, accessed November 17, 2009, http://www.markprindle.com/hell-i.htm.

Hollingsworth, Roy. "You Wanna Play House with the Dolls?" *Melody Maker*, July 22, 1972.

James, Tony. "My Johnny Thunders Story (Part 2)." *Carbon Silicon*, December 31, 2010, http://www.carbonsilicon.com/articles/my-johnny-thunders-story-part-2/.

Kendall, Paul. "50 Years of West Side Story: The Real Gangs of New York. *Telegraph*, July 20, 2008.

Kent, Nick. "New York: Plug In to the Nerve-Ends of the Naked City." *NME*, March 27, 1976.

Kent, Nick. "The New York Dolls: The New York Dolls (Mercury Import)." *NME*, August 25, 1973.

Kolata, Gina. "Virus That May Cause Leukemia Is Spreading Among Drug Addicts." *New York Times*, February 16, 1989.

Laing, David. "It's Been Real: The Real Kids." *Ugly Things*, 1999

Lewis, Emory. "Historic Hotel New Home for Theatre Dream." *Bergen County Sunday Record,* March 12, 1972.

Lewis, O. B., and the *Circus* staff. "The New York Dolls—'Too Much Too Soon' or Too Little Too Late?: *Circus*, August 1974.

Levene, Keith. Interview by Jason Gross. *Perfect Sound Forever*, February 2001, http://www.furious.com/perfect/keithlevene.html.

Makowski, Pete. "Johnny Thunders & the Heartbreakers: D*T*K*L*A*M*F." *Sounds,* June 4, 1977.

Miles, Barry. "They Simper at Times: New York Dolls, Wayne County: The Mercer Arts Center, New York City." *NME*, 1972.

Murray, Charles Shaar. "New York: The Sound of '75." *NME*, November 8, 1975.

National Institute of Mental Health. "HIV Associated Neurocognitive Disorders," Accessed 2015, http://www.nimh.nih.gov/health/topics/hiv-aids/hiv-associated-neurocognitive-disorders.shtml.

Nelson, Paul. "David Johansen Goes It Alone." *Rolling Stone*, May 18, 1978.

Nelson, Paul. "Valley of the New York Dolls." *Village Voice*, May 26, 1975.

Nolan, Jerry, with Doug Simmons. "My Life as a Doll: A Rock 'n' Roll Memoir." *Village Voice,* July 19, 1991

Nusser, Richard. "Once More, Death in Threes." *Village Voice*, November 16, 1972

Parsons, Tony. "Get Your Chinese Rocks Off . . . and End Up like Johnny Thunders." *NME*, May 28, 1977.

Perlez, Jane. "From Riches to Rags." *New York Post*, August 4, 1973.

Philby, Charlotte. "My Secret Life: David Johansen, Musician, 60." *Independent*, April 16, 2010.

Phillips, Binky. "December 19th, 1972: Me, Opening for the New York Dolls 40 (!) Years Ago." *Huffington Post*, December 21, 2012.

Robbins, Ira. "Sid Vicious: Max's Kansas City, NYC." *NME*, October 14, 1978.

Savage, Jon. "The Heartbreakers 'L.A.M.F.'" *Sounds*, October 1, 1977.

Schoemer, Karen. "The Day Punk Died." *New York*, October 19, 2008.

Schwartz, Andy. "The Jerry Nolan Story!!" *New York Rocker*, July 1978.

Simmons, Doug. Calendar. *Village Voice*, November 28, 1990.

Simmons, Doug. "Jerry Nolan 1946–1992." *Village Voice*, January 28, 1992.

Snow, Mat. "Hairspray and Hard Drugs: The New York Dolls." *Q*, January 1995.

Spungen, Nancy. "New Strokes for the Heartbreakers." *New York Rocker*, July 1976.

Stein, Phyllis. "A New York Doll Speaks Out: Phyllis Stein Interview by Mel." Interview by Melanie Smith. *Mudkiss Fanzine,* June 2010, http://www.mudkiss.com/phyllis-stein.htm.

Steinman, Art. "The Story of Art Steinman." FromtheArchives.org, 2016, http://www.fromthearchives.org/nyd/The%20story%20of%20Art%20Steinman.pdf.

Sullivan, Jim. "Spend Mothers Day with Johnny Thunders: Boston Area Debut for Doc on the Late Punk-Rocker, at the Regent May 11." JimSullivanInk.com, May 9, 2014, http://jimsullivanink.com/?p=2840.

Thau, Marty. "Legend of the Lipstick Killers." Popmatters.com, June 25, 2002. http://www.popmatters.com/feature/020625-nydolls/.

Uppal, Gulshan, and Florian P. Thomas. "Meningitis in HIV." *Medscape*, December 29, 2015.

Valentish, Jenny. "CBGB: The Venue from Hell." *Inpress*, January 2006.

INTERNET SITES

Johnny Thunders Cyber Lounge, http://www.thunders.ca/.

Johnny Thunders Rocks, http://johnnythunders.rocks/.

The Kitchen 1971–73, http://vasulka.org/Kitchen/index.html.

FILM, VIDEO, TELEVISION

Amodeo, Rachel. *What About Me.* Oaks, PA: Eclectic DVD Distributors, 1993.

Generelli, Carlo. "Johnny Ramone RAW – Last Interview." Filmed March 2003. YouTube video, 15:16. Posted by "billschannel," Dec. 8, 2010, https://www.youtube.com/watch?v=18i08hEO_xw.

Gruen, Bob, and Nadya Beck. *New York Dolls: All Dolled Up.* Oaks, PA: Music Video Distributors, 2005, DVD.

Gruen, Bob and Nadya Beck. *New York Dolls: Lookin' Fine on Television.* Oaks, PA: Music Video Distributors, 2011, DVD.

Kowalski, Lech. *Born to Lose: The Last Rock and Roll Movie*, 1999.

MTV's "MTV News," originally broadcast October 1991. Used with permission by MTV. © 2016 Viacom Media Networks, All Rights Reserved. MTV, all related titles, characters and logos are trademarks owned by Viacom Media Networks, a division of Viacom International Inc.

O'Dell, Tom. *Punk Revolution NYC*. Essex, UK: Prism Films, 2011.

Thunders, Kane & Nolan: You Can't Put Your Arms Around a Memory. Oaks, PA: Music Video Distributors, 2005, DVD.

Tickell, Paul. *Punk and The Pistols*. London: BBC Arena, 1995.

Whalley, Benjamin. *Once Upon a Time in New York: The Birth of Hip-Hop, Disco, and Punk*. (London: BBC, 2007).

Whiteley, Greg. *New York Doll*. One Potato Productions, 2006.

LINER NOTES

Antonia, Nina. Liner notes to Heartbreakers, *Live at Max's Kansas City Volumes 1 & 2*. Jungle Records FREUDLP117, 2015, 33 rpm.

Antonia, Nina. Liner notes to Heartbreakers, *L.A.M.F.: Definitive Edition*. Jungle Records FREUDCD104, 2012, CD.

Needs, Kris. Liner notes to Heartbreakers, *D.T.K. Live at the Speakeasy*. Jungle FREUD 1, 1982, CD.

Shipley, Ken, and Rob Sevier. Liner notes to Various Artists, *Ork Records: New York, New York*. Numero Group 060, 2015, CD.

OTHER

All Malcolm McLaren quotes, unless otherwise noted, are courtesy of Nina Antonia, *Malcolm McLaren Remembers The New York Dolls, parts 1 & 2*, *Rock's Backpages*, 1997, audio at https://www.rocksbackpages.com/Library/Article/malcolm-mclaren-remembers-the-new-york-dolls-parts-1--2-1997.

All John Perry quotes are copyright and by kind permission of John Perry, via e-mail correspondence with the author July 11, 2006.

"Well, if you know anything about shooting pills . . ." Jones, Barry. "Had a Gig the Night She Died," 1978.

INDEX